To Save
One Life

To Save
One Life

MAX WINDMUELLER AND THE DUTCH
RESCUE-AND-RESISTANCE MOVEMENT

~⟋

Daniel Sachs

Library of Congress Control Number: 2017905933
CreateSpace Independent Publishing Platform
North Charleston, South Carolina

ISBN: 1544679246
ISBN: 13: 9781544679242

To contact the author:
sachs11md@gmail.com

Dedication

To Inge Windmueller Horowitz

*To the memory of Max Windmüller, Metta Lande
(Shulamith Roethler) and the heroic band of
Dutch resistance fighters with whom they served*

Table of Contents

List of Illustrations

Author's Note;
Acknowledgments

～

W hat you are about to read is a work of historical fiction in a story-within-a-story. There is the frame or outer story: for a book about Max Windmüller, a German-Jewish hero of the Dutch rescue movement during World War II, a German woman, Renate Gierecke, interviews Max's lifelong friend, Sigi Kirschner. This frame story is fiction; Renate and Sigi exist only in the author's imagination, as does Hans-Jürgen Heilmann, the publisher who enlists Renate to write the book.

Then there is the story-within-the-story, the story told in the course of the interview. This second story is true, so far as we know. It tells of the central character in the book, Max Windmüller, of his comrades in the rescue movement, of his sweetheart, Metta Lande, of the men and women who helped them, and of those who pursued them. The events described really occurred. The men and women who lived these experiences, those of them who survived, related their stories to authors and historians. The historical record confirms that they took place.

I am grateful to the many people whose assistance, research, and writings made this book possible. Foremost among them is Inge Windmueller

Horowitz of Richmond, Virginia, a distant cousin of Max's. She has been instrumental in the writing of this book on three counts: she was the moving force in having this book written in the first instance; she provided many of the resource materials that were helpful in my understanding of Max; and she made valuable suggestions, both substantive and editorial, after reading the manuscript in its several drafts.

I am also grateful to Klaus Meyer-Van Dettum of Emden, Germany, who blazed the trail with his 1996 biography, in German, entitled *Max Windmüller: Gennant Cor—Ein Retter in Gewaltfreien Widerstand, 1920–1945* (English translation: *Max Windmüller, Called Cor—a Rescuer in Non-Violent Resistance, 1920–1945*). He authorized me to make liberal use of his book, and I have done so, thereby saving me considerable time and effort. My thanks, too, to Anne Marie Perel, who translated the biography into English, and her son, Michael, who transcribed the handwritten translation. I also recommend highly the documentary produced by Eike Besuden, *CODE NAME COR: The Dramatic Life of Max Windmüller.*

I am happy to acknowledge the assistance as well of the late Metta Lande (Shulamith Roethler), who contributed much information about Max and about her relationship with him, and of her son, Doron Roethler. A special thanks to Cornelia Warmenhoven, for her Dutch-to-English translations.

Many people read the manuscript and made helpful comments, and others helped by passing on useful computer-related hints. In addition to Inge Windmueller Horowitz, they include Carole Baskin Stevens, Lee Pittman, Judith R. Klau, and my family: my wife, Ruth, my daughter, Julia Loeb, and my two sons, George and Noah. Kudos to everyone who contributed to this effort!

Daniel Sachs
April 2017

Introduction

_⤶_

. . . . It's easy to say "It's not my child, not my community, not my world, not my problem." Then there are those who see the need and respond. I consider those people my heroes.

FRED ROGERS (1928–2003),
AMERICAN TELEVISION PERSONALITY

I n the annals of history, we reserve a place of honor for those who, when duty calls, step forward, heedless of their own safety and well-being, and say, "I will do it." This book tells the story of one such man, Max Windmüller. For his bravery, we call him a hero. _Hero_—it's a short simple word, just four letters: H-E-R-O, but, oh, the myths and legends that surround it! We are conditioned from early childhood to admire heroes, to aspire to be like them. But what exactly is a hero? Is your favorite sports star a hero? How about that leading Hollywood film star? The President of the United States? No, no, and no. A hero is someone who goes beyond, far beyond, what is expected of him or her, someone who picks up the flag after others have dropped it, someone who exemplifies courage "above and beyond the call of duty."

You don't train to be a hero; you don't intend to be a hero. A need arises in a set of circumstances for a man or a woman to step up and perform acts that he or she would not have dreamed themselves capable of. You don't plan beforehand to pull someone out of a burning car, or, as a soldier, to move from the safety of your foxhole to get a wounded comrade out of the line of fire. Under those circumstances, the hero steps forward and dons the hero's mantle, not because he wants a medal or to have a street named after him. More likely than not, he is driven by his passionate devotion to a cause, by the need to save the lives of others, to create a better world for his children and grandchildren, to respond to cruelty and injustice.

We all have it in us to be heroes, to step outside our comfort zone, to put our lives on the line, but few of us are called upon to be heroes, and even fewer to act decisively to do what it takes to be regarded as a hero.

During World War II, the threat of death loomed constantly over the shoulders of ordinary men and women. Their best and worst qualities came to the fore. There were those who, to their shame, actively enlisted in the enemy's cause and took up arms on its behalf. These were the turncoats, the traitors, the moral weaklings. History remembers them with scorn and contempt.

On the other side were men and women of all ages, all religions, all nationalities, whose every thought was focused on rescuing those who could still be rescued, and doing whatever they could to make that happen. That might have been a farmer and his wife hiding a Jewish family in their barn, or an expert printer forging fake travel documents for a group of people so that they could make their way across the border to safety, or a factory owner convincing the German authorities that his employees were essential to the war effort in an effort to spare them from deportation to the death camps.

At the *Yad Vashem* Holocaust Memorial Museum in Jerusalem, Israel, the names of non-Jews who helped Jews in this way are inscribed on a Wall of the Righteous. There are more than 25,000 names on that wall, of whom 5,413 were Dutch citizens, not Jewish, and that is the highest number, per capita, of any European country. Some of these men and women survived the war; others were discovered, arrested, and killed. Seeing their names on the Wall reminds us that not everyone thought only of his or her own survival; that many risked their liberty and even their lives to protect and save their fellow human beings. These are the moral giants of their time; we will forever honor their memory.

This is the story of one man, Max Windmüller, one man among the millions caught up in the Nazi killing machine. When duty called, he did not step aside and say, "Let someone else do it." He stepped forward, risking his life, to save the lives of hundreds of his fellow Jews. His bravery did, in fact, cost him his life. Max Windmüller can truly be called a hero.

Max was not the kind of hero who leaped out from the safety of his foxhole and, against overwhelming odds, charged recklessly across an open field, bullets whizzing past him, and then killed dozens of enemy soldiers and singlehandedly captured scores of others. His heroism was of the quieter sort, the sort that doesn't make the headlines: Each day he put his life on the line, finding secure hiding places for Jewish children and leading them to safety in neutral countries.

When history books are written, they focus on kings and queens, presidents and generals, leaders of all kinds. All too often we forget that history is made by the small acts of heroism and the sacrifices of thousands of men and women. Max Windmüller was one such man. He deserves to be remembered for his bravery during the war, and for making the ultimate sacrifice of his life. Schoolchildren and their elders should learn his name and learn of his heroism as an example of what each of them has it in him, or her, to do if the circumstances require it.

Prologue

ᐧᕦᐧ

Renate Gierecke was taking her customary afternoon nap in her apartment in the Kreuzberg section of Berlin when the ringing of the telephone at her bedside jolted her awake. She fumbled for the receiver and mumbled her "Hallo?" She would later remind herself that the seemingly mundane episodes in our lives, like this telephone call, end up being the most memorable, the most change-producing.

The voice at the other end was that of her publisher, Hans-Jürgen Heilmann, or "H-J," as he liked to be called. Renate's first thought was that this was some trivial matter relating to that book of hers that was then in production, or perhaps he was calling to explain the delay in the payment of the royalties that were due her on her previous books. She was stretched thin financially; book advances and royalties were her only source of income.

Heilmann cme right to the point. "Renate," he said excitedly, "I have a new project for you, now that your last book has been put to bed. You'd be perfect for what I have in mind."

"And what would that be, H-J?" she asked, wary of new undertakings.

"In February 2000, there's an important anniversary coming up, and I want you to write the book that will celebrate that anniversary."

Renate wondered: A famous scientist? A writer? A politician?

Heilmann continued: "February seventh of that year will mark what would have been the 80th birthday of Max Windmüller."

"Max . . ." She hesitated. The name was unfamiliar; she was sure of that.

"Windmüller." Heilmann spelled it out for her. "Originally from Emden, right here in the northwest corner of Germany. A hero of the Jewish rescue-and-resistance movement in Holland during the war. He deserves to have a book written about his life and about his deeds, and I want you to write it. What I have in mind is a book aimed specifically at the young adult market, and you're the best of our writers in that niche. The anniversary is more than a year away, so there will be enough time to do the research and the writing and go through production."

As if anticipating her next question, he continued. "Don't worry about the financial issues, Renate." But, she thought to herself, would he give her an advance, an up-front payment? She wouldn't start out on this project without an assurance on that score. H-J must have been reading her mind. "You'll be well taken care of. Take my word for it, Renate." He named a sum as an advance that substantially exceeded any previous advance that she had received. "And I've developed a budget that includes reasonable travel expenses to Emden and to Israel, and, if necessary, even to the United States if you need to interview people there who knew Max. Just submit your expenses to us monthly, and you'll get the payment in the next mail."

She had never known Herr Heilmann to be so openhanded with his firm's money. It seemed to Renate that he was prepared to throw his firm's resources and his personal energy and prestige into this project and that she was to be the vessel that he had chosen to carry it out. She was flattered and intrigued, but she still had doubts.

"So many books on the Holocaust, H-J. Here in Germany, in Israel, in America, other countries. Do we really need one more book about the Holocaust?"

"It's true, there has been an outpouring of books over the last decade or two," he replied. "But many of them have been first-person books, written by survivors, now in their old age. This one, as I picture it, would be different, because Max did not survive. He died one week before the war ended, so it would have to be written from another viewpoint. How you do that, I'll leave to you."

Then, the obvious question: "Why me, of all your authors?"

"Why not you?" was his ready answer. "Your sales record shows that you speak the language that young readers understand. You have the ability to gain the confidence of the men and women you interview. Plus, you have a unique perspective because of your background. You're the obvious choice."

Renate, doubtful, needed to be persuaded. "Well, H-J, I'm not sure I have a unique perspective, and I'm certainly not a Holocaust expert. My books haven't been on that subject, and the truth is, I don't know much about it except what we were taught in the schools and what I heard at the dinnertable."

"*Macht nichts* [Doesn't matter], Renate. When you hear this . . ." He paused, searching for the right word, "this eyewitness testimony, when you learn more about Max and his rescue activities, you will feel compelled to share the story with others. Please do this, Renate. For me."

She was pleased with the compliments and honored by the urgent request, having worked these many years for this recognition. She found herself growing increasingly excited. "How much time do I have?"

"Naturally, we would like to have a draft back as soon as possible, but not at the expense of accuracy and completeness. Just check in with me once a month, say, and let me know how you're progressing."

"I'll do it!" she said excitedly. Perhaps, she later realized, she should have deliberated for a day or two, but her emotions had got the better of her.

"Wonderful!" Heilmann exclaimed. "I have collected some material on Max for you to read. It may give you a head start in your research on his life. You'll get it later today. I'll include the author-publisher contract as well." And with that, the call ended. Moments later, she remembered the overdue royalty check and cursed herself for not raising the matter while H-J was on the phone. Ah, well, next time. If he wanted the new book from her, he'd have to settle up on the old one.

Returning from her grocery run later that day, Renate noticed the bulky envelope leaning against the door, evidently delivered by courier. The logo and return address confirmed it was the material that Herr Heilmann had promised to send. "This man doesn't believe in wasting time," she told herself, with respect and admiration.

Renate didn't waste time, either. She opened the envelope right there at the kitchen table. On top of the papers was a piece of yellow memo paper signed "H-J," with two words: "Good luck!" She read the contents carefully: letters, photographs, newspaper articles, and more. It seemed to her in her reading that one name jumped out from these materials as a man who pioneered in preserving Max's memory for future generations. That was Klaus Meyer-van Dettum, a teacher at the *Hochschule* [high school] in Emden. When she had finished reading what her publisher had sent her, Renate came to a quick decision: She would call Meyer-van Dettum later that day and arrange an interview with him there in Emden.

The interview two weeks later exceeded her expectations. Meyer-van Dettum greeted her cordially and told her that he would give her whatever she needed to make this writing project a success. He was eager to cooperate in getting the Max Windmüller story out to a larger audience. He was particularly helpful in giving Renate the addresses and telephone numbers of the four men and women who were close to Max; these are the people, he said, whom she should immediately interview. They were Max's wartime sweetheart Metta Lande, now Shulamith Roethler, living in Tel Aviv; Max's cousins, Gustel and Sophie Nussbaum, who also lived in Israel, in Ramat Gan; and his long-time friend, Sigi Kirschner, now Professor Doctor Shimon Kirschner, who had shared his wartime experiences with Meyer-van Dettum and was now living in Haifa.

"If you like," said Meyer-van Dettum, "I will call Sigi to let him know that he can expect a telephone call from you."

She gratefully accepted his offer. "That's very generous of you."

She ended up spending the afternoon with Meyer-van Dettum, touring the sites in Emden that were important in understanding Max's childhood: his boyhood home at No. 44 *Mühlenstrasse* [Mill Street]; his father's butcher shop, on that same street at No. 4; and finally the site of the synagogue on the *Bollwerkstrasse*. That impressive building no longer existed; it had been destroyed on the night of November 9, 1938, the night we now call *Kristallnacht*—"the Night of the Broken Glass"—and there were not enough Jews left in Emden to justify the rebuilding of it.

Later that evening, the tour completed, Renate Gierecke boarded the plane back to Berlin, filled with affection for Klaus and with lofty expectations of her ability to write this book and do justice to its subject.

PART 1

The First Day

CHAPTER 1

The Story Begins: Emden, Germany, 1933

⁓

Driving in her rental car along Yefe Nof Street on Mount Carmel in Haifa, Renate Gierecke thought to herself, *This has to be one of the most beautiful urban streets in the world.* She was looking for No. 47, the address that Dr. Kirschner had given her over the telephone. Moments later she found it: a six-story apartment building, right there on the crest of Mount Carmel. She parked on the street alongside the building, took the elevator to the sixth floor, and encountered the man whom she had traveled to Israel to interview. "Dr. Kirschner? Herr Professor Doctor Kirschner?"

He smiled. "Please," he replied in flawless German, "we are here in Israel, not in Germany. You can call me Sigi. My friends do. And you are Frau Gierecke?"

"Renate Gierecke," she replied. "But if you are Sigi, then I am Renate. That's what my friends call me."

"Done," he said, cheerfully. His large frame filled the doorway. He stepped aside and motioned for Renate to enter. "Please," he said, showing her the way.

He led her out to the balcony. Standing at the railing, his hands on the rail, he beckoned Renate to join him. The view was stunning: the bay of Haifa in front of them, the teal-blue Mediterranean beyond. Directly below, the residential neighborhood of Mount Carmel and, beyond, the factories, the warehouses, the docks of this world-famous port.

A patrol boat, the Israeli flag fluttering briskly at its stern, was making its way out of the harbor, moving from right to left across their line of view. To Renate it seemed so theatrical; it was as if the scene had been staged for her benefit.

"Very impressive," she told Sigi. "More than impressive, it's powerfully moving, this view."

"Yes," said Sigi, "it is that for me every time I stand here. For me, especially, because this view in reverse is what my dear wife Minna and I saw when we arrived in what was then Palestine in January 1948. Of course, there were not then the high-rise hotels, the luxurious apartment houses, the office buildings and factories that we see now."

Renate looked at him silently, inviting him to continue.

"It hadn't been easy getting here. In our first try—Minna's and mine—we were passengers on an Italian two-masted schooner, converted to hold 647 Jewish refugees, all of us survivors of the Holocaust. As our ship approached the coast, it was intercepted by a British destroyer, forced to change course, and escorted to the island of Cyprus. We spent eleven months there in an internment camp before being allowed to emigrate to Palestine."

"At the first sight of the coast, when we were still a distance away, the cries went out, 'Palestine! *Eretz Israel!*' as we all rushed to the bow of the ship to get our first look. Some of us sank to our knees and cried tears of joy, others, the more religious of us, said an exultant prayer of thanksgiving, others broke out into the Zionist anthem, *Hatikvah.* An hour later, we landed right here, at the port of Haifa. Except for my years in medical school, it's been my home ever since."

Sigi had tried to be casual in welcoming Renate into his apartment, tried not to betray his excitement, his anticipation. But since Minna passed away three years earlier, he had felt keenly a sense of isolation, of life passing him by. Their two children lived their own lives some distance away. The older one, his son Chanan, lived in South Africa, working in bio-engineering. His daughter, Ayelet, was in London, married to a diplomat at the Israeli embassy there. They came to visit once a year at Passover. He had five grandchildren, but he saw them only with their parents, had never spent time with them alone. He tried to remind himself that he had much to be thankful for. In 1948, just months after his arrival in Palestine, he had begun his medical training at the newly established medical school at the Hebrew University in Jerusalem. He had practiced clinical medicine for thirty years; then, in 1979, when the Technion in Haifa established its medical school, he was invited to join its first faculty. Six years later, he had been named dean, and held that post until his retirement in 1990. As a physician and as a teacher, he had aimed high and had achieved everything that he had hoped for.

Then, as he considered the years since retirement and especially since Minna's death, his thoughts turned dark, as when a dark gray cloud moves in front of the sun. *I often feel,* he told himself, *like a piece of flotsam on a mountain stream. Once I was part of that stream, propelled forcefully on the swiftly flowing current. But then I was caught up in an eddy at the banks of the stream and soon I ended up cast onto dry land. Now I am dried out from long exposure to the sun. Yes,* he said to himself, *that's an apt metaphor for the way I feel now. I feel as if my story has ended.*

It wasn't his physical condition that prevented him from leading a more active life. "You're in good shape for a man of your age," his doctor had assured him. At age 78, he told himself, he was certainly not ready to "hang it up." He felt he had many good years left in him.

No, he realized, it was his social life, not his health, that needed attention. He was becoming too accustomed to his own company, to living in isolation here in this comfortable apartment. It seemed as if their friends, his and Minna's, were mostly her friends after all. Yes, yes, if he wanted an active social life, he would have to build it himself, he knew that: give parties, invite people over for cocktails, that kind of thing. But he just wasn't up for that. So his social life now was limited to the twice-a-month get togethers with former colleagues at the medical school, now also retired. He had looked forward to those luncheons, but now they had become stale, even tiresome. *Maybe it's the loner in me coming to the fore*, he thought. Minna was lively and outgoing; she enjoyed meeting new people, mingling with strangers. He pondered, *What would she have me do?* "Sigi, get up off your duff and get out there!"—that's what he heard her saying. He made up his mind to attend the next meeting of the retirees' group at the synagogue, but he had no high hopes that it would lead to anything.

Then his thoughts had turned, as they so often did, to his dear friend Max Windmüller and to Max's brother, Salomon (Salo), and to Schuschu and Nanno and the others, all of them long dead, victims of the Nazis. It had been their passionate dream to set foot on this soil, and they had sacrificed their lives for that dream. Were they somehow less worthy than he was? Of course not! It's been said many times, when speaking of those who had the courage and the strength, first to build this nation, the State of Israel, and then to turn back every attempt of its enemies to destroy it in its infancy, that present day Israelis "stand on the shoulders of giants." *How true*, Sigi said to himself, and, in his mind, that applied as well to Max, and to Salo, and to the others. He reminded himself, "*We who survived stand on their shoulders; for me, they, too, are giants.*"

Those thoughts, in turn, led him to the question he'd often asked himself: Am I worthy? Have I carried out my obligations as a survivor to those who did not survive? Old feelings of self-doubt, of inner conflict, welled up inside him. Had he been good enough as a husband to Minna, as a father to his children, as a citizen of his country? Whenever those questions rose up within him, he had tried to reassure himself: yes and yes and yes, but the disquiet remained.

And then, thinking those dark thoughts, he had received the telephone call from Berlin, from the German woman who introduced herself as Renate Gierecke. She had asked first if he were comfortable in carrying on their conversation in German. Perhaps she had in mind that he might be one of those Jews, formerly from Germany, who had vowed never to speak German again. He had set her mind at ease. "Why not?" he had said. "German is my native language. You don't forget the language of your childhood, but I should warn you, I haven't had the opportunity to speak it often here in Israel. So forgive me if I'm a bit rusty."

"I'm sure that that won't be a problem," she had answered, a laugh in her voice. Then she had explained the purpose of her call: "I'm a writer," she told him, "and I'm gathering material for a book about Max Windmüller. I've been told that you were a school chum of his. Is that right?"

"Yes, that's true," he had replied.

"And that you were at his side, more or less, throughout his life?"

"Yes, that's also true."

"Even when he died?"

"Yes."

"Then we must talk," she had said, with excitement in her voice, "and the sooner the better. You would be my best source of information for this book."

"Perhaps," he had responded. "The best source would have been Max himself, but he has been dead for fifty-three years, and many others who knew him have passed on since then. I'd be happy to tell you what I know about Max and his life, and perhaps I can lead you to others who might also be helpful. We're all getting on in years now."

He found himself looking forward to Renate's visit with mounting excitement. He saw it as a welcome break in his daily routine. He might now become less absorbed in his own life—his isolation—and more important in someone else's life. Maybe as a result of this visit that piece of flotsam that had been cast onto the streambank to dry would once again be caught up and swept forward in the mainstream of life.

Renate's telephone call had not come as a complete surprise. A week earlier, Sigi had received another call from Klaus in Emden, Germany, the city where he was born and had spent his earliest years. He had told Sigi that Renate had called him, knowing that he had a storehouse of information about Max. He, in turn, had put her onto Sigi as a longtime friend of Max's, and had given her his telephone number.

Now, with the two of them seated comfortably on Sigi's balcony, he invited Renate to tell him how she came to be there and where the idea for this book had come from.

"I can't claim to have originated the idea," she told him. "My publisher, Hans-Jürgen Heilmann, it was his idea. He discovered—I don't know where—that Max Windmüller, had he lived, would have celebrated his eightieth birthday on February 7, 2000—a year and a half from now. I guess he felt strongly that this important anniversary should not slip by, that it needed to be commemorated in some fashion. So early last month he called me up, told me over the phone that he had an idea for a book, and that I was the best person to write it."

"So he went on to tell me what he had in mind: a book for young adults about Max. He had surveyed the literature for that age group and found that there had been many books written by survivors, Jews who had been small children during the war and had been hidden by non-Jews during the war. There had been far fewer such books, he concluded, about the men and women who coordinated these hidden-child efforts and brought the children to safety. Max Windmüller had been one of those rescuers, and he felt that the year, 2000, the eightieth anniversary of his birth, would be a good time to bring such a book to market. Herr Heilmann then told me about Max, who he was, and what he had done to rescue young people during the war. It was clear to me," Renate said, "that Herr Heilmann had researched the man's life thoroughly and wanted very much to get this book written."

"But why did he pick *you*?" Sigi asked.

"I asked him that same question. His answer was, 'Frau Gierecke, you are one of our most popular writers. You are uniquely qualified to reach that audience of younger readers to whom we're trying to appeal.' I demurred, telling him that there were several other writers whom I could name, who were just as qualified as I. He would have none of that."

"What did he mean by 'uniquely qualified'?"

"He cited my earlier books, going back to when I wrote my first novel twelve years ago. They had sold well. Herr Heilmann assumed from my publishing history that I had a wide audience of readers who would eagerly await my next book."

"And why a book specifically for those younger readers?" Sigi persisted.

"Because Max was in that age group during the war, twenty years old when the war began, and Herr Heilmann hoped that young readers would identify with him and be inspired by what he accomplished."

"I can understand that reasoning. If I were a young reader, I would want to live as he did."

Renate continued, "I pretended that I was still reluctant to take this project on, but inwardly I was excited by the prospect. So Herr Heilmann, noticing my hesitation, told me that his company would make it financially worthwhile."

"In the end, I said I would do it, not just because of the money, but because Max's story, as Herr Heilmann had presented it, intrigued me. Max Windmüller was someone I could admire, and I agreed with Herr Heilmann that he was someone whom young men and women would look up to, or should look up to."

Sigi tried to appear calm, ready to cooperate. But inside he shared Renate's enthusiasm for this project. In the 53 years since Max's death, there had been only one book written about him, and that one with only limited circulation. By writing this book, Renate would assure that her readers of every age would become acquainted with Max, and understand him and his times, and he, Sigi, was in a position to help her. Finally, he mused with mounting excitement, Max's life story would be in the competent hands of a professional writer, someone who was intent on researching her subject thoroughly, and he would be, perhaps, her most important resource.

For many years, Sigi had wanted to write a biography of Max, but some outside event had always intervened, and the book he had hoped to write still lay, far from completed, in a file drawer in his office. He had given up hope that the story of Max Windmüller would ever be written, by him or by anyone else, and then he had received that surprising telephone call from Berlin. He hadn't wanted to get his hopes up for fear of being disappointed, but now he had a feeling of intense satisfaction that there might be a role for him, a major role, in Frau Gierecke's project.

So now this Renate Gierecke was sitting out here on the balcony with him. His first impression, seeing her in the doorway to his apartment, had been of a young woman, perhaps in her mid- to late-30s, attractive in what he thought of as a Germanic way with light brown eyes and reddish-brown hair worn loose to the shoulders, wearing large round eyeglasses with pink-tinged frames. Casting a discreet glance at her left ring finger, he saw no ring, only an emerald ring on the middle finger. Single then, maybe divorced? He chided himself. Why should he, nearly 80 years old, care about her marital status? But it's all too true: old habits die hard. Then another question came to mind: Was she Jewish? Her name wasn't, he was sure of that. But her coloring, her features? He couldn't rule it out. Maybe, later, there would be a more appropriate time for those kinds of questions.

With both of them seated comfortably on the balcony, Sigi felt that it was up to him to start the conversation. So, he greeted her in what he hope was his warmest, most sociable tone, "Welcome to Haifa, Frau Gierecke!"

She smiled, a bright friendly smile, "I'm delighted to be here, but remember, we are Renate and Sigi. Or do you prefer to stand on formality?"

"Not at all, Renate." Sigi liked that name—Renate. He sounded it out in his head. It had a solid German middle-class ring to it. And he was not surprised by her question about standing on formality. Here in Israel and elsewhere around the world, German Jews had a reputation for exaggerated politeness, for insisting on observing the formalities. Other Jews put them down as "Yekkes," a name said to be derived from the word *Jacke* or jacket, a reference to their supposed insistence on wearing coats and ties when everyone around them was wearing a short-sleeved shirt open at the throat. Sigi took satisfaction now from showing Renate that he didn't fit into that long-held stereotype.

He told her, "I'm happy to help you in your research on Max Windmüller. I have wanted for so many years to write a book about him, but it never happened, and, at my age, it probably won't happen, so I happily pass on the torch to you."

"Let's save the celebrations for when the book actually comes out," Renate replied. "A lot can happen between now and then."

"I take your point," he answered. "I have published several books in my time and started some that were never finished."

"Then we understand each other." Renate paused, then continued with a business-like air: "So let's get started, shall we?"

She went on to explain that the interview they were about to embark on was crucial to her story because of Sigi's close relationship with Max. She didn't say it, but Sigi knew what she was thinking: *I'd better get his story while this man is still alive and thinking straight.* He could understand that; he was Max's age, had celebrated his 78th birthday the past February. He and Max were born just three days apart; they were practically twins. Sigi was pleased to reassure Renate that he was in good health and that his recollection of events that had taken place decades earlier was still sharp.

He thought back now to that unfinished manuscript, stacked now with other papers in his lower-right desk drawer. In the mid-1980s, he had planned to write a book about his wartime experiences, about the rescue operations that he and Max had undertaken during the Holocaust. But right about that time, he had received his long-awaited appointment as dean of the medical school at the Technion, and the pressures of the new job had forced him to shelve his plans to write that book. He had never returned to the writing of it, one of several such projects that were launched but never completed. Now he took the measure of her, assessing her over his eyeglasses. *Does this young woman have the skill and perseverance that I didn't have, to see this project through to completion?* He was optimistic on that score. Certainly he would do what he could to make it happen.

So now she was sitting next to him, her reporter's notepad on her lap. On the coffee table between them was a leatherbound family photo album. He hadn't looked at it in many years, but he had brought it out today, thinking that he'd show the old photos to Renate; maybe she could use them in her book. Also on that table was a small tape recorder. He had given Renate permission to put it there, and to use it. Why not? It was important that she get the story right, and, if she were to quote him, to get the words down just as he had spoken them to accurately convey his message to her readers.

At his feet was a file folder of letters and documents; yes, his memory for those long ago events was good but not perfect, and he would need to refer to the papers in the file from time to time to get the important facts right. Perhaps he wouldn't be able to find in the file folder the exact information that he needed, but still, having it there would be a comfort to him, and it would give Renate the confidence that he took seriously his responsibilities as an informant.

Renate tapped the "On" switch on the tape recorder and, speaking in German, began. "I am Renate Gierecke, and I'm here in Haifa, Israel, speaking to Herr Professor Doctor Sigmund Kirschner, the retired dean of the Technion University Medical School. Today is Monday, April 20, 1998."

Then, continuing in her professional interviewer voice, she began. "So Sigi, please tell us your full name, your age, and your story, from the beginning."

Sigi sat up in his chair and, with as firm a voice as he could muster, began the story.

"I'm seventy-eight years old. My name here in Israel is Shimon Kirschner. At my circumcision, when I was eight days old, my parents gave me Shimon as my Hebrew name, and when I came to Palestine, fifty-one years ago, I simply took my Hebrew name as my new name, signifying the new life I would lead in what was then called Palestine. But my German name, the one I was born with, was Sigmund. Growing up in Germany, everyone called me Sigi, and even here in Israel, I'm still Sigi. So, yes, you can call me Sigi, too."

"Okay, Sigi, so you were born—"

He broke in, not waiting for her to finish. "I was born, as Max was, in the city of Emden, in the northwest corner of Germany, right on the North Sea. I would probably still be there today if it hadn't been for . . ." His voice trailed off, his thoughts reeling back to his childhood, to his parents and grandparents, his sisters, Hannah and Sarah, and to his dear friend, Max Windmüller.

How many times had he thought of them, in good times and bad? Their faces materialized, eerily, before his eyes. They were dead now, these many years, gone years before their time at the hands of the Nazi murderers. Why was he one of the few, the fortunate ones, who survived? Why had God picked him to stay alive and marked them for early death? Why had He not protected them, as He had protected him? Over and over, his thoughts traveled along these well-worn paths. Why was he here, looking out at the sun-dappled waves of the Mediterranean Sea, and they, his family, their bodies reduced to ashes in the camps, and Max, his remains reburied in the 1950's in a common grave with many others on the grounds of a former death camp in southeastern Germany? He asked himself these questions, and knew that they were unanswerable. He had asked them a thousand times over these last 50-plus years, and still the tears welled up in his eyes as the dead came alive once again in his mind's eye.

Renate, seeing the tears, reached over to hand him a clean white handkerchief. He used it to dab at his eyes, trying to collect himself and continue with his narrative. Renate, this attractive, healthy young woman, hadn't come all this way to see him lose control of his emotions. She had come to hear him tell his story, and he welcomed the opportunity to tell it to her and to thousands, maybe hundreds of thousands, of men, women, and children all over the world. So he picked up the glass of Evian water from the table in front of him, sipped from it slowly, meditatively, and took a deep breath, trying to calm his racing emotions.

"Sigi," said Renate solicitously, "I know this is hard for you. Are you up to doing this?"

"It isn't easy, but, yes, I can do it."

"Then please continue."

Sigi was grateful that instead of showing irritation at the delay, this young woman understood completely his state of mind and was giving him time to collect his thoughts.

"You know," he said, "in preparation for this interview, I've given a lot of thought to my life, and Max's, about what we did and didn't do, and how it might have been different if we had made other choices. Life is all about making choices, isn't it? You choose a wife, or you decide that this person is not the right one for you. You choose a career, a place to live, whether to have children and how many, and of course you hope you're making the right choice, but only time will tell, and you have to live with the choices that you make."

Renate interjected, "But surely you will agree that in many cases we can make the most intelligent choices and still find our destiny is governed by outside forces over which we have little or no control. That was true for the Jews who were stranded in Central Europe and were eventually rounded up and killed in the death camps. They had no choice in the matter."

"Of course you're right," Sigi replied. "Free choice has its limits. But to make no choice, to submit to destiny—that's a choice, too. My father told me, resignedly, 'What the Lord tells you to do, you have to do. We must let destiny work its will.' He was one of the fortunate ones. He died before the war. But so many others, young and old . . . Destiny, as they called it, awaited them in the gas chambers at Auschwitz Birkenau."

He paused, momentarily overcome by sadness at the thought, then resumed. "But those of us who were younger, and physically fit, we chose not to submit to the Nazi killing machine. So to live is to choose. Moreover," he said forcefully, "to choose, to make a choice and then act on that choice, is the mark of a free man. A slave has no free will. He does what he is ordered to do by his master."

Sigi pulled out from the folder a copy of a letter that Max wrote to his younger brother Emil in June 1944, and read from it: "I will not bow my head before the scum of the earth. I have the will and I'm obligated to use it right to the end." Sigi added, speaking forcefully, "That principle guided Max's life— and mine, too."

Then, as if to lend moral authority to that position, Sigi continued, "It reminds me of one of the choruses from George Frideric Handel's *Judas Maccabaeus* oratorio. The Greeks of that time, in the second century BCE, were trying to tyrannize the Jews into abandoning their faith. Handel has the Jews sing—and he sang it softly for Renate—"'We never never will bow down we never never will bow down to the rude stock . . .'" As an aside, he said to Renate, "Handel is referring, of course, to the Greeks of that time, but it could easily apply to the Nazis as well." And then he continued, half-singing, half-speaking, and pounding on each syllable for emphasis: 'We worship God and God alone.' Nothing has changed in more than 2,000 years," Sigi mused.

"Yes, I'm familiar with that chorus," says Renate. "I remember singing it in high school. It's an admirable statement, one that might come from oppressed people in every century, and it's especially meaningful coming from Max. Other men and women would have submitted and resigned themselves to their fate."

Sigi felt a warm glow welling up inside him. He was beginning to regard this woman as a kindred soul.

Renate set him on the desired course, *her* desired course. "Why don't you begin by setting the scene for us? Talk about Emden, your early recollections."

It occurred to Sigi that she probably knew more about his home-town, Emden, than she was letting on, but he could take nothing for granted. "You'll want your readers to know about Emden. It's a small city, a seaport, strategically located right on Germany's western border, its border with Holland. It's a coastal town on the North Sea, and it's due north, about 150 miles, from Germany's heavy-manufacturing center, the Ruhr Valley. That's important, because at the end of the nineteenth century, a canal was built connecting Emden with the Ruhr, so that steel and coal could be shipped from the Ruhr to Emden, and from there to every corner of the world. Today Emden is a major manufacturing center, with a Volkswagen assembly plant, and it's also a major shipbuilding center, where ships are built for both civilian and military uses."

"What can you tell us about the Jews of Emden?" Renate asked.

"There was a Jewish community going back to at least the late 1500's," he answered. "Most of them were Ashkenazi—that means they came from Germany and other countries in Central and Eastern Europe—but many came by ship from Spain and Portugal or from across the border in Holland. We referred to them as *Sephardim*—that's the Hebrew word for Spaniards. Many Spanish and Portuguese Jews had come to Holland to escape Spanish persecution during the Inquisition, and their descendants had continued to live there or had migrated across the border to Germany."

"When I was a child, growing up in Emden, we had about 1,000 Jews in the city, out of a total population of 34,000. To put that number in perspective, the Jewish population of Emden as a percentage of the total was the same percentage as the number of Jews in Berlin to the total population of that city before Hitler came to power. We had a large, beautiful synagogue, a Jewish school, and every kind of social club and welfare organization for boys and girls, for men and women, and for the elderly. At the same time, our parents never thought of themselves as isolated from the city around them. We were Emdeners through and through, completely integrated into the political and cultural life of the city."

"What happened to the Jewish community in the Holocaust?"

"In the first year after the Nazis came to power, about half of the community left Emden and emigrated to other countries," Sigi told her. "Another twenty-five percent of them left later in the 1930's. By the time the war broke out in 1939, only a quarter of the former Jewish population remained, mainly the elderly and infirm. They were deported to the East and killed there. Of those who survived, most of us are here in Israel, or in England or the United States."

"Emden is also well-known to Holocaust historians," Sigi continued, "as the site of a displaced persons camp, notorious as the place to which some twenty-five hundred men, women, and children who had been passengers on the SS *Exodus* were returned in November 1947 after the ship was intercepted on its way to Palestine and the passengers brought back to Germany. That camp didn't close down until October 1948, when the last of the Jews interned there left for Israel."

". . . and in Emden today?" Renate asked.

"Almost nothing remains of the once-thriving Jewish community there. A handful of Jewish families, yes, but none of them with roots in our pre-war Jewish community. No synagogue, no regular Jewish worship services, no social institutions. It's very sad."

"Perhaps this book that I'm writing, and the books that others will write, will change that," Renate said.

"Let's hope so. That would be wonderful."

"So, Sigi, you've set the scene, so to speak. Why don't you tell us your story and Max Windmüller's?"

Sigi poured himself another cup of coffee, drank most of it, and took a few deep breaths to calm himself down. He gazed at the wide expanse of the Mediterranean before him and began. He was no longer in Haifa, on the sixth floor of this apartment building, the city below, the bay and the sea beyond. In his imagination, it was April 1933, and he was back in Emden, at the house on *Mühlenstrasse* where he grew up. Max lived two doors away, at No. 44, so they were not only almost-twins, but neighbors and the closest of friends as well. Sigi's father was an accountant, serving mostly lower-middle-class clients—shopkeepers and the like; his mother was a homemaker.

Two months earlier, when he had turned 13, his family had celebrated his Bar Mitzvah, his coming of age ceremony, in the synagogue at No. 50 *Bollwerkstrasse*. Max had been there, too, and his family. Max, three days older than he, had been at the synagogue for his own Bar Mitzvah the previous week. Together they had spent many hours with Mr. Gottschalk, their *melamed*, their teacher, to practice their Torah reading.

After Sigi's Bar Mitzvah ceremony, Max and his family had come to the Kirschner house for a small celebration, just as Sigi and his family had been to Max's house a week earlier. There had been short speeches—Sigi's father had proposed a toast in his son's honor, and the rabbi, Samuel Blum, had come up and told Sigi how proud he was of him. It had all been joy and lilting laughter on that day, people saying kind things to him, and many of the guests had left a small present for him on the table by the front door.

"I have a clear recollection of the little reception at our house on the day of my Bar Mitzvah," Sigi told Renate. "I was a shy lad, bookish, you might say. Max, even then at thirteen, was cheerful and gregarious. He could move comfortably through a crowd and had a way of putting people at ease. So there I was in the living room, standing at the edge of the crowd, watching, even though I was, so to say, the guest of honor, while Max moved from one cluster of guests to another. I remember being jealous that afternoon, wishing I had Max's smoothness with people."

Everything was coming back now, from that fateful spring of 1933, the details crowding in his brain, spilling out into his narrative. So, the words tumbling out, Sigi continued:

"My Bar Mitzvah should have been an occasion for joy and satisfaction, the high point in any young boy's life to that time, but events outside the walls of our house didn't permit us that unbridled joy. Just weeks earlier, on January 30, 1933, President Paul von Hindenburg had named the Nazi party leader, Hitler, as chancellor. With that appointment, the Nazis had gained control of the government apparatus. Earlier, in 1932, we had heard Hitler's rantings on the radio as he crisscrossed Germany by airplane, arguing his case before the German people. He had been telling his enthusiastic audiences that we Jews were not true Germans, that we were an alien growth, a malignant tumor on the healthy German body, that there was no place for Jews in the Germany of the future."

"That can't be true, we told ourselves. For generations, we had thought of ourselves not as German Jews, but as Germans of the Jewish faith, just as our neighbors were Germans of the Catholic faith, or in communion with the Evangelical faith. But we were all Germans to the core! So it wasn't just a question of words, it went to the very essence of who we were. My father and both my uncles had fought for the Kaiser, the German ruler, in the First World War, which ended in 1918, two years before I was born."

Sigi opened a small wooden box that was resting on the coffee table. "Here," he said, "take a look at this." Resting on a blue velvet pad inside the box was the Iron Cross, with its pale blue ribbon, that his Uncle Albert won for bravery at the first battle of the Somme in 1916. "Ten months later," Sigi said, "Uncle Albert was killed in action on the Russian front." Renate looked at the medal appreciatively, then handed it back to him. He continued: "Two years earlier, Moritz Windmüller's brother Max had been killed, also on the Eastern front, at the Battle of Tannenberg. Moritz gave his son that name, Max, to preserve his brother's memory. He and Uncle Albert were among the 12,000 Jewish soldiers who died fighting for their German Fatherland in World War I."

"Among them were ten local boys, Jews from Emden, killed in combat in the Great War. Surely, theirs was no trivial sacrifice! Had they then, died for an ignoble cause? Had they died in vain? You could never tell their families that! But to Hitler and his Nazi henchmen, their heroism was irrelevant—they were, after all, only Jews."

"The Kirschners had lived in Germany for generations. That was true of the Windmüllers, as well. Max had once shown me a letter of protection that his ancestor, Levi Windmüller, had received from the Duke of Sachsen-Anhalt, guaranteeing him and his family the legal status of *Schutzjude,* 'protected Jew'. The letter was dated April 4, 1735, 200 years before! And going back even further, the first list of *Schutzjuden,* Jews under the protection of the Count of East Friesland, was published in 1589! The Jews of that earlier time had to pay a fee to obtain their protection, but they certainly earned it!"

"Max used to say, 'Why should the Emden Jews and Jews elsewhere in Germany be told that their centuries-long history in Germany was of no significance? Why were they being pushed into a particular pigeonhole, identified by their religious belief and not by their nationality? That's what this crazy man was saying—that we weren't true Germans. We were certainly more German than he was—he was born and raised in Austria!"

Sigi recalled, "I remember how, back then, when Hitler was campaigning across Germany on behalf of his Nazi party, our family clustered around our radio, listening intently to still another one of his rants, and how my father exploded in anger, *'Der Mann ist aber völlig verrückt!'"* —'The man is completely crazy!'"

"There were some in our little Jewish community in Emden who, priding themselves on their German-ness, said, 'The German people will never accept this man as their leader; he and his followers are too radical.' That changed on Election Day, March 5, 1933, when Hitler and his Nazi party won a plurality of the seats in the Reichstag, the German parliament, and formed a coalition with other German rightist parties to gain a majority. That gave the Nazis and their allies full control over the country's destiny—and ours. It all came as a devastating shock to my father and to many other Jews. How can it be? they asked. How could so many Germans vote for the National Socialists, the Nazis, and their madman-leader, Hitler? It was incomprehensible."

"So the mood in our community was somber and uncertain. What ought we to do in the face of this threat? Should we ride it out, hoping that the German people would come to their senses and throw this man out? Or should we be realists and start making plans for a life elsewhere, beyond the reach of this man and his fanatical supporters? Were we prepared to pay the cost of going into exile, of starting over in a strange land, of leaving behind our loved ones, our livelihood, and everything we had built up over so many generations? That was an excruciatingly difficult decision to make. So, in those early years of the regime, the prevailing attitude was one of watchful waiting. As my father told us at the dinner table one evening, 'We are not idiots. We Jews know what danger is. But we're not panicking yet. We will wait and see, and be ready to respond in whatever way we need to, when the time comes.'"

Renate broke in, changing the subject. "Sigi, what was it like to go to school in those years? Were you exposed to anti-Semitism from your classmates and teachers?"

"You have to remember," Sigi replied, "that Max and I and most of the Jewish kids of our age in Emden didn't go to the public school that the other boys attended. We went to the *Jüdische Volkschule*, the Jewish school next door to the synagogue. So at least inside our school, we were not exposed to the slurs and the insults that became routine for the few Jewish kids who attended the public school. I had a neighbor, though, a boy my age, who had gone to the public school on the *Bollwerkstrasse* until his parents, responding to his pleas, pulled him out of that school and put him in our school. And he wasn't the only one. There were many others who came into our school like that, so many that our school set up a special program for them, because, coming in at the age of thirteen or fourteen, they had not studied Hebrew as thoroughly as we had, and didn't have the same fluency in it as we did."

"In our classroom at the Jewish school, over the blackboard, there was a large framed photo portrait of Theodor Herzl, the founder of modern-day Zionism, and another one of Rabbi Jacob Emden (1697–1776), the greatest rabbi who ever held the pulpit in our city. Ludwig—the boy who came over from the public school—told me that in his classroom in the *Bollwerkstrasse* school, there had been in former years on the wall over the blackboard a big photo portrait of Heinrich Brüning, the German chancellor, Then, when Ludwig came back to school on a Monday morning in 1933, that portrait had been taken down and a photo of Adolf Hitler was there in its place, with ribbons in the Nazi colors, red, white, and black, draped across one corner of the framed portrait."

"In the schoolyard, where formerly they had practiced soccer and volleyball, Ludwig and his classmates were made to march around with their arms outstretched, practicing the Hitler salute. Every morning, at the start of the school day, they were ordered to stand at attention alongside their desks and sing the German national anthem, 'Das Deutschland Lied.' Then, when the last note had been sung, the teacher, Frau Eberhard, raised her right arm in the Hitler salute, and the students did likewise, shouting 'Heil Hitler!' as they did so. Only Ludwig kept his arm at his side. His parents had forbidden him from raising his arm as his classmates did. That made him a marked man, so to say, in the eyes of his teacher and his schoolmates."

"Matters got worse for him over time. Frau Eberhard took to wearing a swastika pin on her dresses and moved Ludwig from the second row to the back row. When he raised his hand to answer a question, she would pretend not to see him and call on another student for the answer. Worst of all, his classmates, who were formerly friendly to him, didn't speak to him anymore and froze him out of their schoolyard sports. That's when he begged his parents to pull him out of that school."

"We at the Jewish school didn't have to deal with all of that. But you couldn't insulate yourself from what was happening on the outside. After all, Emden was not such a large city, and the Jewish population still smaller."

"We Jewish kids all knew each other, and the boys our age, the ones who weren't Jewish, knew who we were, too. In winter, they would hang around the entrance to our school, and in the late afternoon when we came out, they would pelt us with snowballs and hurl anti-Semitic insults at us. '*Jude, raus!*'"—Jew, get out!—"they would call out, and other words much more hurtful and disgusting."

"And there was no point in filing a complaint with the authorities, I suppose," Renate said.

"We learned that early on. Some of their own sons were the worst of the anti-Semitic bullies! No, the so-called 'authorities' would be the last ones you could rely on to intervene. We Jewish kids learned at a young age what Jews have always known down through the centuries: If you want to get something done, you have to do it yourself. There's no one else to do it for you."

"This new Germany was certainly not the Germany we had grown up in and loved as our native land. Once the Nazis came to power and Adolf Hitler was installed as chancellor, things changed for the worse almost overnight. One hammer blow fell after another. On February 27, 1933, the Reichstag, the German parliament building, was put to the torch. The new Nazi government accused a young Dutch communist of committing the crime and arrested and executed him. Then on April 1, 1933, the Nazis called for a boycott of Jewish-owned stores and businesses. Every day of that first spring after the Nazis came to power, we read of the arrests of social-ists, communists, trade union leaders, and anyone who had spoken against the new regime. Leading citizens of Emden, men who spoke at campaign rallies on behalf of the Socialists, like Victor Mehlmann, were overnight rounded up, forced to stand on the back of a truck like so many head of cattle, and carted off to the concentration camps."

"Suddenly we Jews felt like we had been pushed into a corner, no room to move, no room to maneuver. We could see the change on the familiar streets of Emden. Germans, Jews, and non-Jews alike used to greet each other with a hearty *Guten Morgen* and a firm handshake. Now non-Jews greeted each other with the right arm outstretched and a vigorous *Heil Hitler*! We Jews, when they passed us on the street, were greeted with stony silence. We were forbidden to walk in the streets of Emden and other German cities except on designated days, called *Judentage,* or Jew days, and we had to be off the streets entirely by eight o'clock in winter and nine o'clock in summer."

"On city lampposts where the red, yellow, and black flag of the Weimar Republic had flown, the red and white Nazi flag, with the black *Hakenkreuz*, the swastika, emblazoned in the center, fluttered in its place. The worst for me was that some of the older boys were now wearing the uniform of the *Hitler Jugend*, the Hitler Youth, with a swastika armband. They would all go off together on weekend camping trips. On Saturdays, on our Sabbath, they marched down Emden's main street, the *Neutorstrasse*, singing their vulgar Nazi songs."

"On the walls of buildings along the main commercial streets and on the official bulletin board that stood in front of Emden's

City Hall, there were posters that shrieked out, '*Der Jude ist unser Unglück!*' 'The Jew is our misfortune'! Underneath was a cartoon caricature of a Jew, a man with an enormous nose, thick lips, hairs sprouting from his nose and ears. Sometimes he was shown holding bags full of money, sometimes he was shown leering at or clutching a young blond, evidently pure, Aryan girl. I didn't know any Jew who looked like this caricature, not my parents or aunts and uncles, not my Jewish neighbors, not the rabbi. Back then, when I still had hair . . .," Sigi smiled, a self-mocking smile, "my hair was blond, and I still have the same gray-green eyes. Max's hair was light brown, and he had blue eyes. You wouldn't have been able to tell us apart, just by looking at us, from non-Jewish boys of our age, and we certainly didn't look like the caricature Jew that we saw in those posters or in the Nazi newspaper, *Der Stürmer,* that was now being peddled on the streets of Emden."

Sigi turned to Renate and asked, "Is this a good time to look at the album?"

She said with a reassuring smile, "Of course, if you want. I'd be very interested." So Sigi opened it to the very first photo, a Kirschner family portrait, all of them posing formally in Herr Kondracke's studio on the *Neutorstrasse*. Sigi recalled that his parents had had the photo taken to send to the cousins in London. Sitting ramrod straight in the front row, middle, was his father, Gustave August, with his arms outstretched, one hand on each knee, and, next to him, his beloved mother, Lotte, both of them well-dressed, his mother with her favorite string of pearls around her neck. His sisters, Hanne and Sarah, wearing their Sabbath best, stood behind their parents. At the upper left was Sigi. If the deceased were marked with X's, then every one of these faces, except his, would have an X across it, because they were all gone now; none of them had survived the war. Sigi's mother, of blessed memory, was deported directly to Auschwitz, and was probably killed there immediately on her arrival. His two sisters were taken first to Westerbork, the transit camp in Holland, and from there to Auschwitz.

Sigi turned the pages of the album. He was looking for the photo of the two friends, Max and himself, taken at the beach on the island of Borkum, a short ferry ride away from Emden. Max's family and his, the Windmüllers and the Kirschners, had vacationed there for four days in the summer of 1931. "I'm sure you know, Renate," he said, "that Borkum still today calls itself 'the pearl of the North Sea,' but it was far from that for us, and for other Jews, in those days."

First, Sigi felt that he had to explain to Renate how it happened that they had chosen to vacation on Borkum. Even before the Nazis came to power, Borkum had a reputation all over Germany as a hotbed of anti-Semitism. Jewish organizations had issued travel advisories, strongly suggesting that Jews stay away from that island so as to avoid the hostility of the other vacationers. Twenty years earlier, in 1911, a British travel writer had described Borkum as "the one spot on earth from which Jews are banished."

Sigi picked up the narrative for Renate. "Even though they were aware of this long tradition, our parents decided to go ahead anyway. Because of the economic depression that was then gripping Germany and the whole world, my father's practice had fallen off, our income had dropped sharply, so we could save money by taking our holiday on Borkum, which was nearby, instead of at one of the more remote North Sea islands that we formerly went to. Our parents also calculated that we didn't have Jewish names, and we didn't have the facial features and coloring that other Germans identified as Jewish, so that we wouldn't be calling attention to ourselves as Jews. The larger hotels on the island were known to be unwelcoming to Jewish guests, so the two families, mine and Max's, booked rooms at a small hotel on the outskirts of the town."

"It turned out that the warnings issued by the Jewish organization about what Jews might encounter on Borkum were well-founded. As soon as we stepped off the ferry onto the island, we were greeted by a large sign that announced, "*JUDEN SIND HIER UNER-BETENE GÄSTE*"—"Jews are uninvited guests here." Then, walking with our suitcases from the ferry slip along *Bismarckstrasse* to our hotel, we passed stores with signs in their display windows saying, JEWS NOT WANTED AS CUSTOMERS HERE and NO ENTRANCE HERE FOR DOGS AND JEWS. Not wanting me to see those signs, my mother rushed me past them, telling me that we were in a hurry, but she didn't succeed entirely, and we children, Max and I and our brothers and sisters, did see them."

"So Jews were no better than dogs? Even worse was the song we heard sung on our last evening on the island. We were at a public concert on the promenade that runs along the beachfront, all of us standing under the trees at the edge of the crowd but enjoying the music. Then, at the end of the program, more or less like an encore, the orchestra started playing a few measures of a piece that was unfamiliar to us but very familiar to the others in the audience. The chorus on stage picked up the words, and the onlookers joined in with gusto, the conductor turning sideways to lead the orchestra, the chorus and the audience in the song."

Borkum beachfront, 1930's.

Sigi sang it for Renate, the words coming back easily to him:

> The one who approaches [Borkum]
> with flat feet, with crooked nose and kinky hair
> must not be allowed to enjoy your beach.
> He must get out! He must get out! Out!

"I found out later that the song was known throughout Germany as *'Das Borkum Lied,'* the Borkum song. The government had tried to prohibit the singing of it, but the men and women of Borkum and the non-Jewish guests had continued to sing it in defiance of that order."

"Back then, in 1931, as the *'Borkum Lied'* ended with the last words barked out, *'Er muß hinaus! Hinaus!'* the people on the green dispersed with happy faces, but we, the Kirschners and the Windmüllers, walked quietly and somberly back to our hotel, alone with our thoughts. We were glad to get the ferry back to Emden the next day. Until that holiday on Borkum, I don't think any of us, adults or children, understood the depths of German Jew-hatred.

And bear in mind," Sigi said, "that this was in 1931, two years before Hitler came to power. But it should not have come as a surprise. Jew-hatred had flourished in Germany for centuries, long before Hitler came on the scene."

"Needless to say, we never went back to Borkum. We didn't know it then, but those few days in Borkum were to be our last extended holiday in Germany. But I don't want to leave the impression that our Borkum vacation was a complete disaster for us, that the anti-Semitism we encountered there was all there was to it."

Sigi returned to the photo album to show Renate the photo of the two youngsters, Max and himself, standing arm in arm on the beach, two confident-looking boys grinning broadly at the camera. There was an inscription scrawled across the lower right-hand corner, 'For Sigi—friends yesterday, friends today, friends always—Max.' And it was true. We remained the closest of friends for the rest of his life."

Renate nudged Sigi gently back to the subject. "So, Dr.—."

He interrupted her gently, "It's Sigi. Remember? We're on first-name terms."

"Of course. Forgive me." She went on, "Sigi, you have mentioned Max's father, Moritz, several times. What was his line of work?"

"He was in the meat trade. He had a butcher shop, selling meat at retail, but he was also a middleman, if you will, buying cattle from one farmer and selling it to another. The word for men in that business, for Moritz Windmüller and others in that trade, was *Viehhändler*, cattle deal-ers. That was a very common business for Jews in that part of Germany. Moritz's father and grandfather before him had been in that trade."

"And after your Bar Mitzvahs, Sigi, did you and Max continue with your Jewish education, or did it end there?"

"Both of us continued at the Jewish school," Sigi replied. "But you have to understand that there was a wide spectrum of Jewish beliefs in Emden, as elsewhere in Germany. My family was quite religious. We tried to keep Saturday, the Jewish Sabbath, as a holy day of rest. We kept kosher—that means that we didn't eat pig meat or shellfish, we didn't mix dairy products with meats, and we kept separate dishes and silverware for meat and dairy. We went frequently to the synagogue on Saturday, but not *every* Saturday, and on religious holidays. I myself had, and still have, a strong belief in God, in a Higher Power, who makes himself manifest in everything we do and say. With Max and his family, well, they were more relaxed about their Jewishness. They were Jews—there was never any question about that—but they weren't as observant, as traditional, you might say, as we were. It was rumored in our little community that Max's father wasn't above buying a pig from a local farmer and slaughtering it at his butcher shop, then selling the pork chops to non-Jewish customers at the back door. As for Max, he used to tease me about my strongly held belief in the divine. He would express some irritation with me and then say something like, 'Sigi, remember: God helps those who help themselves, so don't wait for guidance from *HaShem*—just do what you think is right.' That was his philosophy, and it served him well, I must say."

Sigi decided at that point to emphasize his similarities with Max, not their differences, so he changed course. "But regardless of the differences in our religious beliefs, everyone in our families, Max's and mine, were ardent Zionists. From our earliest years, our parents taught us that Palestine was our Jewish homeland, that it should be every Jew's goal to make *Aliyah*—that means, literally, to move up, but in the Zionist world it means to move from wherever the Jew was living, anywhere in the world, to Palestine—because only in Palestine would Jews be free of persecution. But there was more to it than that, as we learned at home and at our school. Palestine was our

Promised Land, the land that God had promised, first to Abraham and then to Moses. So in going to Palestine, Jews were fulfilling that Biblical prophecy."

"Both of us." he continued, "received a solid Jewish education at the *Jüdische Volkschule,* the Jewish School, and we were thoroughly imbued with the Zionist spirit. At the same time, we had strong left-wing political beliefs, even as youngsters. We believed that Socialism offered the only answer to the increasing power of Nazism. We were not going to sit calmly and watch the Nazi mob control the streets. So within a month after our Bar Mitzvahs, we joined the *Sozialistischen Arbeiterjugend* (SAJ), the Socialist Workers Youth. We wore proudly the insignia with the three arrows that showed we were members of the SAJ front-line fighters association."

"So, you actively opposed the Nazi takeover?" Renate asked.

"We sure did," Sigi responded, "and we paid for it in blood."

"How so?"

"As Max told it to me the day after it happened, he and his sister, Ruthi, were standing in the doorway of their house and watched as a man in a black raincoat with a big German shepherd was siccing his dog onto the other Jewish children in the street and shouting, 'Get out, you Jew bastards!' Then the dog lunged at the two of them. Ruthi got inside and slammed the door behind her, but Max got bitten. Ruthi walked the streets of the city for hours, afraid to go home because she thought she had let her brother down, but she finally came home, and Max and their mother assured her that she had done nothing to incur any anger on their part."

"And Max wasn't the only one who got into street brawls with Nazi youth. His oldest brother, Salomon, woke Max up late one night, blood all over his face and his clothes, and told him that he had been in a fight with young Nazis and had come out on top. But, he said, 'They'll be back, and the next time they'll be out to kill me. I'm taking my bike and getting out of here while I still can.' And the next day he packed a bag, said his goodbyes, got on his bicycle, and escaped to Holland."

"So in the weeks and months after the Nazi takeover, the noose continued to tighten as more and more restrictions were imposed on us. The Nazis were doing their best to carve us out of the general German population, to force us to live in our own little ghetto, so to speak, with little or no contact between us and the German population. More than that, they were intent on making life a living hell for the Jews that remained, to drive them out. And in that they largely succeeded."

"Our Jewish friends and neighbors were making serious plans to emigrate, applying for visas to America or South Africa or England, or getting their documents together to leave for Palestine. It was as if we had one foot still in Germany, and the other foot pointed toward some distant land."

"The day of reckoning came for the Windmüllers in April 1933, only a month after the Nazis took power. A month earlier, in one of its earliest edicts, the new Nazi regime had prohibited butchers from slaughtering meat according to *kashruth*, the kosher methods called for by Jewish law. That put a serious crimp in Moritz Windmüller's butcher shop trade. After all, that was his special niche, that's what kept his customers coming back to him."

"If, after that, Moritz still had any illusions that he could continue in the retail meat trade, those illusions were shattered a month later. Max's father was at his butcher shop, and Max and his brothers were at school. Only his younger sister, Ruthi, was at home with a bad cold. At around eleven o'clock on a Friday morning, Jette and her daughter were startled by a loud peremptory pounding on the door.

Jette froze in fear. Only the police knocked that way. Seconds later, from the other side of the door, Jette heard, *'Aufmachen! Polizei!'*— 'Open up! Police!'"

"Jette tried to pull herself together. What could they possibly want? The Windmüllers were not political. They had been careful not to ally themselves publicly with any movement or faction. Opening the door, Jette found two men, dressed identically in black trenchcoats, standing in the doorway. In as calm and even a voice as she could muster, Jette asked, 'What can I do for you, gentlemen?'"

"The man in front, who seemed to be in charge, barked, 'The trade license, and make it quick!' Jette knew that she could not delay or cook up a fake story that the trade license was missing or had been stolen, or was in someone else's hands. She knew that it was where it had always been—in the center drawer of their dining room cabinet. She pulled it out of the drawer and handed it to the police officer, asking, as she did so, 'When will it be returned to us?'"

"The man in front, now with the trade license in hand, snorted derisively, and answered, 'Frau Windmüller, this is no time for jokes.' With that, he pocketed the document and he and the other man turned on their heels and headed back down the stairs."

"When Moritz came home from his shop that evening, Jette told him what had happened. He understood the situation immediately. If he opened the store on Monday, the police would shut him down and perhaps haul him off to a concentration camp. He realized immediately that they had reached the end of the road, that the two centuries' presence of Windmüllers in Ostfriesland was over."

"But if not here, then where? Where would they live? How would they feed themselves and their children? Their thoughts immediately turned to Palestine, but it might take a year or more to obtain the treasured *Certificat,* the document issued by the British authorities granting permission to resettle there. The other countries that Jews were pinning their hopes on to give them entry visas were ruled out also. It would take years to put together the documentation that they required. They couldn't wait that long. With no job for the breadwinner and no other source of income, the family's funds would soon run out."

"With a large family, and now deprived of his livelihood, he had to act quickly. His decision, really, his only alternative, was to move across the border to Holland, to the town of Beilen, where Max's aunt Ruth and her husband, Jakob Van Gelder, lived. That was an attractive alternative if Ruth and Jakob would have them. Beilen was only seventy-six miles to the west. They would be with family, not with strangers."

"The Dutch language," Sigi reminded Renate, "is similar to German—learning Dutch would be easier than learning an entirely new language. And, peering into the future and back into the past, they remembered that Holland had declared itself neutral in World War I. The German armies, respecting that declaration of neutrality, had never once set foot on Dutch soil. If there was to be a war, perhaps Holland would be neutral in this war as well. And if the thunderclouds of war rolled in from the East, there might still be time to find a more secure haven: Palestine, still, or perhaps England or even Australia."

"That night, a Friday evening, the beginning of the Sabbath, the Windmüller family was gathered at the dinnertable, the Sabbath candles already lit at the center of the table. Earlier that week, Max had invited me to share their Sabbath meal with them and, to Max's credit, and his parents', that invitation had not been withdrawn despite the extreme stress that they must have been feeling."

"None of us dared to speak about what had happened earlier that day, although of course it was on everyone's mind. When we had finished eating, Moritz Windmüller was silent, his eyes cast downward as if in deep thought. Then he raised his face, looked at each of us in turn, and said, slowly, 'Children, you know what happened today. They came and took away my business license, and they will not give it back. That means that our life here in Emden is finished. We will have to leave.'"

"'Where will we go, Papa?'" Ruthi asked. Moritz looked at his daughter with great affection. 'We are going to stay with Tante Ruth and Onkel Jakob in Beilen,' he answered. 'I'm confident that I will find a job in Holland, and we will make a new life for ourselves there.'"

"'When will we be moving?' asked Yitzchak, Max's next-older brother. We all called him Isi."

"'There's much to do here before we can leave,' Moritz answered. 'I have to sell the business, we have to sell the furniture, if we can, but, most important, there are exit documents—police clearances, tax releases, and so on—that we have to obtain here to get our exit visas, and then we have to get Dutch entry visas, one for each of you children and for Mutti and me. There's no telling how long that will take, but I'm hoping that, within three weeks, by mid-May, we will be on the train for Holland. There's nothing for us here in Emden, or anywhere in Germany, anymore. In the meantime, you must each try to be as helpful to Mutti as possible, and to sort out your clothes to pick those that you'll be taking with you. Everything else we will try to sell or just leave behind.'"

"Ruthi chimed in: '. . . and my toys and my dolls and stuffed animals? You mean I can't take them with me?'"

"'I'm afraid that you will have to make a very difficult decision, Ruthele. You can take one doll and one stuffed animal—that's all we have room for.'"

"Ruthi cast her eyes downward, as if to hide from the others at the table the tears welling up in her eyes."

"Max's younger brother, Emil, asked, 'Are Onkel and Tante coming with us?'"

"Mutti said, 'No, they said that they won't come with us. Children, this will be the hardest part in all this—saying goodbye to Onkel and Tante, all our friends, and to Rabbi Blum.'"

"'We are leaving, too,' I volunteered.

"'Why?' Ruthi asked. '"Just so you can be together with Max?'"

"'No, it's because they forced my father out of his accounting office, too.'"

"'Are you coming with us?'

"'No, I don't think so,' I answered. 'Probably a week later.'"

"Emil turned toward his father. 'Papa, what about our schooling?' he asked."

"'You will be enrolled in the Jewish school in Beilen, just as you were here. But they will be teaching in Dutch, so it's important that you learn Dutch right away. Mutti and I must learn Dutch, too, so that we can build a new life for ourselves, and for you, in Holland.'"

"The rest of the meal was eaten in silence. Each of them, it seemed, was making a mental reckoning of what might be taken and what had to be left behind, and, more importantly, calling to mind the images of the loved ones and friends from whom they would soon be separating, perhaps forever."

"As we left the table, Moritz spoke once again: 'Children, this is not the time for weakness, for giving in to our emotions. This is the time to show that we can be strong, ready for whatever challenges life has in store for us. Can we all agree on that?' He looked directly at each one of them, waiting for their answer. The four children responded with as much conviction as they could muster, 'Yes, Papa!'"

"'Good!' he said. 'Now let's go upstairs and start sorting through our belongings.'"

"The next day, Jette Windmüller called her sister in Beilen. In a voice that betrayed the extreme stress that she and her family were feeling, she described the latest restrictions imposed on them as Jews. She told her sister how she had been forced to surrender her husband's tradesmen's license, and how he and they were now deprived of their livelihood. Then she came directly to the point: Could they stay with her? They had no place else to go, Jette told her sister, assuring her that their stay would only be temporary, until Moritz could find a position, any position, that would enable the family to stay on its feet financially."

"Jette's phone call, and her desperate request, came as no surprise to Ruth Van Gelder and her husband. They had been watching events on the German side of the border with increasing alarm. It was clear to them that life in Germany was becoming intolerable for its Jewish population. They had already talked together about the real possibility that they might need to offer refuge to the Windmüller family. So when Jette made her plea, her sister did not try to allay her fears, to reassure her that better days lay ahead. She knew better."

"With Jette waiting nervously for her response, Ruth answered, 'Of course!' But she also made it clear that this could not be an extended stay. She and her husband had their own financial burdens. They, too, were having a hard time making ends meet. Jette assured her sister that the Windmüller family would move on well before they had become a burden to the Van Gelders."

"In the following weeks, the Windmüllers did what so many other Jewish emigrés were forced to do: quickly tie up the strands of their life in Germany and start a new life elsewhere. Moritz Windmüller sold his store and business to his assistant, Karl-Heinz Opert. There was no prolonged bargaining. Each of them understood the situation: Windmüller needed to get his money and get it fast. He was in no position to haggle over the last Reichsmark. So they sealed the deal by the following Wednesday, at a price far below the true worth of the business, but Moritz had a certified check from Herr Opert that could be deposited in a bank in Beilen."

"At home, the Windmüller family also had difficult decisions to make. What did they absolutely have to bring with them? And what had to be left behind, however sad that would be? The family jewelry, yes. The Sabbath candlesticks, the menorah, and the prayer books that had come down to Moritz from his father and grandfather before him, yes. Family photographs, some from the middle of the nineteenth century, when photography was still new—those certainly. Each of the children was allowed one favorite toy or doll. But everything else—furniture, bed and table linens, kitchen utensils—would remain. Jette Windmüller sold it all to Frau Hollweg, the landlady, for a fraction of its value."

Reacting to Sigi's narrative, Renate commented, "This was not like the ordinary household move, where you have many weeks to think about what you want to keep, what you want to sell, what you want to give away. All those decisions had to be made almost overnight."

"So true," said Sigi. "The Windmüllers and my family, Jews from Germany, were about to join that massive tidal wave of refugees, down through the centuries, and especially Jewish refugees, seeking to escape from political and religious persecution. We were not moving for a new job, or to be near relatives, or for greater opportunities elsewhere. We were forced out, driven out, fearing for our very lives, just two families among the thousands of Jews who fled from Germany to Holland in the first year of the Nazi regime."

"Although we didn't realize it at the time, we had some advantages that later Jewish refugees didn't have. Most important, we were no longer in Germany in the mid- and late-1930's when the anti-Jewish terror ramped up. When we left Germany, it was still relatively easy to cross the border into Holland. The Dutch government had not yet erected the barriers to immigration from the east, from Germany and Central Europe, which it would later impose."

Sigi paused, peering at Renate to see if she fully understood what he had just said. Satisfied that she had, he resumed. "The worst part of leaving Emden were the goodbyes that each of us had to say to those whom we were close to, who had been woven deeply into the fabric of our lives there. That meant embracing and saying goodbye to our aunts, uncles, and cousins. For Max's father, Moritz, it meant parting from his loyal customers and the local cattle farmers who provided him with his stock in trade. For his mother, it meant sad farewells

Rabbi Samuel Blum

from her neighbors on the *Graf Ulrichstrasse* and from the ladies at the *Frauenverein,* the synagogue's ladies' guild. Finally, for Max, it meant saying goodbyes to his friends and fellow students, our teachers, Julius Gottschalk and Benjamin Abt, and, our rabbi, Samuel Blum, whom we loved and respected."

"The adults were well aware, I'm sure, that these goodbyes might well be final, that they might not see each other again, although they tried to reassure each other that this separation was only temporary. The Windmüllers were among the first Jewish families to leave Emden. They were part of that early trickle of refugees from Hitler's Germany that, in the years ahead, would become a flood."

"So in a way," Renate commented, "those police officers who pulled Moritz's business permit and your father's, were doing them, and your families, a service in forcing them to leave Germany right after the Nazi takeover."

"I hadn't thought of it that way," Sigi responded, "but yes, our parents fared better than those who stayed, thinking that they could wait it out. Those whose husbands had fought and died for the Fatherland in the Great War had thought that they, the wives and widows of heroes, were exempt from the Nazi regime's punitive measures against Jews, but they soon came to realize that they, too, were caught in the net and tried desperately to escape."

"The fortunate ones had family members in the United States, Australia, or England, who had the financial means to fill out an affidavit of support, attesting that the newcomers would not become a public charge. They endured the long wait until their names came up on the visa lists, and then booked passage to their new place of refuge. The Windmüllers, and my family, the Kirschners, did not have those connections. That's why we ended up in Holland, just an hour by train from our home in Emden. We hoped to find safety there, but history proved that our hopes were in vain."

"Two days before the Windmüllers' scheduled departure from Emden, with their bags packed and their possessions—those that they were not taking with them—disposed of, Moritz Windmüller said to his family: 'There is one more farewell that we must make before we leave.'

"Ruthi piped up, 'But Papa, we have already finished doing that.'"

"'Not quite, Ruthele,' he said, smiling indulgently. 'Tomorrow morning, we will say goodbye to those who cannot say goodbye to us, to Oma and Opa and all those who lie buried in the *Friedhof*, the cemetery.'"

"And so, the following day, the Windmüller family gathered in a cluster in front of the house on the *Graf Ulrichstrasse*—the house they would soon be leaving behind—and walked slowly and solemnly the short distance to the Jewish cemetery on the *Bollwerkstrasse*. We—my parents and I—met them at the cemetery gate and walked on to the Windmüller family plot. There, in that one small space, were clustered the graves of generations of Windmüllers. There were men and women who had lived out their normal life span, and others who had died of tuberculosis or other illnesses long before their time. And then there were tombstones, stubby little stones, some of them inscribed only with first names, the graves of little boys and girls stricken in infancy or early childhood with diphtheria, scarlet fever, or some such disease. I was too young to remember any of them, but I'm sure that many of them—certainly the grandparents—lived in the memories of Moritz and his wife and their children, and all of them had to be called upon for a final leave-taking before the Windmüllers could depart from their hometown."

Sigi recalled for Renate the speech that Moritz made as we stood at the graves. Addressing the souls of those who were interred in that place, he had said:

We are leaving, and it may well be that we will never return to this place, but you will always live in our memories. You died before we Jews became the object of the hatred of our German countrymen. Now you lie here in peace, undisturbed, while we must flee for our safety. So we say goodbye, perhaps forever, until, by the grace of God, our souls are reunited in the hereafter.

"And then, with head bowed, he recited the familiar opening words of the Kaddish, the Jewish prayer for the dead—*'Yisgadal v'yiskadash sh'may rabaw'*—'May His great Name grow exalted and sanctified'—and the rest of us—men, women and children, Windmüllers and Kirschners—joined in, closing the prayer with the fervent amen. Then we all—adults and children—walked silently out of the cemetery."

Sigi turned now to face Renate. "It would be thirty-eight years before I returned to that cemetery. The Windmüller graves were still there, almost obscured by the ivy that had grown over them. The cemetery had been left undisturbed during the Nazi regime. It had not been vandalized, as so many others were elsewhere in Germany and Austria. Ironically, though, major damage had been done shortly before my arrival by the skinheads, the neo-Nazis, who had toppled many of the headstones, including the beautiful gravestones in the Kirschner family plot."

Renate shook her head in silent dismay.

Sigi gathered his thoughts and continued the narrative. "The day that the Windmüllers left Emden for the last time started out raw and cold, with rain clouds hanging heavy over the North Sea. They hired a van to get their luggage to the train station. The family had friends drive them in two separate cars the few blocks to the terminal. It was a day that Max would never forget. He spoke of it frequently during our years in Holland, both before and during the war."

"On the platform to see them off, in addition to their small circle of friends, were Rabbi Blum and Moritz's and Jetta's sisters and brothers—Max's aunts and uncles—those that had not already left to seek safety elsewhere. Max's paternal grandparents, Salomon and Friederieke, had already died, Salomon in 1919, Friederieke in 1927. We, the Kirschner family, were there, too, but our days in Emden were also numbered. A week later we would be on that same platform to board the train into Holland. Max and I embraced lightheartedly, knowing that we would soon be reunited in Holland. 'Time to start learning Dutch, old buddy,' he said to me. It was true. The Dutch would get very angry when they heard German spoken in their presence."

"And what of the others, the older ones, who were standing in clusters on the train platform that morning? For them, it was an emotional final embrace. They tried to smile, to put this in a cheerful light, but they must have known that this might well be the final parting, and so it was. Some years after we headed west, to Holland, they took another train, eastward, to the death camps, and never returned."

"With the train already standing at the platform, Rabbi Blum suggested that we recite together the blessing for someone departing on a dangerous journey. We joined in, speaking each word with all the concentration we could muster:

May it be Your will, Lord, our God and the God of our forefathers, that You lead us toward peace, guide our footsteps toward peace, and make us reach our desired destination for life, gladness, and peace. May You rescue us from the hand of every foe and ambush along the way, and from all manner of punishments that assemble to come to earth. Blessed are You, Lord, Who hears prayer."

"After the closing amens, the Windmüllers tearfully said their last goodbyes, picked up their suitcases, and climbed aboard the train. Minutes later, we, those of us who remained on the platform, were still waving our goodbyes as the train disappeared from sight."

Now, sitting on that balcony in Haifa, 2,000 miles from Emden and 65 years later, Sigi paused, lost in thought, then resumed. "It seems that my whole life, Renate, and maybe yours, has been marked by goodbyes. Some people you are happy to say goodbye to, and you don't care if you ever see them again, but most times goodbyes are painful and seem to leave a scar on your heart. You say goodbye to parents and children, to brothers and sisters, to sweethearts and friends, and then you turn your back and walk away, pretending it doesn't affect you, but of course it does. It's the way a tree must feel when a limb or branch is broken off."

"Those goodbyes on the train platform at the Emden station were only the first of many in my life. The goodbyes you never forget are the violent ones in which your loved one, struggling but unable to change his destiny, is literally ripped out of your life, perhaps to be placed on a train to the east, you don't know where. And then, finally, there are the goodbyes that you say, aloud, or in a whisper, to that person who is lying in a hospital bed, in the last moments of his or her life."

"You're right," Renate agreed somberly. "You could say that the chapters in our life-books are all marked by the goodbyes we have to say, until others say their last goodbye to us." After another silence, she spoke decisively. "Sigi, this might be a good time to end this session. Can we pick up again at nine o'clock tomorrow morning?" Sigi agreed readily. In retirement, time was not in short supply.

As Renate rose from her chair and turned toward the door, she paused, looked back at Sigi questioningly, and said, "A last question for today, Sigi. How would you describe your childhood, generally speaking?"

He considered the question, and answered thoughtfully, "For Max and for me and for most of the other Jewish boys our age in Emden, it was an idyllic existence. We were secure in our parents' love and understood our roles in the family. We spent long hours in school on our secular and religious studies, but it seems to me, as I look back, that there was plenty of time, too, for play in the schoolyard and in the street, and for walks in the countryside. Many of my childhood memories are linked to the synagogue, where we came together for religious services, where we marked the holidays, and celebrated milestones: births, circumcisions, weddings, and yes, deaths. It was, I suppose, not very different from the way Jews had lived in Germany for centuries."

"And then it all came to an end," Renate mused.

"Yes, it came to an end, abruptly and violently. The outside world intruded, and we had no say in it. It closed in on us, and brought that happy life to an end."

Standing now, Renate said, with an air of finality, "So, until tomorrow."

Sigi echoed, "Until tomorrow." They shook hands cordially, and said their "*Auf Wiedersehen's*," knowing that they would see each other again the next day. Sigi stood in the apartment doorway, watching as Renate strode purposefully to the elevator.

Returning to the quiet of his apartment, Sigi sank into his favorite chair, feeling emotionally drained. This would not be as easy as he had expected. He had thought that by now, some 65 years later, he would be able to talk about those events as a historian would, objectively, dispassionately. How wrong he had been! Old pains, long suppressed, had come alive again, like an old wound supposedly well on its way to healing, then suddenly exposed, to be dealt with all over again. But, he reminded himself, he had made a commitment to Frau Gierecke and he was honor-bound to carry it through.

Turning off the lamp on his night table that evening and pulling the bedcovers up over him, he told himself that this would not be a tranquil night's sleep for him . . . and it wasn't.

PART 2

The Second Day

CHAPTER 2

Groningen; the
Hachsharah

⎯⎯ᴄ⎯⎯

The next morning, promptly at nine o'clock, Renate Gierecke returned as she had promised. Once again, Sigi invited her to join
him on the balcony; he led, she followed. He poured coffee for the
two of them. Renate clicked on the tape recorder and invited him to
resume his story.

"So, Sigi, when we stopped yesterday, you were telling me about
the Windmüllers' goodbyes on the train platform in Emden. Let's
pick it up from there. Do you remember your feelings a week later
when your family crossed the border from Germany to Holland?
I imagine you felt a deep sadness. After all, you were leaving your
homeland."

"You're asking me to recall emotions that I felt as a youngster
sixty-five years ago. That isn't easy. But I can say with certainty that
there were no such feelings of sadness in me or in any of us as we
crossed the border. Concern over what lay in store for us, yes, but
sadness, no. We were realists. We understood that the Germany that
we had grown up with, the Germany that historians today call the
Weimar Republic—that Germany had been hijacked, it no longer

existed. Any Jew who spent time pining for the good old days was a romantic, one who was blinding himself to the realities."

"No," Sigi went on, speaking with conviction, "I'm quite sure that the dominant emotion when we crossed the border was relief, relief that we had extricated ourselves from mortal danger. We could breathe easily again, knowing that we would not hear again that peremptory knock on the door at midnight and all the other horrors that Jews were encountering in Germany."

"And likewise, I'm sure that there was among my parents and others of that generation a rage, mixed with bewilderment, that the German people who had voted for Hitler and his Nazis, or were just standing by on the sidelines, apathetic, had allowed themselves to be led down the path, a path that would bring them, as we later saw, inevitably to death and destruction. There was more than rage there. They despised the German people for their political blindness, for their willingness to march in lockstep behind a maniac, all in the name of the Fatherland."

Renate seemed offended by that sweeping statement. "You're not saying that every German was blind in that way, are you?"

"Of course not. There were Germans who defied Hitler and his gang. Many of them paid with their lives, standing for their principles. We honor them by inscribing their names on The Wall of The Righteous at the Yad Vashem Museum in Jerusalem and in other Holocaust museums all over the world. There are 587 Germans named on that wall, and we can be sure that there were many more whose names are not listed. But let's face it, they were a small minority."

Renate shook her head thoughtfully, seeming to accept the truth of what Sigi had said. "Go on, Sigi."

"After the Windmüllers had lived for two weeks with the aunt and uncle in Beilen, the aunt, Ruth Van Gelder, told her sister regretfully that it was time for her and for Moritz, and their children, to move on. She gave two reasons: the physical stress of having to accommodate six more people under their roof, and the financial cost of putting that much more food on the table. Jette Windmüller did not try to dissuade her. Her family had felt that same stress."

"So another departure, another farewell, as the Windmüllers boarded the train to Groningen, forty-eight kilometers to the north. Groningen was a much larger city than Beilen. It boasted a university, a thriving Jewish community, and most of all, there would be ample job opportunities for Moritz. They moved into a third-floor apartment on the *Oosterhamricklaan*."

"Three weeks after that parting on the train platform in Emden, Max and I were reunited in Groningen. Naturally, we were excited to see each other again and to share with each other our experiences during those three weeks. My family's journey had been uneventful. Our border crossing had gone smoothly and without a hitch. Max had a different story to tell."

"On the train heading westward, Max and his younger brother, Emil, were sitting across the aisle from their parents. When they reached the border, German border police entered the coach and made their way, row by row, from one end to the other. When they came to the row where Max's parents were sitting, Moritz Windmüller was ready with the travel documents. He handed them to the German border guards, feeling certain that the papers were in order."

"Everything should have gone smoothly, but that was not to be. The German police officer, after scanning the documents, stared coldly at the two of them, husband and wife. Then he said, 'The fox fur—give it to me.' At first Jette Windmüller couldn't believe what she was hearing. She asked the man to repeat it. He said, threateningly, 'The fox fur. You won't be needing it in Holland'. Jette was outraged. The stole had been a Chanukah gift from her husband two years earlier. She would not have parted with it for any price, and now this ruffian was demanding it. No, not just demanding it—he was robbing her at gunpoint, more or less. She was ready to make a scene, but her husband put his hand firmly on hers, sending her a warning. He understood the situation immediately: to be allowed to leave Germany and cross the border into Holland, a ransom had to be paid, and these thugs were demanding the fox fur stole as that ransom. Best to pay it and move on. 'Jettchen,' he whispered to his wife, 'It'll be okay. Hand it over.' Reluctantly, Jette took the fur from her shoulders and handed it to the border policeman. He in turn, passed it on to his assistant. The pair then moved on to the people in the seats behind them, perhaps to extract even more booty from them."

"Jette began to weep silently, while Moritz tried to reassure her. 'I knew why she was crying,' Max told me. 'It wasn't just a fur stole that the man had taken. It was as if a limb had been torn from her body, and she was helpless to prevent it.' In the years ahead, we were to experience often that feeling of futile rage."

"Now, in Groningen, Max and I and our brothers and sisters were enrolled in our appropriate grades in the Jewish school there. We were comfortable in that school, because almost half of the other students were refugees from Germany as we were, all of us having to deal with the sudden changes in our lives."

"Just as we had looked up from our school desks in Emden at the portraits, first of Chancellor Brüning and then of his successor, Adolf Hitler, now we looked up at a large photo portrait of Queen Wilhelmina, and, standing in the corner, at the flag of the Netherlands, horizontal stripes of red, white, and blue. Overnight, we had to forget that we were Germans, born in a neighboring country. Now we were Dutch, and that meant speaking Dutch, a language that was entirely new to us. And it couldn't be Dutch as it was taught in schools, the pure Dutch. We had to learn the local dialect, Dutch as it was spoken in the streets and in the shops."

"We learned it quickly, because we had to and because the local dialect was not very different from the German dialect spoken in Ostfriesland, just to the east on the other side of the border. But we never lost our German accent, and that made us objects of suspicion when we spoke Dutch in public, the marketplace, the public library, or wherever else we came in contact with the non-Jewish Dutch of Groningen. And it wasn't only in the public places in Beilen and later in Groningen that we were marked as *buitenstaanders*—outsiders. Even in our school, our classmates, Jewish as we were, but born in Holland and not in Germany, saw us as 'one of them'—one of those refugees—not 'one of us.'"

"So it should come as no surprise that we Jews, formerly of Emden, clung to each other and to the other young Jews who had sought refuge from Hitler in Holland as we had. And they came not only from Emden and from elsewhere in East Friesland, but from every corner of Central Europe—from other places in Germany, from Austria, Poland, and Czechoslovakia. Everyone was there with the same idea in mind: to escape what they even then foresaw as a grim destiny for Jews if they stayed in place. Eventually some 250 Jews from elsewhere in Europe arrived in Groningen, increasing the Jewish population there by almost half."

"And for the Jews of Groningen and elsewhere in the Netherlands, the grim destiny faced by our fellow Jews to the east became clear early on, even then, in the first years of the Nazi takeover, to anyone who was reading the daily newspaper or listening to the radio. We read the Dutch newspapers avidly, listened to the radio, and honed our English-language skills by listening to the BBC, beamed from

Scotland, just to the west of us across the North Sea. Almost every day brought news of new restrictions imposed on German Jews."

"This affected us—the Kirschners and Windmüllers—very personally. After all, we had left behind in Emden our uncles and aunts, our cousins and our friends, and they were the ones who bore the brunt of these new Nazi edicts. At the dinner table almost every evening these events were the number one topic of conversation. The tragedy as it was playing out on the other side of the border was constantly on our minds."

"There were reminders, too, that in Groningen we hadn't traveled very far from Emden. The Dutch fascist party, the *Nationaal Socialistische Beweging*, used to hold weekly rallies in the *Grote Markt*, the central public square in the city. Its members would march down our street in their black uniforms with orange trim, looking much like the brownshirts whom we had seen parade through Emden. The difference was that in Emden and elsewhere in Germany, the brownshirts seemed to have the full support of the locals, whereas these Dutch fascists were a tiny minority, and their public displays drew no attention from the ordinary Hollanders."

"I don't want to convey the impression that our early years in Groningen were gloomy ones, that we were beset by one new misery after another. After all, we were young teenagers, full of hope and optimism as we tried to imagine what the future would bring. Max and I had a large circle of friends, young people whom we had known from Emden, but also friends newly made from elsewhere in Germany and other countries."

"In school I applied myself diligently to my studies, knowing that the future as I envisioned it depended on the learning that I acquired at this age and on getting high grades on my examinations. Max's brother, Isi, also did well in school. Max, as I've said, never got top grades in school, but that didn't seem to get him down. He was a happy-go-lucky kid, someone who had the self-confidence to believe that he could play the cards that were dealt out to him."

"I remember that Max took up the harmonica and learned to play it quite well, and when he wasn't playing the harmonica he was singing. His favorites were the folksongs that German workers sang on their weekend holidays. He learned how to yodel, too, even though yodeling was something you might hear in the Bavarian Alps, a long way from the flatlands of East Friesland. Soon Max could yodel as well as any man in *lederhosen* from down there in Bavaria!"

Once again, Sigi opened the photo album, this time to another family photo. Standing in the rear were Moritz and Jetta, their daughter Ruthi between them; seated in the second Row were Sigi's parents, his sisters, and himself. In front, kneeling on one knee, the Windmüller boys, Max, Yitzchak, and Emil. Max's oldest brother, Salomon, wasn't in the photo; perhaps he was the one holding the camera. This must have been taken in the summer of 1934, when they were all living in Groningen.

Yitzchak Windmüller   Ruth Windmüller   Emil Windmüller

Looking intently at the photo, Renate said half in jest, "I wouldn't have guessed from the photo that Moritz Windmüller was a cattle dealer and butcher. Somehow you think of people in the livestock trade as big and burly, muscular." Sigi found himself nodding in agreement. Moritz was on the slender side, wore round black wire-rim glasses and looked, if you didn't know him, like a man who might have been a high school teacher, perhaps, or a minor government official.

His wife, Jette, was the lighter-complexioned one; it was obvious from the photo, and he remembered that he had noticed at the time that Max very much resembled his mother.

Jette Windmüller (l.) and
Moritz Windmüller (r.)

She had blue eyes, a face that seemed permanently set in a wide grin (at least it was so back then), and dun-colored hair. Middling in height, she was still taller than her husband by a centimeter or two.

"Do you have any recollections of Moritz during those years that would be helpful to my readers?" Renate asked.

Sigi did his best to answer the question as fully as possible. "Herr Windmüller was not a well-educated man," he finally said. "I believe he had two years at the *Realschule*—that was the schooling for children who didn't plan on going on to higher education—and dropped out when he turned sixteen. Then he went to work in his father's butcher shop and learned that trade. When his father retired, Moritz took over the business. Along the way he became a dealer in livestock. I was told he was an excellent judge of cattle, and that, when there was a dispute involving the value of livestock, people turned to him to help settle the matter."

"Somehow," said Renate, "it never entered my mind that a Jew would be an expert in judging cattle. It's hard to picture that."

"I don't blame you," Sigi told her. "But in Ostfriesland and other rural areas throughout Germany, many Jews were involved in cattle dealing. In fact, it was second only to money lending and accounting as the most popular occupations for Jews."

"What was his attitude toward education?" Renate asked. "Was he one of those men who tells his children, 'I had enough schooling. You don't need more than I had'?"

"Far from it. He was a strong believer in education, specifically a sound Jewish education. That's why his children all attended the *Jüdische Volksschule*. I think Max's older brother, Isi, if the family had stayed in Emden, would have gone to gymnasium—that's a secondary school that prepares students for university—and then on to a university. He was very bright and was motivated to do well in school. Max, not so much. He was more into sports and friends."

"What about Herr Windmüller's political affiliations? Was he politically active?"

"He may have been politically active as a young man. I wouldn't know about that. But when I knew him, he was an ardent Social Democrat, a strong supporter of the Weimar government. I would see him get very upset reading our local newspaper, the *Emder Zeitung*, with its almost daily reports of corrupt and ineffective politicians. But he was never active in the SPD party. He was always on the sidelines, because he was too busy at the store. He may have felt, too, that he couldn't afford to alienate customers whose political views might be different from his own."

"Do you think Max inherited his father's political views?"

"There's no doubt of that in my mind," Sigi replied. "The whole family was very much to the left of center. They despised the right-wing parties that were already causing trouble in the 1920's. They sided strongly with the workingman in every conflict with the bosses. They also had a strong social conscience, and they acted on their beliefs."

Then, as if to drive the point home, Sigi mentioned a pair of long-standing Jewish traditions. "Perhaps you are familiar with our festival of *Purim*?"

"It's a spring festival, right? But what's the connection?"

"Yes, it usually falls in March. We commemorate events that took place at that time of year in Persia, during the reign of King Xerxes. Haman, the vizier to the king, intended to kill every Jew in the kingdom. The king's Jewish queen, Esther, told him about Haman's plans and convinced the king to hang Haman instead. In the Book of Esther, we are told to celebrate that event by singing and dancing and delivering baskets of food to the poor. That's what we did, year after year, at *Purim*-time."

"The rest of the year, every Friday afternoon just before the start of the Sabbath, the Windmüller children would go up and down the *Judengasse* with large bags full of bones, the meat still on them, from Moritz Windmüller's butcher shop. I went along at Max's side. We stopped where the poor Jews lived to deliver those bones to those families who might otherwise not have enough to eat for dinner that night. That was our way of carrying out the commandment of *tzedakah*, the obligation to give to those less fortunate than we."

"Max's father reminded us that we children were doing what the Torah requires of farmers: that they not harvest to the very edges and corners of their fields so that there is food left there for the gleaners, the poor women who come in after the farmer has finished his harvest. That, he said, was what we were doing when we distributed the bones and the unsaleable meats to the poor Jewish families living on the *Judengasse*. As kids, we took that lesson to heart, and we never forgot it."

"And I take it that the Windmüllers were ardent Zionists?" Renate asked.

"That too," Sigi replied. "Max and his older brothers and I were members of the *Blau-Weiss,* the Blue-White. Those were the colors adopted for the Zionist banner, the same colors that were later incorporated in the flag of Israel. We would get together on weekends and go on hikes in the countryside around Emden, or across the beaches and marshes of the *Wattenmeer,* singing Hebrew songs and waving that blue-and-white banner. We stopped doing that, stopped waving our banners, when anti-Semitism got worse in the early 1930's. We wanted to avoid confrontations with the local German teenagers."

"*Blau-Weiss* was, you could say, a Jewish version of the *Wandervogel,* the Wanderbirds, and other German hiking groups that promoted fellowship and a love of the outdoors but excluded Jews. But there was more to it than hiking the countryside and singing Hebrew songs. To be a member of *Blau-Weiss* showed that you supported Zionism and the ideal of a Jewish homeland."

"We understood early on that life in Palestine would be a challenge, that it would be a long way from the comfortable life we enjoyed in Germany. If the Zionist experiment was to succeed, the *chalutzim,* the pioneers—and we considered ourselves pioneers—would need strong bodies, and a dedication to working the land, to making it fruitful again. We would need to acquire skills that were new to Jews, especially German Jews, because for centuries we Jews had not been allowed to own land and be farmers. We could be the middlemen, like Moritz Windmüller, people who dealt with the farmer, bought their livestock and their produce from them, and took it to market, but we could not own land and farm it ourselves."

"So *Blau-Weiss* was about teamwork, about working together and enjoying the outdoors together, a specifically Jewish camaraderie. It was also very much a Socialist movement—there was little or nothing of observance of religious rituals or discussion of what was required of us as members of the Jewish faith. But, at least in our part of Germany, the *Blau-Weiss* didn't reject that element, they just downplayed it."

"To us, that conflict, between the religious and the secular, didn't matter, because we were thoroughly imbued with the religious element of Judaism in our homes and our synagogue and our religious school. So in our minds, we had the best of both worlds: a home permeated with Judaism, and then, in *Blau-Weiss* the fun of socializing with other Jews. The supposed conflict between those who wanted to emphasize the religious elements and those who attached greater importance to the political side—well, we left that conflict and its resolution to others who were much smarter than we were and more deeply involved."

Pointing again to the photo of Max and Sigi with their parents, Renate asked about Max's temperament. "In the photo Max looks like a cheerful, well-adjusted kid. Was he?"

Sigi's response came easily. "No question," he said. "As I've already said, he enjoyed life, had a very easygoing nature. He did not dwell on life's little setbacks as some kids do. He was always upbeat. There was an impish side to him—he loved to play jokes on his brothers and sister and on his friends. That's why I enjoyed his company, because he was fun to be around."

"And his brothers?"

"I didn't know Emil, because he was younger, and the oldest one, Solomon, was already out of the house, living independently. But Max's older brother, Isi—he was different. He was always more serious, very studious, and had a strong sense of purpose. He and Max made a good team. They complemented each other."

"So," Renate said, trying to get back to the thread of the story, "Tell me more about Max and his brothers and sister in the 1930's before the war."

"Those were difficult years, and they must have left their mark on Moritz and the other members of the Windmüller family. Moritz could not re-establish himself in Holland as the independent businessman that he had been in Emden. After many months of unemployment he hired himself out as a butcher's assistant at a much lower income than he had been accustomed to."

"Everyone understood that they had to help out to put food on the table, and they did. Max got a job as a delivery boy, bringing groceries from the store to the people who had ordered them. I used to see him on the street, cheerfully riding his bicycle, in front of the handlebars a large wicker basket full of breads and meats, fruits and vegetables. Jette worked as a seamstress, doing alterations and other such work, and Ruthi helped her out. As I said, everybody pitched in."

"And *your* family?" Renate asked. "How did they manage in Groningen?"

"We were financially better off. My father's accounting firm was bound by contract to pay him according to a fixed formula on leaving the firm. The formula worked out to a decent settlement with him, so money was not as much of a worry for us as it was for Max's family. Still, we had to pare down. Our apartment in Groningen had two bedrooms: my parents slept in one, my sisters in the other, and I ended up sleeping on the living room sofa. That's how it was in those days—everyone had to manage the best way they could."

Renate urged him to continue with his narrative. "So tell us more about the years after you left Germany."

"In the years that followed our arrival in Groningen, we children, now teenagers, grew in height, put on weight, gained in strength, grew in our understanding of the world, and prepared ourselves for the lives that lay ahead. We learned to speak Dutch fluently, but at home we still used that Low German that we had grown up with."

"We became increasingly concerned about the future of Jews in Germany, and, specifically, in our native city of Emden. When we received letters from our aunts and uncles, they were couched in vague terms, because all mail that crossed Germany's borders was heavily censored. Despite the censorship, we quickly came to understand just how badly things were going for them. Life was a living hell for the Jews of Emden and for Jews everywhere in Germany. That was confirmed for us every day by reading the local newspaper, *Nieuwsblad van het Noorden*, and listening to the Groningen radio stations. That flow of information strengthened us in our Zionist convictions and in our determination to move to Palestine, the Jewish homeland."

"And your education?"

"You could say that Max and I continued on the tracks leading to the destination that fate had prepared us for. We both completed our education, at least as much of it as we could get in those turbulent times. I applied myself diligently to my studies, while Max . . . well, over the course of the next five years, Max threw himself more and more enthusiastically into his Zionist work, into doing everything that he needed to do to qualify for *Aliyah*, for emigration to Palestine."

"And what did one have to do to qualify?"

Sigi paused, then jumped in. "Let me answer that in a roundabout way. As you probably know, the League of Nations in 1922 gave Great Britain what was called a mandate, or administrative control, over what was then called Palestine. One element of that control was a rigid limitation on the number of Jews who could immigrate into Palestine. The British authorities did that through the issuance of *Certificats,* documents that were like entry visas. It's safe to say that, especially after the Nazis came to power in Germany, the number of Jews who were trying to enter Palestine far exceeded the number of *Certificats* that the British Mandate authorities were willing to issue."

He glanced at Renate, as if to decide whether she was following the thread, then continued. "The British assigned to the Jewish Agency the task of deciding who among the thousands desperate to enter Palestine should receive the precious *Certificat.* The Jewish Agency gave priority to Jews from Germany, Austria, and Poland, because it felt that those Jews faced the most immediate danger from Hitler and the Nazis. But you could also get a priority if you could show that you had had two years of training in agriculture. That was how Max and I, and many other young Jews in Germany, Austria, and Holland, tried to gain an advantage, to obtain that priority."

"Why was agricultural training so important?" Renate asked.

"Because farming was seen as crucial to the success of the Zionist enterprise. The leaders had a vision that Jews would turn the wilderness of what was then Palestine into green pastures and farmland, groves of fruit trees and olive trees, that kind of thing. Their objective was what they called the 'reversal of the pyramid.' As I've already said, the broad base of the Jewish pyramid had for centuries consisted of intellectuals, artists, merchants, and traders, and the other occupations that one would find in a city. In countries all over Europe,

Jews had been barred from owning farmland and working the land, so Jews who knew farming were rare indeed. They were, in terms of their numbers, the tip of the pyramid."

"The Zionists sought to turn that pyramid upside down. In Palestine, the bulk of the population would be engaged in agricultural work, and the young people who now dreamed of emigrating to Palestine would need to learn the specific skills that one had to have to turn the wasteland into a new Garden of Eden."

"Young people like Max and me could meet the agricultural training requirement in one of two ways. One way was to work on a farm, getting hands-on experience as a farmhand, an agricultural worker. The problem with that was that we young Jews, coming from cities in Germany or Austria, didn't know any Dutch farmers. Some of us got on our bicycles and rode the country roads, going from one farm to the next asking if the farmers needed help on their farms until we found one who said yes."

"Another way of getting placed on a farm was to ask for help from the Zionist coordinating organization, the Central Deventer Organization. The director, Rudolph (Ru) Cohen, had a roster of farmers who were willing to take on young Jews and teach them the ropes. Cohen was an ardent Zionist who believed passionately in the dream of a Jewish homeland in Palestine. He was clear-headed about the type of young men and women who were needed to build that Jewish homeland. They had to be healthy, strong, muscular, and ready for back-breaking work."

"If you expressed interest in having him assign you to a farm, he called you in for an interview at his home in Deventer and sized you up in an instant. If you met his picture of a person who would succeed as an agricultural worker in Palestine, you passed his test."

"But oftentimes he would put you on probation. He would assign you to a farm where the most difficult work was required, where you might have to work sixteen hours a day, and the accommodations were primitive. That was his form of 'basic training.' It was only after you had shown you could pass that test without caving in that he might agree to move you to another farm where the workload was lighter and you might have a bed to sleep on instead of a bale of straw."

"And how did Max meet that requirement?"

"Max was one of the fortunate ones who didn't need Ru Cohen to find a job as a farmhand. He found one on his own. In April 1937, he hired himself out as an agricultural worker on Schloss Slangen, an estate in Doetinchem, a hundred and twenty-five miles south of Groningen, almost at the border with Germany. I didn't see much of him during the two years he was there, but evidently he acquired the strength and the skills there that he would need later on. He also grew hugely in self-confidence, because that was the quality that made him stand out in the years ahead."

Sigi lifted the coffee cup to his lips, took an extended sip, then continued. "Then in February 1939, Max moved to another farm, this one called Koekoek, or Cuckoo, located outside of Hengelo in Overijssel province. While he was there, he came in contact with other young Jews who were working on nearby farms to qualify for a *Certificat* for Palestine. Many of them he would later come to know well after the war had begun and they became active together in the rescue-and-resistance movement."

"After the Germans had overrun the Netherlands, Max's identity card had on it that large black J that stamped him as a Jew. So when the police came to the Koekoek farm, as they sometimes did, he and the other Jewish farmworkers hid in a freshly dug drainage pit. Once they were all safely inside the pit, the farm owners slid the concrete lid into position over them and pushed a milk cart onto the lid. The hiding place was pitch-dark, damp and with an unpleasant smell, but it served its purpose. Max and the other hiders were never found."

"I learned later that it was during his time at Koekoek that Max came to be known to Ru Cohen and the other leaders of the Central Deventer Association as a disciplined worker and as an excellent organizer. So you could say," Sigi commented, "that Max's years at Koekoek were the seed-time for what came to bear fruit in the years ahead."

"If you wait just a minute," he said, "I can show you the towns that we're referring to." He took a map of the Netherlands from the folder at his feet and showed Renate the towns and cities that he had mentioned so far: Groningen, Doetinchem, and Hengelo. They formed a triangle: Groningen to the north and the two other towns at the base of the triangle, just 28 miles apart.

Looking back up at Renate, he explained, "Max's experience during those years—working in near-isolation from other Jewish *chalutzim* on a farm owned by a non-Jew—was the exception. Most Jewish youth of his age, if they were preparing to make *Aliyah* to Palestine, were assigned to a *hachsharah*. . . ."

Renate looked puzzled. "*Hach*—?"

Sigi repeated it, slowly. "*Hach-sha-rah.*"

"That sounds like a Hebrew word. Am I right?"

Sigi seemed pleased that she was listening so intently and went on to explain. "Yes, it's a Hebrew word meaning 'training' or 'preparation.' The plural—more than one *hachsharah*—is *hachsharoth.*"

He went on to say, "Preparation to move to Palestine and build a new life there"—he seemed to be searching in his mind for a comparison—"well, it wasn't like moving from Berlin to Hamburg or across the border to Denmark. Except for a few cities like Jerusalem, Tel

Aviv, and Haifa, and the few towns that earlier generations of Jewish settlers had established, Palestine at that time was an undeveloped place. The Zionist leaders realized that if the Jews were to build a strong nation there they would need agricultural skills, construction skills, mechanical skills."

"We *chalutzim*—that's the Hebrew word for pioneers—were not blind to the difficulties that we would face if we were to succeed in Palestine. There would be major public health problems to deal with: the fresh water supply, waste water, and so on, and the ever-present danger of an outbreak of infectious diseases. We assumed, and accepted, that the high quality of medical care that we were accustomed to in our cities would not be available in *Eretz Israel*, the Land of Israel. We were well aware that backbreaking work was in store for us if the desert was to be turned into fertile and productive land."

"Finally, we were told that we would be surrounded by hostile Arab neighbors, that our safety required that fences be erected around the kibbutz, and that watchtowers be erected and manned around the clock by armed guards to prevent Arab infiltration."

"And yet," Sigi peered over the tops of his eyeglasses at Renate as if to make sure that she was not missing his point, "knowing these things did not diminish our enthusiasm for the Zionist enterprise. This would be our land, a land where we, and not some outside authority, whether it be a czar, a Führer, or a king, would make the weighty decisions that affected us. For the first time in 2,000 years, Jews would become a political force to be reckoned with."

"Finally, the most important consideration was our personal safety, our very lives. We *chalutzim* were well aware that here in Holland, and in almost every other country in Europe, there were thousands of people who measured success by the number of Jews they had killed. In Palestine, we could at least have the opportunity to defend ourselves, to meet force with force."

"The Jewish leaders of the time, those who called themselves Zionists, understood that by and large, Jewish youngsters did not have the skills that were needed to build a Jewish homeland. They didn't understand how water had to be brought into a field to irrigate the new seedlings, or how to join two electrical wires together to create a circuit. They had never had the experience of working sunup to sundown in grueling heat. So the idea behind the *hachsharoth* was that young Jews, men and women, would spend two years at these workshop/camps, doing classroom work to keep up with their education and also getting the practical training in the fields."

"Our intention, our hope, was that, at the end of two years, we would qualify for a *Certificat*, and then, after arriving in Palestine, we would make our way to a *kibbutz,* or communal living farm, to put into practice the skills that we had learned at the *hachsharah*."

"But of course, there was more to it than that. The *hachsharoth* tried hard to instill in us a sense of pride and self-respect as Jews and a love of that land that would ten years later declare its independence as the new State of Israel. It was also about learning cooperation. I'm sure you agree with me, Renate," Sigi said, turning toward her, "that cooperation is something you have to learn. It's not a trait that we're born with. You watch little toddlers in a nursery school, maybe here in Haifa. Say that little Yigal has a toy, a red wagon that Yaacov wants. Does Yigal willingly share it with Yaacov? Does he say 'I had my turn, now it's your turn'? Chances are he doesn't. Nine times out of ten, Yigal pulls it away beyond Yaacov's reach, and little Yaacov cries in frustration. You would see that same scene played out in Berlin—it doesn't matter where it takes place. As we get older, many of us are like that: We protect what we have and don't let the other guy have it. We're also about proving that we're better than the next person, that there's a natural pecking order, and that we belong right up there at the top."

"But that's not the Zionist way. Our ideal, which had been instilled in us since we were small children, was that Palestine was to be a Socialist utopia, a place where each member of the group put the well-being of the group ahead of his or her own good. That's what was drummed into us every day at the *hachsharah*, and, of course, we young people were very receptive to those ideals. We had been trying to live them ever since our days in the *Blau-Weiss*. You could say that the *hachsharoth* were like small *kibbutzim*, where everyone's talents were appreciated and everyone was respected as a contributor to the common good."

"So the Zionists in Holland and other countries began early on to acquire rural properties in their countries where these skills could be taught. Even before the outbreak of World War I, and in the years immediately after, the leadership was acquiring hostels, orphanages, summer camps, and other such places. They turned them into *hachsharoth*, places where young people could get ready for their new life as pioneers in Palestine. In fact, in Holland, the first *hachsharah* dated back to 1910. It was started by a Jewish banker, Hendrik Jacobus Kann. He called it the *Joodsche Tuinbouw Veeteelt en Zuivelbereidings Vereeniging*—the Jewish Horticulture, Livestock Farming, and Dairy Processing Association. The more religious Jews, most of them from Eastern Europe, had a separate organization, called *Agudas Israel*, which operated its own *hachsharoth*."

"So," Renate commented, "it wasn't a new concept, a response to the conditions in the 1930's?"

"Not at all, but the exodus in the 1930's of young men and women from Germany and elsewhere in Europe made them much more important than they had been. Max and I and our families didn't realize it at the time, but we were part of that mass migration from East to West, out of Germany and Central Europe. We were different from many of the others in that we came out of Germany with our parents, our brothers and sisters. Many of the young people whom we came to know at the *hachsharah* had boarded trains in Vienna, Cologne, Berlin, and elsewhere, leaving their parents and other relatives on the station platform, in many cases never to be seen again."

"As young people began to arrive in Amsterdam and other large Dutch cities in the mid-1930's, the Zionist representatives met them at the train station, and if there was no one else at the station to see to them, steered them to one or the other of these *hachsharoth*. That served the objectives of the Zionist organization, of the Jewish young people arriving in Holland, and equally important, of the Dutch government."

"The aim of the Dutch Zionist organization was to keep the immigrants together, in an all-Jewish environment, in a setting which fostered *Aliyah*, their further migration to Palestine. Moreover, if the new arrivals from Central Europe were diverted to the countryside, away from the cities, they were less likely to encounter anti-Semitism than if they joined the other Dutch Jews in the major cities. It furthered the immigrants' objectives, too, in that in the *hachsharah* setting they would acquire the essential skills that they would need in Palestine."

"Lastly, it served the objectives of the Dutch government in that it kept these immigrants away from the major centers of Jewish population and underlined that these new arrivals were in Holland only as temporary guests, who were to view Holland as a way station on the road to Palestine, and not as a permanent home. The new arrivals were to understand that they were visitors only and not on the road to Dutch citizenship."

"Why was it so important to the government to keep these Jewish newcomers out of the cities?" Renate asked.

"You have to remember that those years in the mid-1930's were marked by high levels of joblessness and social unrest. The Great Depression affected the Netherlands no less than other Western European countries. So the channeling of some of the refugees to *hachsharoth* in the countryside also enabled the Dutch government to reassure its people that it was doing everything within its power to keep Dutch jobs for Dutchmen."

"You know," Sigi added, "that's how the young Jewish idealists who were flooding into Holland saw it as well. They had arrived in Holland because it seemed to offer a haven from Nazi oppression. Very few of them saw Holland as a place to settle permanently. For them it was a way station on the road to that ultimate place of refuge, whether that was Palestine, England, America, South Africa, or elsewhere—to any place that would have them."

"And that attitude suited the Dutch people as well. Many elements of Dutch society resented that their little country was being 'overrun by those foreign elements from the east' who didn't fit into Dutch society and seemingly were making no effort to do so. To them, the Dutch government could say, and did say, that those outsiders, the *buitenstaanders*, were in their country only temporarily, and that it would not be necessary to make any efforts to integrate them into Dutch society."

"In fact, when the Nazis first came to power in 1933, the Dutch government posted six hundred additional guards along the border with Germany to keep people like us from crossing the border illegally. But later on, the pressures mounted until the number of applications for asylum increased to more than 50,000 annually."

"Eventually, in response to that pressure, the Dutch government issued residence permits to several thousand Jews from Central Europe, with conditions: They had to dwell in the countryside and not in the major cities, and the Jewish organizations had to speed these refugees on their way to permanent havens outside of Holland."

"Beginning in March 1938," Sigi went on, "the Dutch government also clamped down on Germans and Austrians who were entering the country on short-term and tourist visas and then staying beyond the expiration of those visas. The Dutch government mandated that the holders of those visas return to their own country and apply at the Dutch consulates in those countries for the longer-term visas. Of course, that was the last thing that those families and individuals were likely to do—to return to Germany and Austria to meet that requirement."

"Was it anti-Semitism that was behind all those restrictions?" Renate asked. "The government and the people just didn't want to be flooded with all those Jewish refugees from the East? 'Dutch jobs for Dutchmen,' as you put it?"

"That was part of it. But it was also that the Dutch government was still trying to placate Nazi Germany, and it thought it could do that by forcing these desperate refugees to comply with the strict letter of the law. The officials also reasoned that, by going along with the Nazis and their anti-Jewish edicts they were acting in the greater good. That is, they were making sure that if they took these measures the Germans would keep their hands off the non-Jewish Dutch population."

'Thank you for filling me in with the historical background," Renate said. "But let's get back to the main story, the story of Max Windmüller. What was the connection between Max and the *hachsharoth*?"

"As I said, Max worked in those years on his own, on farms owned by non-Jews. That system, young Jews working as individual farmhands on farms owned by non-Jews, was referred to as the *Einzel-hachsharah*, the one-person or stand-alone *hachsharah*. Men and women like Max, working alone on farms, had to have a focal point, a place where they could overcome their isolation by meeting other young Jews, learning Hebrew, participating in Jewish religious and cultural activities, and so on. So they were attached for those purposes to the largest and oldest of the *hachsharoth*, the Central Deventer Association."

"That *hachsharah*, the one that Max was affiliated with, was organized in 1918, so it was one of the early ones. It was housed in what had been a youth hostel before it was acquired by the Zionists. The new owners renamed it the *Beth Chalutz*, the Pioneer House. The director was Rudolf, or Ru, Cohen, the man whom I've already mentioned as the coordinator of the *hachsharah* movement. He was later to play an important role in Max's life and mine."

"And how about you, Sigi? Were you also working in an *einzel hachsharah*, on a Dutch farm, during that time?"

"No. I was living in Loosdrecht, a town in central Holland southeast of Amsterdam in a *hachsharah* there, called, in Dutch, the *Paviljoen Loosdrechtse Rade,* or Loosdrecht Youth *Aliyah* Pavilion. It had been built and operated originally as a home for troubled children whose families couldn't raise them in their own homes. Then it was acquired by a Jewish family, the Deutsches, who donated it to the Youth *Aliyah* movement."

Renate changed the subject. "Let's get back to Ru Cohen. Can you give us some background information on him?"

After consulting his notes, Sigi continued, "Ru Cohen was born in 1889, one of six children. He and his family owned a furniture store in Deventer. The Cohens were a large Dutch-Jewish family, all of them very accomplished. They all made a name for themselves before, during, and after the war. His older brother, David, had been for many years a leader in the Jewish community."

He paused, seeming to choose his words carefully. "I would consider Ru Cohen one of the key figures in Dutch Zionism. Keep in mind that the Jewish leaders in Holland were not keen on the Zionist ideal. They felt that they had a secure place in Dutch society, and they saw no need to encourage Dutch Jews to pull up stakes and to move to Palestine. Why give up their comfortable existence, they reasoned, to move to a primitive land where they would have to struggle just to meet their basic needs?"

"Ru Cohen was cut from different cloth. Seeing the need for a Jewish homeland, he had the courage to fight for the Zionist ideal. Sadly, he and his wife Eva died in the Bergen-Belsen concentration camp on February 27, 1945."

"You must understand," Sigi said, "that the conference held in Basel, Switzerland, the one at which Theodor Herzl kicked off the Zionist movement, was held in 1897. So in 1918, when the Central Deventer Society acquired that former youth hostel for use as a *hachsharah,* the movement had not yet taken hold. The idea of a Jewish homeland in Palestine, a place where Jews, regardless of their present nationality, would want to spend the rest of their lives—that was still a relatively new notion in 1918."

"And I imagine," Renate mused, "that the Zionist leaders and the rank and file got renewed energy for the movement from the First World War, with all the turmoil and the huge loss of life that it brought everywhere in Europe."

"You're certainly right about that," Sigi responded. Then, returning to the story, he went on: "Those two years at Loosdrecht, before the war started, were the happiest days of my life." He pulled out a photo album from the bag at his feet and quickly found what he was looking for: a full-page group photo. "This was taken at the *hachsharah* in May 1941, shortly before we all disappeared into hiding."

"The Loosdrecht building," Sigi continued, "housed only sixty men and women, both staff and trainees. In this photo you see about fifty of the *chalutzim*, the pioneers, about equally divided between men and women. Metta Lande, the young girl who was to play such an important role in Max's brief life, is among those in the photo: she's number thirty-eight, the girl with the long dark hair, at the far left in the second row. Another pioneer who was to be significant in this story was Menachem Pinkhof. He's in the front row, third from the right. Max's younger brother, Emil, was also a member of the Loosdrecht *hachsharah,* but he came only later, after this photograph was taken."

Residents of Loosdrecht Pavilion *Hachsharah*

Renate looked intently at the faces in the photograph. These young people all looked so healthy, so confident of the future. Did they not know that the locomotive was coming down the track at full speed, and that they were in front of it, tied to the tracks? They must have known, but in this photo they seemed to be brimming with confidence, enjoying the vigor of youth.

"Are you in this photograph?" Renate asked.

"I was one of the few members of the Loosdrecht pavilion who were not there for the photo, either because we were sick or away from the Pavilion for some reason."

"And am I right, that the mood was one of optimism and confidence?"

"Maybe for some of us," Sigi replied. "But believe me, we were worried and had good cause to be. We missed our parents terribly, and we were deeply concerned for their safety. Would we ever see them again? Would they be able to escape the Nazi onslaught? And we stayed awake at night, lost sleep, thinking about our own future. Would the Netherlands be overrun? If so, would we live to see the end of the war? Yes, we had each other for support and took great comfort from that, but would that be enough? So there was a strong undercurrent of concern, which we didn't hide from each other or from ourselves."

Sigi continued, "To you and to your readers, the people in this photo are just faces and names. To me they were best buddies. We were a unit, almost as if we were welded together." Identifying the leaders first, his forefinger landed on the images of Joachim (Schuschu) Simon, Menachem Pinkhof, and Kurt (Nanno) Hannemann.

Joachim (Schuschu) Simon

Kurt (Nanno) Hannemann

His finger moved across the photograph. "Harald Simon, Siegbert Pinkus, Hans Eisner, Herbert Levy, Ferencz (Schraga) Engel—thirty-three of these young men and women survived and achieved their dream of *Aliyah*. But these others"—his face took on a somber cast as he named them—"Kurt Hannemann, Erwin Schwab, Manfred Schwab, Juda Pinkhof, Harald Simon, Joseph Rolf Kalmanowitz, Esra Jurovics—twenty-three in all—did not survive. They died in the camps, of typhus maybe, or of starvation, or they were shot or gassed. Hardly a day goes by when I don't think of them, especially Esra. He was only seventeen when he died."

And then Sigi pointed to the image of Metta. "That's her . . . Metta Lande. She became Max's sweetheart."

Metta Lande

"You'll tell me about her, I hope?"

"Yes, but we're not there yet. Their relationship didn't bloom until four years later in Paris."

"Where is Max in this photo?"

"Max was never part of the Loosdrecht pioneers. As I told you, he was working independently at the farm in Hengelo."

"Young men and women living under the same roof . . . there must have been many intense romances at Loosdrecht," Renate mused.

"Not that I can remember," said Sigi. "It's fair to say that the leaders—the administrators and instructors—frowned on us boys and girls coupling up. They felt that these relationships led to conflict and distracted us from the mission of the *hachsharah*. But yes, it's likely that nature and hormones prevailed."

"Do we know how Max and Metta came together?"

"Yes, I was there that weekend. Max already had a girlfriend, Edith Kaiser. She was originally from Aurich, a town in Ostfriesland not far from Emden, and she was working on a farm near his. Learning that Max was planning a trip to the Loosdrecht *hachsharah,* Edith asked Max to deliver a message to Sophie and Auguste (Gustel) Nussbaum, who were already living there. Sophie and Gustel were Max's cousins and also friends of Edith's. She also asked Max to look out for Metta, who had only recently arrived at the Loosdrecht Pavilion."

"Where had she come from?"

Sigi hesitated. "I can only tell you what I learned from her and from others while we were at Loosdrecht."

"Please," said Renate urgently, "tell me what you know."

"Metta's father had been sent to the Buchenwald concentration camp just days after the outbreak of anti-Jewish violence on *Kristallnacht*, the night of November 9–10, 1938. After nine months in the camp, he was released when he showed the prison authorities a forged American entry visa. On December 10, 1938, a month after *Kristallnacht* and while Metta's father was still in Buchenwald, her mother put Metta on a *Kindertransport* train to Amsterdam. Many Jewish parents at that time were sending their children to Holland, thinking that if there were to be another war, the Netherlands would remain neutral as it had been in World War I, and that their children would be safe there."

"So Metta was met at the train station by the Zionist representatives and steered to Loosdrecht?"

"No, it didn't happen that way," Sigi answered. "She lived first in Rijswijk, near the Hague, at the home of a wealthy Jewish woman, Mrs. Hartog, who was also sheltering other Jewish children in her home. Then she lived briefly with another couple, the Wentinks, in Zutphen. They brought her back to Loosdrecht, where she lived briefly with the Doetses, Dirk and Petronella, before moving into the Loosdrecht Pavilion in January 1941."

"What happened to Metta's parents?"

"They were among the fortunate ones," Sigi replied. "Both of them and her older brother managed to get to Palestine on an illegal transport before the war broke out, but Metta was unable to join them."

". . . and Edith?"

"Max and Edith parted company soon after, and she met someone else. But I can say that from that, one visit, Max fixed a picture of Metta in his mind, and was completely smitten by her, even though it would be four years until he would see her again."

"The people whom he was to meet that weekend as a visitor at Loosdrecht," Sigi added, "were to change Max's life. That was where he first set eyes on Metta, and where he was introduced to the two men with whom he would be working closely later on in the child-rescue movement: Joachim (Shuschu) Simon and Menachem Pinkhof."

After Sigi closed the album. Renate allowed him a few moments of silence to be alone with his thoughts, before urging him to continue his story. He returned from his reverie to that time and place and resumed his narrative. "So yes, Renate, you want to know more about Max . . ."

She nodded encouragingly. "Yes, of course . . . and in as much detail as you can give me."

"In May 1937, when Max and I were still in school in Groningen, our little community of Emden Jews experienced the first of the many hammer blows that were to strike us in the next eight years, and it fell specifically on Moritz Windmüller, the patriarch of the Windmüller family. Max told me after it happened that his father had complained of stomach pains but dismissed them as indigestion and took a heavy dose of antacid pills. Then three days after he first felt those pains, he woke up in the middle of the night doubled over in pain. His wife, over her husband's objections, called the ambulance and had him brought to the hospital. There the blood tests confirmed that he had a perforated stomach ulcer. The doctors performed emergency surgery, but they could not save his life. On Friday of that week, Moritz Windmüller, age fifty-seven, passed away with his family at his bedside. Before he died he exhorted his wife and children to *'Hab' Mut! Sei stark!—*'Have courage! Be strong!'"

"The funeral was held the following Sunday at the gravesite in the Jewish cemetery on what was then the *Winsumerstraatweg.* A light rain was falling and a strong wind gusting from the north. We mourners held our umbrellas in front of us to keep the rain and the wind from our faces. The rabbi from the Groningen synagogue, a man who hardly knew Moritz, presided at the funeral service. We recited in Hebrew the traditional payers for the dead and confirmed our belief in the restoration of the soul at the coming of the Messiah. Then the rabbi gave a brief eulogy in Dutch. I'm sure his words were well chosen, but we exiles from the east understood hardly a word because of our limited knowledge of Dutch and because the brisk wind seemed to blow his words away as soon as he uttered them."

"I was there with my family, and of course Moritz's wife and children. There were only five others present, German Jews whom we had come to know, refugees from the east, as we were. Moritz was laid to rest in a remote corner of the Jewish cemetery, an exile, an outsider, even in death. He had requested on his deathbed that he be buried with his parents and Windmüller ancestors in the Jewish cemetery in Emden. His dying wish could not be fulfilled because the family could not travel back to Emden for the interment and then resume its life there in Groningen. They would have been turned back at the border and their fates forever sealed."

"As the gravediggers lowered the coffin into its resting place, Ruthi, standing under her mother's protective arm, broke out in wracking sobs, which continued even as Max and I and the other mourners tossed our shovel loads of dirt onto the casket, signifying the finality of death. Then we trudged slowly away from the open grave, huddled against each other for warmth and for protection against the randomness, the cruelty, of our earthly existence. No doubt the Windmüller family was even then asking themselves what the future had in store now that their mainstay—husband and father—was no longer there to guide them."

"Moritz's death came as a shock, too, to my parents and to other Emden Jews of that generation. So young and so suddenly! He had been a contemporary of theirs, and for him to die so young was unfathomable. How could that happen? I stayed behind to be a comfort to my parents, just as Max was then staying with his mother, newly widowed, and his brothers and sister. They surely needed him, and he was there for them."

"After the *seudat havra'ah*, the traditional mourners' repast that follows the funeral, Max called me aside. He had the air of someone who had important information to impart. I followed him out the backdoor into the little backyard. All was silent between us for a few moments, and then Max turned to me and said, 'Sigi, I have a favor to ask of you.'"

"'Of course, Max. What can I do for you?'"

"'On my way back from the cemetery, I made a promise to Vati that whatever I do in this life, I will do it to honor his memory. I will do nothing that would make me ashamed before him.'"

"'And how can I help?' I asked.

"''If you ever see me heading in the wrong direction, I want you to remind me of my promise and pull me back onto the right path. That's what good friends are supposed to do for each other. Will you do that, Sigi?'"

"'You have my word on it, Max.' I embraced him, as if to seal my vow."

"I remember that conversation so clearly," Sigi went on, "because in my opinion everything that he did in the few years he had left was done to carry out that promise that he had made to his father. And I can say with complete confidence that I never had to pull him back from the wrong path."

Renate was much moved. "How many of us will be able to look our parents in the eye and be able to say, when we arrive in whatever afterlife awaits us, that we were true to their teachings?"

"That's certainly true, Renate," said Sigi, "but it's a noble goal nevertheless. Am I right?"

She nodded in agreement. "Please continue."

"In the weeks and months ahead, it seemed to me that a profound change came over Max. He was no longer the jokester, the happy-go-lucky kid yodeling his way through life. It was as if God had put a hand on his shoulder and said, 'Max, put the foolish ways of childhood behind you. Now is the time to be a man. I expect nothing less from you.'"

Sigi went on. "I noticed in my friend a new seriousness of purpose that hadn't been there before. You could say that he had consciously donned the mantle of leadership. It must have been so, because the younger boys and girls at the *hachsharoth* looked up to him with admiration and respect, and the adult leaders consulted him when there were important decisions to be made. Our friendship, at the same time, remained steadfast. Max considered the two of us to be a team, and so did I."

"So we completed our secondary education and moved on to our *hachsharah* training. But it seems to me, looking back, that we did so with a new focus, a higher level of intensity. The work we did couldn't just be good enough, it had to be very good, and that wasn't just to please our instructors, but to satisfy ourselves that we were excellent in what we did. Max was motivated by the vow that he had made to his father on his deathbed, and both of us by centuries of Jewish history: Jews had been held in contempt over the centuries because we were not rooted in the land, we didn't have that love of the land, that connectedness with it, that the non-Jewish peasant had."

"Of course, that wasn't our choice. The laws had forbidden it and forced Jews into occupations that were barred to non-Jews by their religious authorities, such as money changing and money lending. But Palestine would be different. There we Jews had bought the land from the Arabs, we owned it, and we were extracting a living from that ownership, and that's what we were training ourselves to do. Then came *Kristallnacht* in November of the following year, when the Nazi pigs burned down our synagogue in Emden."

"Renate noticed that, after sixty years, the memory of that event still brought an expression of contempt to Sigi's face. He continued: "Five years earlier, Max and I had stood on the *bimah*, the raised platform in the front of the synagogue, facing our family and fellow Jews, and we read from the Torah and delivered our Bar Mitzvah *Rede*, our little speech. Now, in my mind's eye, nothing of the building remained but piles of charred wreckage."

Emden synagogue before *Kristallnacht*

"We learned after the war," Sigi continued, "that the Nazi chief in Emden was given instructions on the evening of November 9, 1938, that every synagogue in Germany was to be destroyed later that night, and that it was his responsibility to burn down the Emden synagogue. He mobilized the local SS to get the job done. He alerted the firefighters that they were to turn out to keep the fire from spreading to nearby houses, but that they were not to interfere with the torching of the synagogue. The police were also alerted to cordon off the synagogue to prevent Jewish men from entering the building. The SS men sloshed five gallons of gasoline around the synagogue and then set the building afire. And that was the end of a centuries-long chapter of Jewish history in my hometown. That pogrom—,"

"'Pogrom'? I'm not sure of the meaning of that word," Renate said.

"It's a Russian word originally, and it means an organized violent attack on a particular religious or ethnic group. It referred originally to attacks on Jews in nineteenth century Russia, and still today it usually refers to attacks on Jews."

"Okay, please continue."

"So that pogrom, directed at Jews and Jewish institutions, made it clear to us, and to Jews in Germany and everywhere, that this was the start of a planned effort at the highest levels to destroy what was left of German Jewry, that Jews who remained in Germany were targeted for internment and, what was more and more likely, for death."

"It was also becoming clear to us in the *hachsharah* that it wasn't only the Jews of Germany and Austria who were under siege, but that no place in Europe was safe for us, that Hitler and the Nazis had territorial ambitions extending beyond Germany's borders and that we in the Netherlands, with its long border with Germany, were especially vulnerable. Max and I both felt that we had mastered the agricultural skills—Max on his farms and I at the *hachsharah*—that we would need and that we were ready, now more than ever, to leave Holland and make *Aliyah* to Palestine. That had been our dream and our goal since we were children. Seven months after *Kristallnacht*, we were to have the opportunity."

At that point, Renate closed her notebook, turned off the tape recorder, and ended the interview, telling Sigi that she would return at nine o'clock the following day. It seemed to Renate that Sigi was much relieved that the stress of recalling these events was over, at least for that day.

PART 3

The Third Day

CHAPTER 3

The S.S. *Dora*

‿❦

At nine o'clock on the following morning, Renate was standing in Sigi's apartment doorway, pleased with herself that once again she had had the discipline to arrive on time. Sigi greeted her, beaming broadly. "Typical German punctuality!" he chuckled.

The fine weather that they had enjoyed the previous day had changed overnight. Now a light rain was falling, and the western sky as they viewed it from Sigi's living room window showed itself in menacing shades of gray, with low scudding clouds.

After hanging her raincoat in the hall closet, Sigi said, "Renate, it looks like we will have to sit inside today." He gestured toward a comfortable upholstered chair next to the sofa. Renate saw at a glance that coffee cups, a coffee pitcher, and croissants were already neatly in place on the coffee table. She took her seat. Sigi took his.

As they sat down, Sigi told her, "My dear wife, Minna, picked out this furniture suite when we first bought this apartment twelve years ago. I was not enthusiastic about it at the time—too contemporary for my taste—but she had her way, and the placement of the furniture was her choice as well. I have to admit that over the years I have become used to this furniture. On the rare occasions when I have guests, I like to think that they are impressed with my good taste."

He poured coffee into her cup, Renate's second cup of the morning, and another for himself. Renate readied herself with the tape recorder turned on and the notepad in her lap. Sigi sat at the edge of his chair, eager to begin. "Where would you like to start today, Renate?" he asked.

"Yesterday you talked about the training that you and Max got—Max on his farms and you at the Loosdrecht *hachsharah.* You must have felt at the end of the two years that you had acquired the skills that you would need in Palestine and that you were ready to make *Aliyah.*"

"Absolutely. In our minds we were ready, and even more important, the leadership at the *hachsharoth* told us that we were ready—ready, as they put it, to make important contributions to *Eretz Israel* once we arrived there."

"And yet, it never happened. Tell me about that."

And so he did. He spoke in a flat voice, as if trying to suppress the emotions that he felt, even now, almost 60 years after the events that he would be describing.

"It was on June 17, 1939, a Saturday night. It was our custom at the Loosdrecht Pavilion to celebrate the close of the Sabbath with *havdalah,* the short prayer service marking the end of the Sabbath and the beginning of the workweek. Our leader, Lodi Cohen, remained standing after the final amen and held up his hand. When the hall had quieted down, he began in a serious tone:

Chaverim, friends, the day has arrived that we have dedicated ourselves to for the last two years, the day that we have worked so hard to prepare ourselves for.

"We looked at each other, our faces showing a mixture of excitement and concern. Lodi continued:

By noon tomorrow, those of you who are of age and quali-
fied will be taken from here and brought to destinations that
I cannot identify right now. The following day, you will be
brought by launch to a ship that is waiting in the harbor at
Amsterdam, and that ship will, please God, bring you to *Eretz
Israel*, the Land of Israel.

"Amid the ensuing hubbub, the raised voices, the enthusiastic shoul-
der-claps and embraces, one of the pioneers raised his hand and
asked, 'What does "qualified" mean?' Lodi answered, 'Qualified'
means that you are eighteen years old or older, that you have had
two years of training here or at another *hachsharah*, and that you
are in good health. A doctor will be here tomorrow to make that
determination.'"

"I looked around at my fellow *chalutzim*. Many of them were
overjoyed that their stay in Holland was ending and that they would
soon be at sea and on their way to Palestine. At the same time, there
were others at the tables who were somber, even sad, and I saw not a
few whose faces were turned down so that we might not see the tears
in their eyes. I understood their reaction, understood it well—indeed
I had some sympathy with it."

"Some in that group were not yet of age to leave the *hachsharah*.
Others were of age but had not spent the requisite two years of training at the *hachsharah*. And then there was that physical fitness issue.
In our excitement, very few of us had heard that last word of caution.
But I did. Could I somehow get past that physical hurdle? I felt a
nasty choking sensation in my throat. Those years of preparation . . .
were they now to be for naught?"

Renate interrupted Sigi's narrative. "And Metta? Was she among
those who were too young to make the trip?"

"You're forgetting, Renate. At that point, in June 1939, Metta had not yet arrived at the Loosdrecht *hachsharah*. She was still living with Mrs. Hartog near The Hague. But even if she had been with us, she was then only fifteen, too young to make the voyage."

"And even among those who were old enough, healthy enough, and fully-trained, there was the sobering realization that this voyage would require another round of painful goodbyes—goodbyes to the families who had brought us out of Germany to this temporary haven in Holland, and goodbyes to our fellow *chalutzim*, the ones who would be left behind. Why is it, I asked myself, that these moments of joy seemed always to be tempered with a tinge of sadness? I tried not to picture the parting from my parents and my sisters. I looked across the table at Isi, Max's brother. If he had any doubts about this adventure, he hid them well. I saw only a look of intense satisfaction, as if he were saying to himself, 'This is it, and I'm ready.' It's like those war movies where the commander tells the troops in his unit to synchronize their watches, and, moments later, at the agreed-upon time, he calls out, 'Let's move out!' At times like these, you want to be fully focused on your objective and to push away the thoughts of the family and the sweetheart back home."

"'What was your thinking, Sigi? Do you recall?'"

"I shared in that general feeling of excitement. These were my adopted brothers and sisters, so to speak, and now we would be traveling to the Promised Land together. Of course I was excited. You would have been, too," he said, looking in Renate's direction.

"But I had some gnawing doubts. How would I make a living in Palestine? Where would I be living? And would I personally have to confront the Arabs who had been raiding the Jewish settlements? I'm sure that all of us, even if we wouldn't admit it, shared those same questions, the same doubts."

"Of more immediate concern was my health. Would I pass that physical examination? And if I passed that hurdle, was I physically up to the strain of the voyage? There in Loosdrecht, for the last few months, I had had that same feeling of congestion in my chest that I had had years earlier in Emden, a shortness of breath, a flushed feeling in my face. I dared not let anyone know about it. At night I took aspirin when no one was looking. I was desperate to get on that ship to Palestine, and my greatest fear was that if my condition were known I would be medically disqualified from sailing."

"I can imagine that you didn't get much sleep that night," Renate suggested.

"You imagine correctly," Sigi answered. "When Lodi had finished, he invited questions, but many times he refused to answer, explaining that the less we knew about this operation, the better. Of course, this was not reassuring to those of us in the room. It was obvious that we were being asked to launch ourselves into the unknown, putting our trust in the adults who were organizing this emigration."

"So, yes, we hardly slept at all that night. The next morning we stood in line, men in one line, women in the other, for the physical examination. When my turn came, I moved into the little cubicle where the doctor sat, an elderly man, probably retired from medical practice. I stripped to the waist. He asked about my general health. I lied, said I was in excellent condition. He assessed me thoughtfully. He took my blood pressure, felt for my pulse, checked my nose, ears, and throat, then examined me with a stethoscope. I got dressed again, and he dismissed me with a warm smile."

"Our leaders had suggested that we spend the afternoon writing letters to our families, assuring us that the letters would be mailed that same day. We assembled in the dining room for that purpose, our places set with blank paper and pens instead of plates and cutlery.

I pictured my family reading my letter, and the tears that they would shed, but I was convinced that in time. they would come around to see that this was all for the best."

"In the middle of the letter writing, as I hunched over the letter-paper deep in thought, I felt a tap on my shoulder. It was Lodi Cohen, our director. He asked me to follow him into his office. I knew, even as I followed him, what he was about to tell me. 'No tears,' I said to myself. When we were together in his office, Lodi confirmed my worst fears. 'Sigi,' he said, 'Doctor Wolff has informed us that you have a serious case of influenza. He recommends that we not allow you to board that ship. It's best, the doctor told us, that you undergo a period of hospitalization to regain your health.'"

"As much I had anticipated this, Lodi's words hit me like hammer blows. I put my hands to my face, rubbing my eyes to keep the tears inside. 'Why?' I asked, knowing the answer. 'He says your influenza is highly contagious. The ship will be very crowded, one body close up against another. The Zionist leadership in Amsterdam can't take the chance of a major epidemic on board the vessel that could possibly threaten the success of the journey and safe arrival in *Eretz Israel*. It's just not possible.'"

"I mumbled my thanks to Lodi and got up from the chair, wanting nothing but to be alone with my disappointment. But Lodi put a consoling hand on my arm. 'Sigi', he said, 'we have arranged for you to spend time in a sanitarium not far from here, where, hopefully, you can get your health back and then rejoin us. We will drive you over there tomorrow morning.' So the leaders would be looking after me, had my best interests in mind. I was grateful for that, even as I was resentful that my chances of ever getting to Palestine were effectively now at zero."

"The next morning, those that had passed muster were downstairs hugging each other, joy on their faces. Those that were staying behind because they were too young or because they had not had their two years of training, stood along the walls, watching the hubbub, wishing that they were among those scheduled to depart. I was there, too, with my bags packed. My destination: a tuberculosis sanitarium in Hilversum, just three miles away. There was no joy on my face, for sure. One by one, those who were leaving for Amsterdam came over to me to offer their condolences. I tried to be gracious, but it was hard."

"Within an hour the buses arrived. You may be picturing tourist buses, brightly painted, such as you see on the roads nowadays, with clear markings on the outside identifying the owner or operator and the destination. Far from it. These were painted a gun-metal gray, with no markings to indicate who owned them, where they were coming from, or where they were going. The *chalutzim* who were leaving received a cheerful send-off from the leaders who were staying behind—from Lodi Cohen, Menachem Pinkhof, and Schuschu Simon. The three of them were still there, a half-hour later, when the car arrived to bring me to the sanitarium. 'You'll get the best of care,' they assured me, 'and you'll be back here in no time. Just cooperate with the doctors and nurses, and you'll have your health back. Be strong, Sigi,' they said. 'You'll be out on the next ship!' I was pleased with their reassurances, even though I knew, as they probably did, too, that there would never be a next ship."

"And Max? Where was he during this time?"

"Max was among those who had been selected for the journey, but he left for Amsterdam directly from the farm where he had been working."

"So you came to the Hilversum sanitarium. What was that like?"

"I received the best of care there. But mainly, I think that what put me on the path to recovery was the good food, plenty of sleep, and hours and hours of lying on the terrace, soaking in the warmth of the sun."

"Three weeks after my arrival I was on that sun-soaked terrace, dozing as usual, when a nurse came over, nudged me awake, and said, 'Mr. Kirschner, you have a guest.'"

"Who would be visiting me?, I wondered. Someone from Loosdrecht, no doubt. I was wrong. Through the doorway onto the terrace came . . . Max Windmüller, smiling with that ear-to-ear grin of his. I sat up in shock. 'Max, it can't be! Is it really you?'"

"'It's me, in the flesh, come to make sure that my dearest friend is getting the best of care.'"

"'Sit down, sit down! I was sure that you were on the high seas right now, approaching *Eretz Israel*. Didn't the ship leave when it was supposed to?'"

"'Oh, the ship left, yes, two weeks late. Isi boarded it, but I didn't.'"

"'What happened?' I asked. Had he been medically disqualified, as I had been?

"'They needed me here,' Max said with a shrug of his shoulders. 'I made a commitment, and the ship sailed without me.'"

Renate broke in. "You'll tell me that whole story?"

"I'll tell it to you just as Max told it to me," Sigi said, "The best that I can remember it. The buses left Loosdrecht and headed westward toward Amsterdam, as they were supposed to. But instead of heading toward the docks, as Max had reckoned they would, they skirted the city and continued westward. At that point, the leader on the bus, Erich, got up—"

Renate broke in. "'Erich,'" she repeated, "'Do you know his last name?"

"Zielenzieger," Sigi replied, "'Erich Zielenzieger.' He spelled out the name, letter by letter. "He survived the war and ended up in New York City. He may still be living there."

"Okay, please continue."

"He told the *chalutzim* on the bus that, as the ship would not leave until the next day, they would be dispersed in villages around Amsterdam. He told them, also, that when they arrived at the place where they were to spend the night, they were to go straight to the room where they would be sleeping and stay there, leaving only to use the bathroom. Their meals would be left at the door, and there would be three knocks at the door to tell them that the food was waiting. Then the next morning, a car would come by to pick them up."

"'When'? someone in the back of the bus asked."

"'I can't tell you for sure,' Erich answered. 'Just stay in your room until the lady of the house tells you that it's time to go.'"

"So that's what they did. Max and Isi were taken to the village of Assendelft, fifteen miles northwest of Amsterdam. Max was dropped off at a farmhouse at the edge of the village, and Isi was put up somewhere else farther on. In any case, the one day that they were supposed to stay there in that town stretched out, first to two days, then three, then more. It was two weeks later that they were finally picked up and brought to Amsterdam. Those two weeks seemed like an eternity, and it must have been so for Max's host family as well. They were the van den Heuvels, Piet and Wilhelmina, like the queen's name, but everybody called her Willi."

Sigi turned to Renate, interrupting the narrative. "When I went back to Holland in 1982, I went to Assendelft, hoping to find them.

Both of them had passed away, but their daughter Annieke still lived in the town, took me back to where they had lived, and showed me the room where Max had been cooped up for those two weeks."

Renate asked, "Did Max ever learn the reason for the two-week delay?"

"The only explanation he received was '*bureaucratie*'—Dutch bureaucracy."

"And do we know now what the real reason was?"

"That *was* the real reason, more or less. When you've lived in Holland, even if only briefly, that's all the explanation you need."

"Okay, Sigi. Continue with the story as Max told it to you. What happened when he and the others in the group were finally brought to the quay in Amsterdam?"

Sigi took a deep breath. "We're at a turning point in the story, one in which Max made that life-altering decision, a decision that ultimately cost him his life, but a decision also that elevated him into that pantheon of Jewish and non-Jewish heroes who sacrificed their lives to save others during the *Shoah*, the Holocaust."

"First, some background. Since the time when the Nazis had come to power, the Netherlands had taken in about 15,000 Jewish refugees from Central Europe, but only a fraction of them, 1,000 in all, were on *hachsharoth* preparing for a new life in Palestine."

". . . and the others?" Renate asked.

"The majority of the refugees were absorbed in the existing Jewish communities in Amsterdam and the other large cities." Sigi resumed. "As I said before, the Jewish Agency gave most of its allowance of *Certificats* to Jews from Germany and Austria because those Jews were seen as exposed to the greatest danger. That meant that only a trickle of Dutch Jews was able to emigrate legally in the late 1930's. As a consequence, many of the German and Austrian Jews who were living on the *hachsharoth* and training there were forced to stay there longer than they had anticipated, waiting to receive the *Certificats*. That, in turn, prevented other young Jews then living in those countries from crossing the border into Holland and securing places on the *hachsharoth*."

"Another consequence was that the young Jews who had been training on the *hachsharoth* for emigration to Palestine, when their efforts to get the *Certificats* for legal entry were frustrated, started thinking about entering Palestine illegally. Those were the years in which a flotilla of hardly seaworthy ships was assembled in ports everywhere in Europe for the risky voyage to Palestine."

"Like the S.S. *Exodus*, in Leon Uris's book, right?" Renate suggested.

"More or less," Sigi answered, "but the *Exodus* sailed after the war, and my point is that many such ships—fifty of them, in fact—were already trying to reach Palestine in the years before the war. A group of Zionists in Holland, with the help of Zionist organizations in Palestine, took matters into their own hands. They decided that they would use the *Haganah*—'"

"—the '*Haganah*'? Can you explain what that was?"

"'*Haganah* means 'the defense' in Hebrew. It was the military arm of the Zionist movement, of those who had successfully arrived in Palestine and were now trying to help their fellow Jews get out of Europe. The *Haganah* developed the plan to buy old ships, refit them, and use those ships to smuggle Jews out of Europe. They sent Giora Josephthal to Holland to tell the Dutch Zionist leaders of the plan. But those men, most notably the Cohen brothers, David and Rudolf (Ru), did not want to be party to any illegal methods of helping Jews to emigrate. So the *Haganah* proceeded with its plans without their assistance or support."

"The Haganah's point man in Paris, Shmarya Zameret, was put in charge of making the arrangements for the illegal immigration to Palestine from European ports. As an American citizen, he carried an American passport identifying him as 'Mr. Grey', his name at birth. With that American passport, he could move freely from one European country to another. Moreover, he could speak English fluently, and did so when the situation required it. He traveled to Denmark on that passport to look for a ship that might be suitable for the purposes he had in mind and found just such a ship riding at anchor in the Copenhagen harbor. The ship was then named *Tjaldur*. Zameret renamed it the S.S. *Dora,* and that's the name that we, and later the entire world, would know it by. The *Dora* had been a coal-carrying vessel, built in Glasgow, Scotland, forty years earlier, but when Zameret saw it, he judged the ship was well-built and seaworthy, more than adequate for its intended purpose."

The S.S. *Dora*, formerly the S.S. *Tjaldur*

"On June 21, 1939, Zameret bought the ship from its Greek owners, and he and they, working together, proceeded to refit the ship with 175 bunkbeds, a kitchen, lavatories, and showers, with adequate lifeboats and life-vests. They also set out to hire a Danish crew, which was told a cover story about the ship's destination: They weren't told the real purpose of the *Dora's* voyage."

"All of this refitting and the recruiting of a crew took more time than expected. The Zionist leadership and the young men and women who were then living in those villages outside of Amsterdam were getting increasingly nervous as the days slipped by. If word leaked out of the *Dora's* illegal mission, the Dutch navy might prevent the ship from leaving the Amsterdam harbor."

"There were further delays when the *Dora* finally arrived in Amsterdam. The Danish crew found out the ship's mission, decided that the voyage was too risky, and walked off the ship. A new crew of Greek sailors was brought on board. Coal and provisions had to be ordered and delivered."

"Despite the strenuous efforts of Zameret and the others on the team to keep the ship's destination a secret, word leaked out. The men who were loading coal onto the ship noticed all the beds crammed into the hold. This was clearly no coaling vessel. They passed the word to the local Communist newspaper, which published a headline story attacking the government for allowing this derelict ship, with hundreds of 'slaves' aboard, to set sail. Other Amsterdam newspapers picked up on the story, referring to the *Dora* as the *Dodenschip*, the 'ship of the dead', and news photographers encircled the ship in little boats to get pictures of it. Responding to the publicity that the ship was getting, the government ordered the harbormaster to inspect it."

"Zameret had to disclose to the harbormaster the real reason for the *Dora's* voyage and its true destination. Fortunately, the harbormaster did not quash the entire expedition: He ordered only minor adjustments to comply with maritime safety codes. The Dutch government had to issue a statement explaining that the *Dora* was not a 'slave ship' or a 'death ship',' and that the passengers were leaving of their own free will."

"Finally, after those weeks-long delays, the ship was ready to set sail. On the evening of July 14, 1939, the brothers, Max and Isi, and the other young people who had been living from day to day in the villages outside of Amsterdam were brought into the city. They were put up for the night at the Lloyd Hotel, right there on the quay. From the hotel room window they could see the *Dora* riding at anchor in the harbor. In the early morning hours of the next day, the pioneers assembled at the dockside where the launch stood ready to take them out to the ship."

Renate interrupted. "What can you tell us about the Windmüller brothers' goodbyes from their family when they were about to leave for Palestine."

Sigi replied, "I asked Max that very question. He took his time answering, as if he was still grappling with the pain that he felt when he recalled those events."

"The Windmüller family had lived for a long time with their sons' passion for Zionism, and that brought with it the knowledge that they would someday emigrate to Palestine to make *Aliyah*. Then, as the brothers prepared for their voyage on the *Dora*, they shared that information with their mother, now a widow, and with their brothers, Emil and Salo, and their sister Ruth, who were staying be-hind. Even so, Max told me, the actual day of the leave-taking was one he would never forget. It was made especially painful because they all knew, although they didn't voice it, that they might not see each other again."

"Another gut-wrenching separation," Renate commented.

"Exactly so. For Max, his parting from his mother, Jette, was the hardest. His brothers and his sister were young and healthy, and he could reasonably assume that they could make their way to safety. But Jette hadn't been the same since her husband's death. She was still, two years later, emotionally distraught, and had many physical problems to contend with. She hardly ever left her apartment and depended on a network of German and Dutch Jewish women to help her out."

"I know that she was fiercely proud of Isi and Max and of their accomplishments. She may have felt like the mothers of legend who sent their sons into battle knowing that they might not come back."

"How did Max describe her emotions on that day?" Renate asked.

"He could see that she was fighting hard to keep her self-control," Sigi answered, "but yes, when it actually came time for Max and Isi to leave, she threw her arms around them and wept silently, while Max's brothers and sister tried their best to comfort her. As Max was leaving, she pressed a silver *mezuzah,* on a chain, into his hands."

"*Mezuzah?* Explain that for my readers, please."

"It's the cylinder that contains the parchment on which is written the Lord's injunction to the Israelites from Deuteronomy Chapter 6, to believe in Him and to remember His words. It's affixed to the doors of Jewish homes and is often, as in this case, worn on a chain around the neck."

He continued: "Max wore that *mezuzah* around his neck every day for about two years, but then he took it off because anything of a Jewish nature would have made him a marked man if he had been caught on the street wearing it."

"Now go back," Renate urged, "to what happened the day that Max was leaving Amsterdam to board the *Dora.*"

"He told it to me this way," Sigi said, and commenced to tell the story to Renate as Max had told it to him, that day on the terrace of the sanitarium in Hilversum.

"'I was standing at the dockside with my knapsack on my back, my bags at my feet, waiting for my turn to get into the launch. You can imagine my state of mind. This was the moment that I had prepared for, had worked so hard for, for the past two years. I had no idea, as I prepared to step into the launch, that within minutes I would come to that fork in the road that we all encounter at some point in our lives, when we would be called upon to make decisions that are likely to change our lives forever.'"

Renate leaned forward to catch every word Sigi was saying, making sure that the tape recorder was likewise in full working order. "Go ahead," she said urgently.

"As the two of us, Isi and I, stood there at the water's edge, a familiar voice called out from behind us: 'Max! Max!' Turning around, we saw Ru Cohen, gasping and trying to regain his breath. 'Max, I need to talk to you. May I?' Isi and I started to walk back to where Ru was standing, but he gestured to Isi, indicating that he wanted to speak only to me. Isi and I looked at each other then, sharing an unspoken understanding that this turn of events did not bode well for us as passengers on the *Dora*."

"Complying with Ru Cohen's request, I walked the few paces to join up with him. Ru began to speak, in an urgent voice. 'Max,' he said, 'I know you have your heart set on making *Aliyah* to Palestine, on boarding this ship that will bring you there. I understand that. I understand your passion. But I have a passion, too. War is coming, Max. You know that. And when it comes, Jewish lives will be in peril. We are vulnerable, very vulnerable, especially our children and young people. They will need our help to escape from the Nazis. I am dedicating my life, Max, to making this happen. But I can't do it alone. I'll need help, *your* help, Max. Yes, the Jewish state needs you in Palestine. I know that. But we need you here even more.'"

"Ru went on: 'Max, I've learned in life that the path we have set out upon isn't always the one that we get to follow, that we run into many bumps in the road, many detours, so years later we look back in wonderment because we arrive at a point that's very far away from the one that we had started out on.'"

Renate interjected, thoughtfully, *"Mann denkt, Gott lenkt."*[Man proposes, God disposes'].

"You can certainly say that," Sigi agreed, and continued in his retelling of Max's story.

"So Max addressed to Ru the question that was uppermost in his mind. 'Why me, Ru? You have many capable people still here with you in Amsterdam, Rotterdam, the other big cities. So, again, why me'?'"

"Ru responded, 'Max, we've been watching you for the past two years. You've impressed us with your hard work, your enthusiasm, your leadership skills. We've noticed how you have been able to convince the farmers around Hengelo to take young Jewish refugees like yourself as farmhands. There aren't so many here with those qualities. That's why we need you, that's why I am asking you to stay here.'"

"Hearing this, I asked, 'Max, what was going through your mind when Ru was speaking'?"

"That Ru was like a military officer, asking me—no, demanding—that I not abandon my post, that I not take the easy path, that I belonged here.' He seemed to be saying that, if I boarded that ship, I would be deserting my comrades and allies here. When he put it in those terms, how could I turn him down? I would lose all my self-respect and I would be carrying this guilt for the rest of my life.'"

"So, meeting his intent gaze, I said, 'Ru, I'll do it, I'll stay here with you.'" Ru broke into a wide grin, threw his arms around me, and said, 'Welcome to the cause, my brother.'"

"At that point, Ru suggested that I call out to Isi and tell him of my decision. So I did that, gesturing to Isi to come over and join us. Isi walked the few paces over to where we were standing, locking his eyes on mine, as if he had a foreshadowing of what I would be telling him. With a slight movement of his head, Ru invited me to speak. 'Isi,' I said, 'Ru has asked me not to go with you. He wants me to stay behind to help him in his efforts to bring Jewish children to safety.'"

"'and you—,'" Isi broke in, impatiently.

"'I said "Yes."'

"Isi stared, speechless, first at Ru and then at Max. His face flushed with anger. Then he turned toward Ru and burst out, 'Ru, this is not fair! It's not fair that you should put Max in this position.'"

"Ru responded, 'It's a decision that didn't come easily, believe me. We know very well Max's passion to make *Aliyah*. But in the end we decided that we needed Max for this work. In my mind, this work, the work of saving Jewish children, must take priority over any other task.'"

"'Yes, yes, yes,' said Isi impatiently. 'But if anyone stays, it should be me. I'm the older one. It's my role to take on this responsibility.'"

"At that point, Max broke in. He told his brother, 'Isi, Ru left the decision to me, and I willingly and without pressure from him agreed. You are needed in *Eretz Israel*. That's where you belong, Isi. Think of the thousands of men, women, and children who will be entering Palestine in the next few years. You need to be there to help them. That's very important work, just as important as the work I'll be doing here.'"

"Isi responded, 'Max, have you considered the danger, the possibility that—'

"Max cut him off. 'Isi, you know me. I'm no fool. But this is my duty. This is where I belong.'"

"A resigned look came over Isi's face. Turning his hands palms upward in a gesture of finality, he said, 'It's *beschert;* it's God's will.' He invited the three of them to join hands in prayer, and he went on, in a low, emotion-charged voice: 'I pray that, with the help and guidance of *HaShem,* each of us will carry out the mission that He has entrusted to us, and that we survive and thrive, in full health and vigor. Amen.' They embraced warmly. With tears in his eyes, Isi picked up his suitcase and turned to board the waiting launch. With a last look back, he faced his brother and said softly, 'May God be with you, Maxl', and descended the ladder into the launch."

"The S.S. *Dora,*" Sigi told Renate, "cleared the Amsterdam harbor on July 16, 1939. And that was it: she was the last ship to sail from Holland to Palestine before the war broke out. For the two brothers, Max and Isi, that was their last goodbye. The two men never saw each other again."

"Another one of those heartrending goodbyes that you spoke of when we first met," Renate commented.

"Not the first one, and certainly not the last."

Renate asked. "Did you see Isi after the war?"

"I did, and on more than one occasion, here in Israel. He lived in Ra'anana, just north of Tel Aviv."

"Tell me more," Renate said, "about your conversation with Max at the sanitarium."

Sigi picked up the story: "So Max picked up his belongings and left the quayside with Ru at his side. Max told me that as they walked back to Ru's car, Ru said to him, 'I'll be forever grateful to you for doing this, Max. You've stood fast on your principles, and you will, I'm sure, make a huge difference in the lives of these young people.'"

"Max smiled. 'Huge difference'? I'll be satisfied with just a tiny difference. That would be enough for me."

"It was more than just a tiny difference, wasn't it?" Renate mused.

"Agreed," Sigi answered, then returned to his retelling of his encounter with Max at the sanitarium.

"And then I said, 'Max, Ru was asking you to make an excruciating choice. What was going through your mind when Ru was trying to convince you to stay?'"

"I was thinking of my father, Sigi, and of the promise that I made to him, the one I told you about on the way out of the cemetery after his funeral. What would Vati want me to do? I asked myself. And the answer was right there in front of me. He would be telling me: 'Max, don't take the easy way out. Do what is right for others, for the Jewish people, for *tikkun olam,* repair of the world. Make yourself an instrument for God's will.' So you see, the choice was made for me, really."

Sigi noticed a look of admiration, of wonderment coming over Renate's face. She commented, "Many men and women would have said, when Ru Cohen made that request, 'Give me a day or two to think about it.' Or they would have responded immediately. 'Ru, please find someone else to do it. I'm leaving.' But Max didn't ask for time to think about it; he made his decision right then and there, to take on the responsibility that Ru asked him to assume. Max's actions in that moment showed his great strength of character. That willingness to take these heroic steps to help others in need, without regard to his own health and safety, is what separated him from ordinary people."

Sigi nodded his agreement, and Renate resumed her questioning.

". . . and what happened to Isi? Did the *Dora* arrive safely in Palestine?"

"We learned about that in the letter that Isi sent to Max after he arrived, and of course, we know even more now, from the historians. The ship cleared the harbor with 350 young Jewish refugees on board, most of them, like Isi, from Germany and Austria, but twenty Dutch Jews as well. In the sleeping quarters, two cots were pushed together, side by side, each pair of cots sleeping three."

"So one person had to sleep on the crack between the two beds?" Renate asked.

"Exactly. So the *Dora* left the harbor and everyone—the passengers and crew, the Dutch Zionists who remained behind, and the Dutch government—breathed a collective sigh of relief. The problem represented by the *Dora* was someone else's; it wasn't theirs."

"The ship then moved on to Antwerp, the most important Belgian seaport, and there it took on another 150 passengers, Jews who had assembled there from everywhere in Europe. The ship cleared the English Channel without a mishap, but in the Bay of Biscayne the *Dora* encountered heavy seas. Everyone got sick, with people throwing up over the railing, in the sleeping quarters, and in the corridors. You can imagine what that was like, as overcrowded as the ship was. There was a doctor on board who should have been giving out anti-nausea pills, but it turned out that he was a drug addict and was down in his cabin the whole time in a morphine-induced haze. He was worse than useless."

"As the seas calmed and the passengers recovered, the ship approached the Straits of Gibraltar, which were, and still are, controlled by the British navy, because Gibraltar is a British possession. As the ship approached the straits, a British patrol boat intercepted it. The head of the boarding party demanded that the captain turn over the ship's papers. Fortunately, the *Haganah* had already prepared for this turn of events. The captain explained to the British naval officer that the ship was headed for Thailand, via the Suez Canal, and that was the destination listed on the ship's documents as well. The British government had also been told that Thailand was the ship's destination. Since the papers were in order, and were verified by the British Admiralty, the naval officer had no choice but to let the ship proceed."

"It's a miracle that the British inspectors did not ask to be taken below to the passengers' quarters," Renate commented.

"Yes," Sigi agreed, "the story would have ended very differently, even tragically, if they had insisted on going below-decks. Of course," he continued, "the passage through the straits was not the last of the dangers facing the *Dora*. As the ship negotiated the Mediterranean between Sicily and North Africa, it had to avoid the Italian navy as well. Finally, as it neared Palestine, it had to elude the British warships enforcing the blockade against illegal immigration. They would not hesitate to fire their guns at the *Dora* and leave it in flames in the water."

"The *Dora*'s next stop was at Mersin, on the southern coast of Turkey, where it took on water, fuel, and provisions, but the Turkish authorities there allowed no one off the ship. The *Dora* remained off the Turkish coast, awaiting further instructions from the higher-ups to move on to Palestine. The delay in arrival caused substantial difficulties. The Greek crew mutinied, demanding more pay because of the delays in the voyage. The men were finally convinced to return to their duties only after the passengers raised enough money among themselves to meet the crew's financial demands."

"Finally, on August 11, 1939, the *Dora* arrived in Palestinian waters, moved into position for the landing, and began to offload the passengers and their belongings. After a month at sea, the 500 men, women, and children on board had realized their dream, they had reached *Eretz Israel*."

"By two o'clock the next morning, the off-loading was completed—the last passenger had waded onto the beach at Sh'fayim, a kibbutz north of Herzliya. The *Haganah* people, waiting on the beach to receive the passengers, were able to radio the agreed-upon message to their representatives in the Netherlands: "The delivery was successful and the patient is healthy." The coded message was passed on later that day to the Netherlands government, and then to the rest of the world. The voyage of the *Dora* had ended successfully. There was satisfaction and joy in many circles: in Jerusalem and Tel Aviv, yes, but also in Amsterdam, Antwerp, and Paris. Needless to say, there was jubilation, too, among the families and friends of those who had reached shore that day."

Sigi took a deep breath, signifying that he had come to the end of the narrative. Renate commented, "That's a truly amazing story. They should have made a movie of it, and not wait for the voyage of the *Exodus*." Then she asked, "And what about Isi? What was his life when he arrived in Palestine?"

"He had a career in education, first as a teacher and then as a high school principal in Ra'anana. Many of the Dutch *chalutzim* settled there after the war. In July 1943 he married Rosel Silbiger. They had two children, Aryeh and Yaron. You will want to interview them as well. Isi passed away on July 14, 1990."

"Did he ever return to Emden?" Renate asked.

"Only once, in 1982. He was one of a group of former Emdeners who came back for a first postwar reunion of Emdeners and former Emdeners now living in Israel. And after that he was in ongoing contact with the Emdeners who came in a steady stream to visit him at his home in Israel."

"One more question before we break for the day," Renate said. "About that life-changing decision that Max made that day in Amsterdam: Did he ever express regret about the choice that he made that day, to stay behind and let the *Dora* leave without him?"

"Well, of course, if he had considered only his personal health and well-being, to say nothing of his very life, he would have been better off, much better off, if he had turned his back on Ru and sailed on the *Dora*. But then, I always come back to the good that he accomplished in his short lifetime, the many Jewish children and young people who survived because of him. So, in answer to your question, no, I never heard Max express any regrets, or rue his decision."

Sigi paused, weighing his words carefully, and continued: "You know, Renate,"—a smile came over his face as if he were trying to soften the impact of what he was about to say—"when you are convinced that you have received a call from Above, that God's will is acting through you, any talk of regret is beside the point. It just doesn't matter. When the young Isaac allowed his father to bind him, there on Mount Moriah, when Abraham picked up the knife with which he was to kill his son, did either of them ask themselves if they regretted what was about to happen? Does the Bible tell us that Jacob tried to retract his decision to wrestle with the man/angel at the place he called Peniel (Genesis 32)? No, there were no second thoughts in any of them. They did what God commanded them to do. That's how it was with Max. He was fully committed to delivering on the promise that he had made to Ru that day on the dock."

"And you, Sigi? What happened after you left the sanitarium?"

"They discharged me after a four-week stay, with two different medications that I was told to take twice daily. By some miracle, my symptoms never came back, even as people took sick and died around me."

"Did you link up with Max again?"

"I did. After our conversation there in the sanitarium, I was convinced that God had a mission for me, too, that my taking sick just as the ship was leaving was His way of showing me a path other than the one that I had planned for myself, and that was to stand shoulder-to-shoulder with Max to help Jewish children in their time of need. So when I left the sanitarium, I immediately joined up with Max and told him that I was ready to take on whatever assignments he wanted to give me."

"What did he say when you told him that?"

"He embraced me warmly and simply said, 'Sigi, I knew I could count on you. You've always been there when I needed you.'"

"Beautiful," Renata murmured. There was an interval of silence, while Renate took in what Sigi had said "And then, just a few days later, the Germans invaded Poland."

"Right," Sigi repeated, "Germany invaded Poland, World War II began, and our wartime activities, mine and Max's, began in earnest."

"This might be a good time to end for today," Renate suggested.

Sigi could have easily continued, but he could see that her suggestion was more like a demand—that she was telling him that it was time to stop for the day.

"That's fine with me," Sigi answered. "I'm ready for a nap."

"Good! See you tomorrow. Same time?"

"Same time."

Sigi retrieved Renate's raincoat from the closet. She placed it over her arm and, with a cheerful *Bis Morgen*!"—"Until tomorrow!"—slipped out of the door.

PART 4

The Fourth Day

CHAPTER 4

The War Begins, the Mission Gets Underway

~~

Seating themselves once again on the balcony of Sigi's apartment on this, the fourth day of their interview, Sigi awaited Renate's first question.

"Sigi," she began, "go back to September 1, 1939, the day that the Germans invaded Poland. What was it like when the young people at the training center in Loosdrecht heard the news?"

Sigi had a ready answer. "Shock . . . shock and horror . . . and fear. The shock was not a reaction to the invasion. That came as no surprise to us because Hitler had been making menacing gestures toward Poland for many months. The shock was at the speed with which Hitler's Wehrmacht overran Poland. It's a big country, and the Poles fought back—it wasn't as if the Poles invited the Germans to take over, and welcomed them in. But within five weeks the Germans had the entire country under their control. And the horror—that was at how, everywhere in Poland, as soon as the army had gained military control of that area, the SS and the special *Einsatzgruppen* moved in behind them to round up civilians who might resist the Occupation, and liquidated them. 'Liquidated'—that's a fancy way of saying 'killed' them'. One day they're leading active, productive lives, surrounded by family and friends—the next day—pouf!—dead!"

"That would include Jews, is that right—especially Jews?" Renate asked.

"No, in the beginning, they were not targeted as a group. The repressive measures were focused on those who the Germans thought would resist the Occupation—teachers, university professors, priests, Communists, Socialists, labor union leaders and the like. It was only later, in 1941, that the organized effort to slaughter Jews got underway. But Jew or non-Jew—it didn't matter: Our Dutch newspapers fed us a steady drumbeat of information on the atrocities that were being committed against the Polish civilian population. Anyone with brains and foresight knew that if Germany were to invade the Netherlands, they would commit those atrocities there, too. We never doubted that."

"So, in that state of mind, how did the leadership respond? Did the German attack on Poland change anything for Max and for you?"

"Not immediately. After leaving the sanitarium, I returned to Loosdrecht. Max went back to his farm, Koekoek, near Hengelo."

Renate invited Sigi to continue: "And then the Nazi hammer fell on Holland . . . ?"

"Yes," he said, "on May 10, 1940, the Germans invaded the Netherlands. You could say that that day marked the opening of the final chapter of Max's life, that part of his life that he had willingly stepped forward to take on at the quayside in Amsterdam that day in July, ten months earlier."

"How did you become aware of the invasion?" Renate asked.

"We woke up in the early morning hours of May 10 to the steady drone of aircraft engines, the planes flying low from the east, from Germany, toward the main Dutch cities to the west of us. We knew in our bones that those were German planes and that the war in the West was underway. We learned later from news accounts that the German planes first continued to fly west, out over the North Sea, to lull the Dutch into thinking that they were intending to attack England, and then doubled back to their intended targets in Holland. They bombed the airfield south of Rotterdam to make it unusable by Dutch warplanes. The next wave of German planes carried a battalion of paratroopers who landed at the airfield once it had been secured. And then more planes flew over, this time toward Dordrecht, to land more paratroopers to secure a vital bridge there."

"The Dutch military—the army, the air force, and the navy—fought bravely, giving us hope that the Dutch would prevail, or, at the very least, that a long, drawn-out campaign would result in a deadlock. But then, three days later, we got word via the BBC that a British destroyer had evacuated Queen Wilhelmina and her family and brought them to England, and we knew that the game was up. And it was. Two days later, on May 15, 1940, the Dutch surrendered."

"Surely the attack was no surprise to you," Renate ventured.

"Of course not," Sigi replied, "We knew it would come, because in October 1939, five weeks after the invasion of Poland, Hitler had spoken of attacking the Netherlands, Belgium, and Luxembourg in preparation for the further attack on France and Great Britain."

"But once again, we were unprepared for the force and swiftness of the attack. The Germans overwhelmed the Dutch with the sheer superiority of numbers of infantry, their armor, and their warplanes. For years, even as the Germans were rebuilding their army and their navy, and building modern warplanes, the Dutch government sat on its hands, spending much less money on its military than it should have. As a result, when the attack came, the Dutch military was outmanned and outgunned. Even so, the Dutch fought back courageously."

"Then on May 14, 1940, the Luftwaffe destroyed the city of Rotterdam, Holland's second-largest city, killing 800 civilians. Hitler threatened publicly that if Holland did not surrender, the city of Utrecht would likewise be attacked and destroyed. The following day, May 15, the Dutch government decided to avoid further losses, civilian and military, and surrendered."

"So the military phase of the war lasted only five days," Renate reckoned.

"Correct," Sigi replied. "But for Jews that was only the start of the bad times. The worst was still to come. You can imagine our terror," he said, "particularly the terror induced in the many Jews who had entered the Netherlands in the 1930's from Germany, Poland, and other points in central Europe, because it had seemed at that time to offer refuge from Nazi anti-Semitism. They now realized that that had been a false hope. Many of them committed suicide by drowning in the Dutch canals and waterways or by other methods."

"In those first days," Sigi continued, "a rumor reached Loosdrecht that it was still possible to escape by sea, that a flotilla of small boats was waiting at IJmouden to take us across the North Sea to safety in England."

"Just as a few weeks later," Renate put in, "another such flotilla would take thousands of British soldiers off the beach at Dunkirk in Belgium."

"That's right. So that evening, during the regular after-dinner announcement time, our leader, Joachim Simon—we called him Schuschu—stood up and said:

You may have heard the rumor that boats are standing ready at IJmuden to take Jews to England. Some of you may be thinking of packing up and heading west to IJmouden. If you go, we won't stop you. But I'll tell you this: This would be a terrible mistake. If you leave, you will not get to IJmouden. The roads will be clogged with people like you, all desperate to get to the departure point. And, if by some miracle you get there and get on one of those boats, do you really think that the Luftwaffe will let those boats reach their destination? You will be sitting ducks there out there in the open water.

"Then he pounded forcefully on the table and shouted, '*Chaverim*, we must stand together. That's the only way we will survive, by standing shoulder-to-shoulder as a body, determined to support each other!'"

"Everybody in the room called back, '*B'seder*'! That's the Hebrew for 'Okay' or 'Agreed'!"

"Did any of you leave for IJmouden?"

"Not a single one of us. You have to remember, Renate, that most of the *chalutzim* were teenagers who were too young to make mature independent decisions. They had been conditioned to believe, and they did believe, that their best chance of survival lay in unity, in sticking together. So they did what their leaders, who were themselves mostly in their mid-20's, instructed them to do."

"And, on the whole, that worked out well for them," Renate commented.

"That's my belief, and I believe that that is the verdict of history." "So," Sigi continued, "with the Nazi occupation of Holland, all the contingency plans that the Dutch Zionist movement had developed had now to be put into effect. Max received from Ru

Cohen the assignment that he had agreed to take on there at the dock in Amsterdam. He became what you might call an area coordinator, making frequent visits to the Loosdrecht Pavilion and the other *hachsharoth* in the area, and to the training center at Werkdorp Wieringen in North Holland. That was a school, not strictly speaking a *hachsharah*, where 300 young Jews from Germany were being educated and trained."

"All of this effort must have required a lot of money to sustain it, to support the people in the field," Renate said. "How did they manage that?"

"The worldwide Zionist movement contributed funds, as did the American Joint Distribution Committee," Sigi replied. "So did wealthy Dutch Jewish families and others who could afford it. But much of the money to run the centers in the end had to come from the young people themselves. The money that Max was being paid as a farmhand barely covered his own costs. He couldn't afford to give financial support to the movement. So in December 1940 Max left the farm and joined me in Assen, a nearby town, to work in the paper mill there. Max had grown fond of the farm's owners, and it was emotionally wrenching to have to leave."

Max and friends in Assen

"Another one of those difficult goodbyes," Renate commented.

"That's right. On leaving, Max wrote a letter to Gerda, the farm's owner,"—and here Sigi pulled a copy of the letter from his folder—"in which he closed by asking, 'May God be gracious to you in the coming year, may He return Willem [her husband], and grant the entire world peace.'"

"In Assen Max and I shared a room at No. 3 Javastraat, the home of Josef Van Tijn, one of the leaders in the town's small Jewish community. Our jobs at the paper mill had been arranged through the Deventer Association. Part of the pay that we received from our jobs at the mill went to its support, enabling the Association to place more young *chalutzim* on nearby farms. It was during this period that Max started to receive assignments from Ru Cohen to move among the many sites in Holland where young Jews were being trained to make *Aliyah*. In that capacity, he came to the *hachsharoth* in Gouda and Loosdrecht and Elden and to the big *Werkdorp* in Wieringen that I mentioned earlier. So he came to be known to the staff and the *chalutzim* in those places and earned their respect."

"Once the Germans had overrun the country and the Netherlands government had surrendered, how did that affect you?" Renate asked.

"In the first months of occupation, it affected us hardly at all. You have to remember that most of the Jews in Holland lived in the big cities—Amsterdam, Rotterdam, Haarlem, and The Hague. That's where the Dutch Jews were concentrated, as well as the Jews originally from Germany and elsewhere in Europe who had sought refuge in Holland."

"The first anti-Jewish edicts issued by the Germans fell most heavily on those big-city Jews. Early on, those of us who lived in Loosdrecht and the other small towns and in the countryside, and especially those of us who were refugees from elsewhere, had only the loosest of ties with the Dutch Jewish community. Yes, we were living among them, but we never felt that we had a common destiny with them."

"And the feeling was mutual: Before the war, the Dutch Jewish community had looked down at us. They were well integrated into Dutch society, or so they believed, and we were outsiders. Yes, they provided help to us, but they still kept us at arm's length. Now that the war was on and the Germans began issuing their anti-Jewish decrees, the shoe was on the other foot: We outsiders felt no obligation to comply with those decrees, and they were not enforced as strictly in the countryside as in the large cities."

"At first, there were few signs around Loosdrecht that the new order was now in effect. We hardly ever saw German uniformed soldiers on the streets. That raised a lot of false hopes in many people, even in me. Once during that period I mentioned to Lodi Cohen that the occupation might not be as bad for us as we had feared. Lodi rounded on me, and in retrospect, I don't blame him. He said,

Sigi, you're being ridiculous. You don't know what you're talking about. Hitler hates Jews—it's that simple. To the Nazis, we're like insects underfoot. They're looking to crush us, to get rid of us once and for all. You saw what happened to our community on November 9, 1938, in Germany and Austria, and then last year in Poland. Don't for a minute think that it won't happen here in Holland. It will, and for sure we had better be ready for it. And don't count on the Dutch government to save us. We have to save ourselves."

"He looked me squarely in the eyes, waiting for my reaction. I was mute, thinking of some appropriate response, some argument that I could make in opposition, but nothing came to mind. I had spoken out of a head-in-the-sand optimism, which even then was completely unjustified. In the end all I could do was nod my head in silent agreement."

"Even as we were speaking, the machinery was being put in place to carry out the Holocaust to devastating effect in Holland in the years to come."

"How so?" Renate asked

"Immediately after the surrender, Hitler appointed Arthur Seyss-Inquart to be Reichs-Kommissar for the Netherlands, in essence, its governor. Seyss-Inquart had held similar posts in his native country, Austria, after the Nazi takeover in 1938, and in Poland, too, after the Germans conquered that country in October 1939. Hitler knew that Seyss-Inquart could be depended upon to carry out the Nazi policies, including those that were aimed at destroying the Jewish population. Early on, Seyss-Inquart made his intentions quite clear. In a radio address he told the Dutch people, 'We shall hit the Jews wherever we find them, and those who side with them will bear the consequences.'"

"His military counterpart was Hanns Albin Rauter. He had been an obscure SS officer who, in that same month, May 1940, was named chief of the SS in the Netherlands. If you're looking for individuals who personified the Nazi evil in the Netherlands, it would be these two men, Seyss-Inquardt and Rauter. It was under Rauter's direction and supervision that the three notorious concentration camps in the Netherlands were operated, at Vught, Amersfoort, and the best-known of them, Westerbork. That was the camp to which Anne Frank was sent before she was deported to Auschwitz."

Feeling the need to be more specific, Sigi continued, "The camps at Westerbork and Amersfoort were already in existence. The one at

Amersfoort, on the heath southeast of Amsterdam, had been built originally as a Dutch army post. The Westerbork camp was near Holland's eastern border with Germany. The Dutch government had opened it in the summer of 1939 to house the thousands of Jewish refugees who were then pouring across the border to flee Nazism. The third camp, at Vught in the south near the Belgian border, was the only one built by the Nazis, opening in late 1942."

"And then, gradually, the noose tightened on the Jews in Holland, like in the other European countries that the Germans had occupied," Renate commented.

"Exactly. I liken it to the medieval torture instrument, the thumbscrew. When your thumb was first inserted in the thumbscrew, you felt only discomfort, very little pain. But with each twist, the thumbscrew tightened and the pain increased, until with that final turn, the pain became unbearable. Similarly, in Holland the earliest anti-Jewish decrees were harmless enough, but each additional decree chipped away at our freedoms, until, at the end, our fundamental human rights, including the most basic right, the right to life itself, was taken away from us."

"Can you be more specific? How were they stripped of their rights?"

In response, Sigi launched into the chronology of the anti-Jewish measures taken by the Nazis. "On July 1, 1940, six weeks after the Germans conquered the Netherlands, Dutch Jews were barred from serving as air-raid wardens, and we were excluded from conscription in the forced labor teams that were being sent to Germany."

"They were comfortable with that exclusion, I'm sure," Renate commented.

"Of course. But then over the next six months through the end of 1940, the bans and restrictions came thick and fast, sometimes only days apart. July 31, ritual slaughter, the killing of animals in accordance with Jewish law, was prohibited. August 28: Jews were banned from the Dutch civil service. Other decrees followed rapidly, and increasingly they affected Jews living in the countryside as well as those living in urban areas."

"In the summer of 1940 the Germans shut down several *hachsharoth* elsewhere in the Netherlands, but not ours. Many of the young men and women ousted from these *hachsharoth* sought shelter at our Loosdrecht Pavilion, many more than we could reasonably handle. Additional beds had to be brought in. Now four of us were squeezed into a room originally intended to hold only two, with hardly any space between the beds. There were terrible difficulties that following winter—inadequate heat, frozen pipes, lack of food—but the heaviest burdens were the emotional ones."

"Keep in mind, Renate, that many of us were teenagers, we might never before have been away from our parents for any length of time. Now they were hundreds of miles away, and there was grave concern in our minds whether we would ever see them, and our siblings, again. The physical problems, the distance from our loved ones, those were bad enough, but now there was the dawning awareness that our parents' best efforts might have been in vain. They had placed us on the *Kindertransport* trains thinking that we would be safe in Holland, but it seemed likely that we were no safer now than our parents who had stayed behind. As much as we feared for their safety, we had to start thinking of our own survival as well. Finally, our dream and our goal in undergoing the *hachsharah* training had been to make a new life for ourselves in Palestine, and that goal now seemed more and more remote. Under the burden of these pressures, many of the *chalutzim* became moody, depressed, and withdrawn, susceptible to sudden crying jags. You can imagine the burdens that these psychological issues imposed on our leaders and on the rest of us. Gloom is contagious, after all."

"What kept us from falling apart emotionally was our leadership. They were our substitute fathers and mothers, teachers, mentors, advisors. We could pour our hearts out to them, because we had complete trust in them. We knew that our well-being, our safety, our very lives, were uppermost in their thinking."

"Still, in that first year of the Occupation, there was uncertainty at the highest levels of the movement over what the proper response should be to the Occupation, because the full scope of the Germans' intentions was not yet known. Should we stay in place, carry on as before? Go into hiding? Active resistance? Emigration, legal or illegal? Each of these alternatives had its perils, and each had its advocates and its very vocal opponents."

"These questions—what were the Nazis' intentions and how were we to respond to them?—were answered in the new year 1941. On January 10 of that year, the Nazis decreed that all persons 'wholly or largely of Jewish blood' had to register with the local authorities." Here Sigi consulted his notes again. A total of 159,896 persons registered, including 19,561 persons born of mixed marriages. The total included some 25,000 Jewish refugees like us, originally from Germany and Austria."

"And the *chalutzim* of the Loosdrecht Pavilion complied with that order?"

"Of course not! If we had, I might not be sitting here with you now. We in Loosdrecht and at other *hachsharoth* knew better than to comply, because our leaders had seen the consequences of similar decrees in Germany, Austria, and Poland. They knew that complying with this order would be a dangerous mistake."

"How so?"

"Now the Germans would have in one file cabinet, so to speak, the names and addresses of every Jew in Holland. That was certainly not in our best interest."

"But weren't your names already on file in many different places?" Renate asked. "For example, the Dutch immigration authorities must have had your visa applications on file."

"That's true," Sigi replied, "but nowhere, so far as we knew, was there a single consolidated file on every Jew in Holland."

He went on "If we needed confirmation of the dangers of registration, those fears were confirmed in the following month. The Jews in Amsterdam had set up a self-defense group, called the Jewish Action Group (JAG), with headquarters at an ice cream parlor in the Jewish quarter. On February 19, 1941, German police raided that ice cream parlor, and were met with strong resistance from members of the JAG. In response, the police brutally arrested and detained 425 young Jews and sent them to the Buchenwald and Mauthausen concentration camps. Only two of them survived."

"To protest those arrests and deportations, the local Communist Party sponsored an open-air public meeting, which led to a call for a general strike. Heeding the call, the Amsterdam transit drivers stayed home from work the next morning. Other municipal employees followed their example. And the strike wasn't confined to Amsterdam: It spread to other Dutch cities as well. But the strike leaders were unable to get the Nazis to cease or to modify their anti-Jewish measures. They put the strike down after two days by arresting the strike leaders and deporting them. So the work stoppage ultimately failed, but it still goes down in history as the first organized mass protest against Nazi mistreatment of Jews."

"It was after that general strike and after it was so brutally put down, that the Germans called a meeting of the Zionist leaders and the top rabbis and demanded that a *Joodse Raad*—a Jewish Council—be set up, which would represent the Jewish community and transmit orders from the Germans to the community. Similar councils had been set up in Warsaw, Lodz, and other Polish cities with large Jewish populations, at the insistence of the German occupiers."

The Amsterdam *Joodse Raad*

"In March 1941, the SS brought Jakob Edelstein, a Czech Jew, to Amsterdam to assist the. Dutch Zionists in setting up that *Joodse Raad.*"

"A 'consultant,' we might say today," said Renate with a wry smile.

"Perhaps, yes, but his importance to us lay in the urgent message that he brought. In a meeting with the Zionist Federation of Holland, Edelstein told the Jewish leaders what Dutch Jews could expect in the months and years ahead. Remember that Czechoslovakia had been under German occupation since March 1939, so Edelstein could speak with authority on this subject.

Jakob Edelstein

He told the Dutch Jewish leaders how Czech Jews were suffering at the hands of the Nazis, and warned them that 'the Germans intend to kill us all. The most important thing we can do,' he told us, 'is to hold on.' Edelstein's warning came just a few weeks after that first roundup and deportation of Jews from Amsterdam. He was telling his audience that that deportation was not a random occurrence, that it was the first round in what the Germans intended to be the systematic destruction of the Jewish population in Holland."

Renate was skeptical. "You were not present at that meeting. How do we know all of this?"

"The minutes of that meeting with Edelstein were preserved, and there was testimony at the trial of Adolf Eichmann in Jerusalem in 1961 from a witness who had been there at the meeting."

"Moreover, at our leaders' invitation, Edelstein came to Loosdrecht, to our Pavilion, and, speaking in Hebrew, passed on to our *Youth Aliyah* leaders the same message that he had transmitted in Amsterdam: that we Jews, every one of us, were in mortal danger."

"We did not dismiss his warnings as so much scare-talk. In fact, early on in the Occupation, well before that meeting with Edelstein, our leaders understood that as Jews we were the Nazis' prime targets. In 1938, Joachim (Schuschu) Simon had been interned by the Nazis at the Buchenwald concentration camp and then released. From that experience he knew what we could expect if we were to be 'resettled' at Buchenwald, or Mauthausen, or Dachau, or the other internment camps. He urgently confirmed what Edelstein was telling us: Under no circumstances, he told us, could we allow this to happen."

"If we did nothing, we faced arrest, deportation, detention, and death. The alternative was to disappear, and that meant to go into hiding so that when the Germans came for us we would not be found. The leaders decided that this would be their strategy for the young people in their care, recognizing that it was only a temporary solution. But if hiding was to be the solution we would need help, two different kinds of help. We needed, first, advance warning that the Nazis were planning a roundup of the Loosdrecht pioneers, and second, we needed hiding places, non-Jewish people who would take our Loosdrecht pioneers into their homes."

"The solution to the first problem was found in Erika Bluth, a former member of the Loosdrecht Pavilion, now working in Amsterdam. Her husband was a high-ranking official in the *Joodse Raad*, the Jews' Council. She agreed that as soon as she learned from her husband that the Loosdrecht pioneers were to be targeted for arrest and deportation, she would call the Loosdrecht leaders with a coded message to that effect."

"The second problem—finding places to hide for the fifty young men and women then living under the Pavilion roof—was harder to solve. How would we find non-Jews willing to take us in on short notice? The Loosdrecht *Youth Aliyah* had been almost entirely self-sufficient. We had prided ourselves on that, on our ability to survive and prosper without being dependent on the surrounding non-Jewish community. And we hadn't gone out of our way to build bridges to the Dutch Zionist leadership, either. As I've said, to the leaders of Dutch Jewry, even to those who supported the Zionist movement, we were *buitenstaanders*—outsiders—, temporary guests and not an organic part of Dutch society."

"But now that independence, that outsider status, became an enormous disadvantage. Whom could we reach out to? Whom could we trust? If we approached the wrong person, that person might be an informer for the Gestapo and roll up the entire Loosdrecht community. Our freedom, our very lives, depended on the good judgment of our leaders."

". . . and then Fate intervened," Renate commented.

Sigi smiled. "Call it Fate, call it luck, call it good planning. I call it two heaven-sent rescuers. The first one was a young Dutch-Jewish woman, Miryam Waterman. She had been a teacher at the *Werkplaats*, a progressive school in Bilthoven, but she had lost her job in 1940 when the Nazis barred Jews from teaching at non-Jewish schools. Miryam had grown up in Loosdrecht, and so, after losing her job at the *Werkplaats* school, she had

Miryam Waterman (l.), shown here with Menachem Pinkhof, whom she later married

come back to her hometown to teach at the *hachsharah* there. From her childhood in Loosdrecht, she had contacts in the non-Jewish community there. She volunteered to call on people whom she knew and could trust to take some of the younger Loosdrecht children into hiding. Her efforts were successful up to a point, but many more children remained to be taken care of."

"Our second angel was Johan (Joop) Westerweel. He was one of those beautiful souls whom one encounters so rarely in life—a man with strong beliefs, but more than that, a man who is prepared to act on those beliefs regardless of the cost. He and his wife, Wilhelmina, were convinced pacifists."

Johan (Joop) Westerweel

"At the outbreak of the war, he was the head of that progressive school, the *Werkplaats* school, where Miryam Waterman had taught. With that background, Westerweel was an outsider, as we were. He was, to be sure, born and raised in the Netherlands, a Dutch citizen, but he was a conscientious objector, had not served in the military, practiced no religion, politically he was a committed socialist. The Dutch educational establishment was hostile to the progressive principles that guided the *Werkplaats* school. So he was, again, an outsider, even as an educator."

"That made the Westerweels, husband and wife, a good fit with the Loosdrecht Pavilion," Renate commented.

"They were heaven-sent angels in our time of need." Sigi continued. "Outraged at the way the Germans were treating the Jews, Joop and his wife began to shelter Jewish children in their home. Another man might have said to himself and to those who asked: 'I'm already taking a risk by hiding Jewish children. I'm doing more than my share.' But Joop felt compelled to do more, much more. Knowing Miryam Waterman from her days as a teacher at the *Werkplaats* school, Joop asked her what he could do to help Jews in their time of need. She told him about the Loosdrecht *hachsharah*, and he and his wife stepped up to volunteer their services to us."

"That opportunity came soon after. On Wednesday morning, August 15, 1941, the call came from Erika Blüth: 'I regret to inform you that Uncle Robert will be operated on tomorrow towards evening. The doctors can no longer postpone his surgery. Goodbye!' At this, the Loosdrecht leadership sprang into action, because this was the agreed-upon coded message informing them that the Gestapo would be raiding the *hachsharah* within the next few days. That meant that a convoy of cars and trucks would arrive at the front door, soldiers would be posted around the property to prevent anyone from escaping, and men in black leather coats would round up everyone, adults and children alike, and load them onto trucks to be taken away for deportation and certain death."

"That same evening," said Sigi, "our leaders called an emergency meeting. We all crowded into the dining room to hear the dire news."

"Who were the leaders at that point?" Renate asked.

"The overall leader was Lodi Cohen. Menachem Pinkhof was second-in-command; he was later to marry Miryam Waterman. There were also two women leaders: Hannah Aascher and Adina Simon, who was married to Schuschu Simon. They weren't much older than we were, in their mid-twenties. Also present at the meeting, standing off to one side, was Joop Westerweel."

"Speaking for the leaders, Heinz Moses stood up and, in an urgent voice, spelled out the situation:

Eliezer (Lodi) Cohen

Chaverim, we have learned today that the deportation order has been issued for the occupants of our Loosdrecht pavilion. We are to be sent to Poland, along with other Jews living elsewhere in Holland who are every day also being sent there. *Chaverim,* we have made sure that these commands will not be carried out. For several months, we have been working on a plan, to ensure that none of us will surrender to the authorities. Many good and courageous Dutch friends are ready to help us. It isn't necessary that I burden you with the details. What is certain is that none of us need voluntarily comply with the enemy's command. Tonight, the first group of *chaverim* will be picked up by friends and taken to their new address.

Now listen closely so that I can make you aware of how you have to behave in your new living circumstances. If you should be picked up by the Nazi authorities, just tell them that the men in charge of this Pavilion forced you to go underground, and that's all you know. Just put all of the responsibility on me and the other Loosdrecht leaders.

You must adjust completely to your new environment, doing everything that is asked of you. You will have to live under very difficult conditions. The people who open their houses to you are good people, but they are after all only human. You must never be rebellious, and you have to accustom yourself completely to their lifestyle. We will try, with the help of our Dutch friends, to stay in constant contact with you. You can bring with you only those things that you absolutely need: no letters from home, no photographs, and of course, no identity cards or anything else that will give away your identity.

Chaverim, out struggle is now underway. How long the war will last, we do not know. How many of us will survive it, we do not know. But one thing we do know: We, the *chaverim*, the Dutch *chalutzim*, we will not walk meekly as sheep to the slaughter. That should give you the strength to endure!

Sigi returned to his narrative. "It seems now, looking back, that Joop Westerweel and Miryam Waterman had performed a miracle. They had, on very short notice, found a hiding place for every one of the Loosdrecht *chalutzim*. Schuschu and Menachem had organized us into groups—each of us older ones had been assigned eight younger children. They would be our responsibility, and it was our job, our sacred trust, to keep them safe in their intended hiding places. Granted, for many of the children, that first hiding place was just a way station on the way to someplace else, someplace more secure, but it worked."

"After that, each of us was taken aside and given the name and address of the person with whom we were to go into hiding. On the following day, we stripped off our Jewish star and received our false identity papers. We were also assigned to smaller groups and clustered in those groups, waiting for our turn to leave for our assigned destinations. When the Gestapo agents arrived the following Monday, August 20, they found only two barking dogs and had to turn back empty-handed. For the time being we had eluded our tormentors."

"What was your state of mind during this hiding operation, do you recall?"

"Of course, we were nervous, moving from the known to the unknown. Had our leaders made the right choices for us? Would we be well-hidden? Would we get along with our hosts, both the adults and the children? Could they be trusted? On those issues, we had to rely on our leaders' good judgment, that they had found the right place for us. But more than the nervousness, there was joy—joy that we were no longer passively waiting to be arrested and deported, joy that we were taking our destiny into our own hands, thumbing our noses at the Nazis. But it wasn't only the Nazis whom we were defying. It was also the *Joodse Raad*, the Jewish Council in Amsterdam, those self-anointed leaders who had been advocating cooperation with the German occupation as the best strategy and who had opposed our going into hiding. Resistance—non-violent resistance—would be our strategy for survival."

"None of the *chalutzim* acted independently to find hiding places on their own?"

"A few of them had made inquiries about escaping on their own, but in the end everyone stayed. When the leaders presented their plan to us to go into hiding, some of the *chalutzim* expressed doubts. The war would surely end soon: Was it necessary to go into hiding? Couldn't we live openly with our false identity cards and without the Jewish star to give our identity away? But finally, when our leaders asked for a vote on the plan, up or down, the plan was approved with not a single dissenting vote. As I said, we had been conditioned to rely on the judgment of our leaders. So when our elders, even if they were our elders by only a few years, told us to go into hiding to places that they had found for us and then to follow their further instructions, that's just what we did."

Renate was silent, absorbing what Sigi had just told her. Then she asked, "In this hiding operation, how much support did the Loosdrecht *chalutzim* have from the larger Dutch Zionist organization?"

"None," Sigi answered promptly. "Of course, we had no time for consultations, the whole operation had to be carried out overnight.

But even if there had been ample time for consultation and collaboration with the Zionist leadership, we probably would not have discussed it with them beforehand. Remember that the Zionist leadership and its membership in Holland was concentrated in Amsterdam and the other major cities; they didn't have much of a presence in the country towns like Loosdrecht. In the second place, the leadership's power base was concentrated among native-born Dutch Jews. We were living in Holland, to be sure, but we were from Germany and Austria, and had no strong connection to the Dutch Zionist movement."

Seeing that Sigi still felt strongly about this issue, even after all these years, Renate encouraged him to continue.

"The biggest reason that we didn't consult with them was that early on, the leaders, and here I'm referring to the Cohen brothers, David and Ru, believed in playing by the rules, working within the system. They were firmly opposed to the idea that Jews should go into hiding, to become *onderduikers*,"

"*Onderduikers?*" Renate asked.

"That's what we called ourselves," Sigi explained. "It means 'divers'. Going underground, we were just like divers going underwater."

Renate asked Sigi to pick up where he had left off.

"They did not believe in moving our people across borders illegally, and they certainly did not approve of moving people to Palestine illegally, evading the British blockade. We on the other hand believed that desperate times required desperate measures. Looking back now, it's clear to me that our approach was the right one, that 'working within the system' would have led to the complete annihilation of Dutch Jewry. So our leaders felt that if they let the Cohen brothers in on our plans, there would be Gestapo on our doorstep before we had a chance to fully evacuate the building. I have to say though, that when Ru Cohen finally understood what was at stake—that those who were caught were deported to the east and killed—and that going into hiding was the only way of avoiding that fate, he did everything that he could to help us in our *onderduiker* activities."

". . . and Max?" Renate asked. "Did he go into hiding, too?"

"Yes, he did." Sigi replied. "That first Saturday night after the evacuation, Max met up with us, and he and I, and Max's younger brother, Emil, traveled to a small village in south Holland, near Breda. We had been assigned to a hiding place in that village in a small house occupied by two unmarried sisters. We were grateful to these two women for the risks that they took on our behalf. There was a problem, though: One of them was strongly attracted to Max, which made our day-to-day life very difficult. Eventually, the tension in the household reached a point where we decided that we had to move. So we packed up our gear and moved to Amsterdam, to the Jewish quarter there."

"How about Metta," Renate asked. "Where was she hidden?"

"She was brought first to Zutphen, a city some sixty miles due east of Loosdrecht. Joop Westerweel's parents lived there, and connected her with friends of theirs, the Wentinks. She stayed with them for about nine months, and then when her hosts feared that she would be betrayed, she was brought back to Loosdrecht, to a family whom she had known during her previous stay there. Eventually, in January 1944, she was brought out of Holland altogether and taken across the border, first into Belgium and then into France."

"What was happening with Max during this time?"

"Now that he was in hiding in Amsterdam, he had another critical decision to make. He could have stayed hidden, taking on the life of the *onderduiker,* as the other Loosdrecht *chalutzim* were doing. Of

course his survival depended on his ability to stay hidden, and that depended, in turn, on non-Jewish Dutch families who would take him in and hide him. He could have easily reckoned that this would be the safest path to take and then emerged, alive and unharmed, when the war ended. But was that what he had committed to do that day in 1939 when he had accepted Ru Cohen's request that he step back from the quay? Certainly not! Ru had asked him to stay behind and accept a responsibility, and he had freely agreed to do so. Max was not one to shy away from a commitment once made, and he would not do so now when Menachem and Schuschu and the other *chalutzim* were looking to him for direction and leadership."

"So Max linked up with Joop Westerweel, Schuschu Simon, and the two Kurts, Kurt Hannemann and Kurt Reilinger, to provide the leadership services that the *chalutzim* in Loosdrecht and elsewhere would need if they were to remain in hiding and avoid detection."

"Can you be more specific," Renate asked, "about those services?"

"You can break them down into the services that we provided at the outset, when the young boy or girl first moved in, and then the ongoing services that were expected of us, either from the hosts or by the children, and finally, the crisis services, the services that we would need to make available on a moment's notice."

"First we had to arrange the marriage, that is, we had to find Dutch non-Jews willing to hide our young boys and girls. Yes, we had a network of friends and friends of friends who were willing to take a Jewish child in. But our network wasn't large enough to take in all the children who had to be placed, so in the end we resorted to cold-calling, like door-to-door salesmen. We got onto our bicycles and pedaled down country roads, and whenever we saw a large barn where children might hide, we knocked on that farmer's door and pleaded with him to take a child in. Most of the time, we got 'No' for an answer, but occasionally, we found a willing farmer."

"Sometimes they would take our young people for only a brief period of time, and then we would soon have to find someone else to take them in, a week or two later. Once we had found a non-Jewish Dutchman willing to take one of our people in, he might provide us with the names of friends and other people whom he knew who might do the same. In that way, a network of hiders was formed."

"And before we made the decision to place a boy or girl with the non-Jewish family, we had questions: Did they have a secure hiding place? In an emergency, did they have an exit that the *onderduikers* could use, a second staircase or other such escape route? Could the hosts be counted on to be discreet and not blab all over town about their new 'guests'? Was there someone in the household, or in the extended family, who was unreliable, who might, accidentally or intentionally, spread the news about the new arrivals or even, God forbid, report them to the police?"

"You know, Renate," Sigi said as an aside, "the Germans paid a reward, a bounty, you might call it, to Dutch men and women who betrayed Jews to the Germans: seven guilders per head, or $50.00 US. That could be very tempting to a cash-strapped Dutchman."

"Then, when the marriage had taken place, when the boy or girl had been brought to the hiding place, we had to make sure that the marriage would endure. A constant flow of information, from us to the *onderduiker* and his or her host and from them back to us, was essential. How to maintain contact with the boys and girls in our care? We fixed a time when we would visit, usually late at night, and then we would get on our bicycles and go to those houses. Or the hiders would meet Joop at a designated place and give him a report. We had to make sure that the host family got ration cards for the *onderduiker* so that he or she could be fed as well as the host family was."

"Where did the ration cards come from?" Renate asked.

"We had several sources, some more reliable than others. The best way was to enlist one of our non-Jewish comrades to lift blank ration cards from the registrar's office at the town hall. Another way was to get the ration card of someone who had died or had emigrated, and then carefully cut out the photo of that person and substitute the photo of the person who received that card. If those sources were unavailable, the other alternative was to forge the necessary documents."

"We had friends in the Dutch Resistance who were engravers and could forge identity cards and ration cards so beautifully that you couldn't tell them from the genuine article. Or we might turn to one of our Loosdrecht *chalutzim* who had been an artist in Berlin before the war. She could forge ration cards expertly, too. But sometimes, there were no ration cards, or even with ration cards there was no food to be had, and then the *onderduikers* would have to walk the country roads, going from one farmhouse to the next, begging for food, even if it was just a sack of potatoes."

"Money was a problem. To take in an *onderduiker* had a financial impact on the host family: the cost of additional food, medical care, higher utility costs, and so on. So that those costs wouldn't deter a family from taking a young person into hiding, the leaders offered a generous housing allowance: fifty guilders a month."

"Where did that money come from?"

"Sometimes the pioneer had his or her own resources. If they did, they would have to contribute some portion of that. The assets of the

Pavilion were also sold off to raise money. Later on, Jewish organizations and individuals, not only in the Netherlands but elsewhere, stepped up to contribute."

"And then we had to think about the medical care for the *onderduikers*. If one of them took sick, was there a reliable doctor who could be called on to treat him or her, a hospital to which they could be taken without being betrayed? And what about their schooling? We didn't want these boys and girls to fall too far behind. Of course, their survival came first, but it was always good if someone was available who could help them in their studies or who could at least provide them with textbooks that they could study on their own."

"Communications were also a problem. We didn't want our youngsters to feel that they were isolated, that they had been stuck in some farmhouse in the country, never to be heard from again. We encouraged them to write letters to their loved ones, and we encouraged their families to write to them, so it was part of our job to pick up and deliver those letters."

"Psychological support, you might say," Renate commented.

"That's right. And," Sigi continued, "these so-called 'marriages' didn't always last. Someone might find out, and then the hiding place would no longer be secure. Or maybe the *onderduik*er and the host family, or one member of the family, had some kind of conflict, or there was a clash of personalities, and the host family would demand that another place be found for that boy or girl."

"Like the tensions that Max and Emil and you encountered at that first hiding place with the two sisters."

"Exactly," Sigi replied. "There could be dozens of reasons why the place might no longer be suitable, and then a new place would have to be found, often on very short notice."

"What were Max's specific duties?" Renate asked.

"His job duties as a coordinator were 'all of the above.' At the front end, you might find a cooperative family even in your own home, or next door, or as far away as the other end of Holland. The hider might be a Christian woman who had worked for years for a Jewish family; perhaps she herself took the family in, or she prevailed on a relative to do so. Or a non-Jewish employee took in his employer and his family, or the other way around: a Gentile employer took in the Jewish employee and his family. Geographically, Amsterdam and urban areas generally were not good places for hiding: too many Jews and too many Germans, SS, or police. On the other hand, the Northern provinces—Friesland, Groningen, and Drenthe—were regarded as especially good places to hide. Why? Because that was largely farmland, sparsely populated in comparison to the rest of the country, lightly garrisoned by the Germans, and—" Sigi paused, trying to find the right words.

"and . . . what?" Renate asked.

"Those northern provinces had always had a strong streak of independence, going back to the 16th century, when they led the fight that the Netherlands waged to throw off the shackles of domination by Spain. There were religious reasons, too. The Dutch Reformed church was especially strong in those northern provinces. Its lay people and the pastors saw it as their religious duty—a call from God—to shelter Jews. If you took in a Jewish family, you would be securing for yourself and your family a place at the right hand of God in the Kingdom of Heaven. Dutch Reformed pastors—they were called 'black stockings'—drummed it into their parishioners that what the Germans were doing to the Jews was immoral, that they had a duty to resist. Those preachers spoke their truth, and they lived their truth. They hid many Jews, adults and children, in their churches, their parsonages, their schools, and their orphanages. Their parishioners listened and responded, even though many of them had never seen or encountered Jews except in the Scriptures."

"One of the Dutch Reformed hiders, Hetty Voute—we know from her testimony after the war—kept a quotation on her refrigerator door that should be a motto, a watchword, for every one of us:

I am only one, but I *am* one. I cannot do everything, but I *can* do something. What I *can* do, I *should* do, and, by the grace of God, I *will* do.

"We should all memorize those words and live by them," Renate commented.

"The world would be a far better place, certainly. But," Sigi went on, "I don't want to leave the impression that the Dutch Reformed Church was the only church that expected its parishioners to provide assistance to the Jews. The Roman Catholic archbishop of Utrecht, Johannes deJong, sent out a diocesan letter to every church in his jurisdiction asking that they take up a special collection to raise money to support Jewish refugees. And he also cautioned his priests that they were not to baptize, convert, or teach Catholic doctrine to the Jewish children who had been placed in Catholic homes in the Utrecht diocese. We know now that 40,000 Jews were hidden by the Dutch church and that forty-nine Catholic priests were killed for their work in protecting Jews."

"Coming back now to the leaders' plan for saving the *chalutzim* of the Loosdrecht Pavilion, please spell out for me what was at stake if the plan failed, if members of the Youth Alijah were discovered and arrested."

"What was at stake?" Sigi repeated. "Everything. For the young men and women who were arrested, their liberty, even their life. But it went beyond that. If a member of the group were arrested, there was the ever-present danger that he or she might, under torture, disclose the names of their comrades in the group, leading to their arrest, deportation, and death. These were the consequences that the leaders had to weigh in making their decisions for the rest of us."

"But to do nothing and wait for the mass arrest of everyone in the group was even worse, right?" said Renate.

"Knowing what our leaders knew about the fate of other young Jews who had been sent to the east, yes, it was unthinkable," Sigi replied. "Renate, have you ever been in someone else's gunsights and knew that you were? Have you ever lived with the certainty that you are being hunted down, that someone out there will find it personally satisfying to capture or kill you, and experience that feeling of triumph that a hunter has when he brings down a stag or other game? I'm sure you haven't."

Renate was silent as she considered the questions, then answered, "You're right. Thankfully, no."

"You should be grateful to your God that you have not been in that situation. That's what we faced every day and every night, we the rescuers and the children whom we were hiding. We and they could never be sure when we went to bed at night that we would be able to sleep through the night, or that someone would wake us and tell us that within minutes we had to collect our possessions and be on the move, down the back stairs, or across roofs, to another safe place, or maybe, that this would be our last night of freedom and that we would be picked up in one of the *razzias*—roundups—before the sun came up the next morning."

"That was the Germans' way of operating, to conduct their roundups, whether of dozens of people or only of a handful—to carry out their raids at night, when the Jews were sleeping and would not have time to escape and when their Dutch neighbors would be sleeping and unaware of what was going on next door or across the street. To live in constant fear that our luck had run out and that we would be on the next train to Westerbork, to live life on the edge, with the nerves frazzled—you had to have a special kind of strength to stand up under that kind of pressure, and Max Windmüller, without question, had that self-confidence, that courage."

Sigi resumed his narrative. "In late 1942 there was another big roundup in the Amsterdam Jewish quarter. Max was among the hundreds who were caught up in that *razzia,* arrested, and brought to Westerbork. That was the camp that I've already mentioned, the one that the Dutch government had built in 1939. By then Jewish refugees were streaming across the border, and the Dutch government, despising the newcomers, did everything it could to keep them from integrating into Dutch society. Twenty-six sites, everywhere in Holland, were identified where these refugees could be held against their will. Westerbork was one of those sites. When the Germans took over, they used those same camps as detention centers where Jews and other prisoners were held until they were deported to the death camps in Eastern Europe."

Sigi continued: "While Max was at Westerbork, he learned of the tragic fate of the members of his family who had not gone underground. His widowed mother, Jette, and Max Kornblum had fallen in love. He was the father of Ruth Kornblum, the woman whom Salomon Windmüller, Max's oldest brother, had married. Jette and Max Kornblum were engaged to marry, but before they could wed, they were arrested and taken to Westerbork. From there, they were brought to Auschwitz and were killed there on December 15, 1942. Jette was so ill that she had to be brought into the gas chamber on a stretcher. Max's oldest brother, Salomon, met the same fate."

Salomon and Ruth Kornblum Windmüller

"He and his wife, Ruth, with their nine-month-old son, Maurice, were deported and all three killed in Auschwitz, also on December 15, 1942. On hearing this tragic news Max felt deep grief for his losses. At the same time, the death of his mother, brother, sister-in-law, and infant nephew deepened his hatred for the Nazis and steeled him in his resolve to do everything in his power to prevent other Jews from falling into the enemy's hands."

"We know that Max wasn't deported, as so many others were, from Westerbork. How did he get out?" Renate asked.

"This was another instance of Max's good luck and 'street smarts' working together. Knowing that the prison's laundry was taken in trucks through the prison gates to a laundry outside, he hid himself in one of those trucks under those bags of dirty laundry and escaped that way. On the Westerbork prisoner log dated August 18, 1943, Max is listed as 'missing'. By that date, Max had already made his way to the home of his friends, Frans and Henny Gerritsen, in Haarlem. Another *onderduiker,* Paula Kaufmann, was already living there. Within days after Max's arrival he was joined there by his brother, Emil."

"Frans Gerritsen . . . you haven't mentioned him before," Renate interjected. "What role did he play, other than to shelter Max?"

Frans Gerritsen

"To me, Frans Gerritsen was one of the heroes of the rescue movement. In 1964 he was rightly recognized at the Yad Vashem Museum in Jerusalem as one of Holland's 'Righteous Gentiles.' He had been trained as a graphic artist, and now during the Occupation, he became one of those forgers whom I mentioned earlier who duplicated the documents that the movement needed if we were to move around freely. Frans could produce identity cards so well-crafted that you couldn't tell them from the government-issued cards. Every time the Germans made changes to the cards to make them more secure and forgery-proof, Frans figured out how to keep up with those changes. And the identity cards had to be tailored to the country that they were used in: Cards that were valid in Holland were not valid in Belgium, cards that were good in Belgium could not be used in France."

"Frans made the little modifications that were needed to make 'genuine' cards in each of those countries. He also printed ration cards that were unrecognizable from the real thing, and that was vital because you couldn't get food at the markets without them. Later on Frans forged *Marschbefehle*—travel orders—bearing the message: 'The German Army is kindly asked to provide the bearer of this document with every help and protection necessary.' Showing those travel orders whenever the situation called for it enabled us to travel freely on German troop trains and to stay at hotels otherwise occupied by German soldiers."

". . . and Paula Kaufmann?" Renate asked.

"Paula was born in Poland and grew up in Vienna. She had escaped to Holland like so many of us and ended up working as a nanny for Frans and Henny Gerritsen. Later on in Paris she played a leading role in our Resistance efforts, and she was with us in the last months when we were all sent back to Germany."

"Did she survive?"

"Yes, she did. She and the other women in our group, those who were arrested, ended up in Theresienstadt, and were there when the Russians liberated the camp."

"Okay, Sigi. Can we return to Max's story?"

"Of course," Sigi replied. "To carry out our responsibilities as rescuers, we had to blend into the non-Jewish population, and to do that, we had to shed our obviously German-Jewish names and take on the identities of non-Jewish Dutchmen, and not just their identities but their personas, too. So with Frans Gerritsen's help, Max became Cornelius Andringa, a name that Max gleaned from looking at the names of Dutchmen who had emigrated to the United States years earlier. And I, likewise, became Piet de Vilbiss, with the documentation to prove it. We owe Frans Gerritsen a tremendous debt of gratitude for using his unique skills on our behalf."

"Now, with our new good-as-gold identity cards in our wallets, Max and I recited our new names back and forth to each other until we could say them without hesitation as readily as if they had been our birth names. Before long Max started calling himself Cor, the

Dutch nickname for Cornelius, and that's what we called him from then on."

"And you were 'Piet' to Cor and the other *chalutzim*, right?"

"Yes, from then on I was 'Piet', and, even after the war, that's what many people called me. And we adopted a new name for our little group of rescuers. We took on the name of our leader, Joop Westerweel. From then on, we were the Westerweel group, and that's the name that others knew us by."

"In the year following that overnight dispersal of the Loosdrecht *chalutzim*, several of them were arrested and deported to the east. They were caught up in *razzias*—round-ups—or picked up in some random encounter with Gestapo agents, or their hiding places were betrayed."

"Just as Anne Frank's was, in Amsterdam," Renate observed.

"Exactly so." Sigi replied. "The way that the Loosdrecht *chalutzim* were being picked off, one by one, confirmed for the leaders that hiding in the homes of non-Jews was what they had feared it would be: a temporary response to an acute need and not a long-term solution. There were many reasons: the number of Jews seeking shelter far exceeded the number of people willing to hide them; there was too much movement required from one address to another because of the time limits often imposed by the hiders; and, of course, every time a pioneer was moved from one house to another, there was the danger of discovery. Some of the pioneers had medical issues that required reliable treatment; there were personality conflicts between the pioneers and their hiders; and there was the ever-present risk of betrayal. Finally, we didn't have in the Netherlands the natural features that made hiding easier in other European countries: we had no mountains, dense forests, caves and so on, where humans might find shelter."

"So our leaders came to realize that real safety would come only when our youth were brought out of Holland and across the borders to neutral countries—either Switzerland or Spain. But that strategy presented problems, too, the biggest one being geography, the location of the Netherlands in the northwest corner of Europe, to be exact. To reach safety meant crossing three strongly guarded borders, between Holland and Belgium, between Belgium and France, and then between France and the destination, either Switzerland or Spain. At each of those borders we risked detection, arrest, and immediate death or, worse, to be turned over to German custody."

"Faced with this crucial choice—to move out, to take our destiny in our own hands with the confidence that you could face the risks and deal with them—or on the other hand, to do nothing and wait for the day when you were picked off, one by one, and delivered, like sheep, to the slaughter, Joop and the other leaders of the Westerweel group chose to act."

"I have a clear recollection of Joop, Schuschu Simon, and Max, in late August 1943, just after Max's escape from Westerbork, poring for hours over maps of Belgium and France, trying to identify the best places at the borders to move from one country to the other and the best ways to get to those border-crossing locations."

"Looking back," Sigi said reflectively, "you could understand why our leaders thought the escape route to Switzerland was the winning strategy. Switzerland was much nearer to the Netherlands than Spain; there would be no problem in learning a new language, because German, the native language of the *chalutzim,* was also the dominant language in Switzerland. And, because Switzerland was neutral in the conflict, we expected that the other side of the French-Swiss border represented safety and freedom, if we could reach it."

"Once the best border-crossing locations had been identified, Joop and Max set about to contact the underground resistance in Belgium and France to build a chain of safe houses in those countries, where our people could spend the night. We had to be so very careful in picking reliable safe houses. We felt the pressure to make quick judgments so that the children for whom we were responsible would have a place to sleep that night, but hasty judgments were dangerous—we learned that early on. But after all the questions had been asked and answered, you had to call on your sixth sense, that feeling in your gut that this person was reliable or wasn't."

"Finding reliable families who would take in refugees in the first instance was hard enough, but there was no guarantee that a 'safe house' would stay safe. If the Germans or the Vichy French police found out about a safe house and raided it, they would keep the seizure quiet and use the house as a *'sourcière'*—that's the French word for 'mousetrap'"—to capture refugees and resistance members who were unaware that the house wasn't 'safe' anymore. So it was critically important that if a safe house had been turned into a *sourcière,* the word get out quickly to everyone in the Resistance network that this house was no longer a reliable link in the chain."

"And of course we couldn't find the way across the borders on our own. We needed professional guides who knew their way across the mountains and past the unguarded border crossings. But those stretches along the border that were lightly guarded, and therefore offered the best opportunities for escape, were also the most challenging. Along the French-Swiss border, for example, the way to safety would take the refugees along high mountain trails that were challenging even for experienced hikers. Now the *chalutzim* would need to use those same trails, perhaps in rainy, snowy, or windy weather that made the trek even more difficult. That would be true, too, if they tried to cross the border between France and Spain. That line runs through the Pyrenees, a mountain range that extends from the Mediterranean on the east to the Bay of Biscayne on the west, ranging in width from six miles on the Mediterranean to eighty miles at the midpoint, and over 11,000 feet at its highest point."

"Even after the decision had been made to move us across borders to Spain and Switzerland, our leaders soon realized that, between Spain and Switzerland as destinations, there was no real choice: it had to be Spain. The Swiss authorities were intent on keeping the undocumented—that means illegal—immigrants out, turning them back at the border, often into German custody. A few courageous Swiss border guards allowed Jewish refugees into the country without proper documents, but they were the exception. If they were caught, they lost their jobs. The Spaniards, on the other hand, if you could get across the border, were actually welcoming to the illegals."

"The men and women who helped out in that way, leading the *chalutzim* across the French-Spanish border—were they motivated by patriotism or a desire to outwit the Nazis?" Renate asked.

"Only in the storybooks, dear lady," Sigi answered, smiling. "For the men who led the *chalutzim* across the French Alps toward Switzerland or across the Pyrenees to Spain, this was an occupation that required immense skill and experience, to say nothing of the risk involved if the band met up with German border patrols. For using those skills, these guides—they were called *passeurs*—demanded and received healthy sums of money, $1,250 to $2,000 per person, to be paid up front, before the party set out on its journey."

"And of course there was no guarantee that the journey would end in success. Sometimes the weather was so bad that the refugees had to turn back, and that could happen two or three times before they could finally cross the border. Sometimes there was a medical emergency that would force the band of refugees to turn back. And sometimes the *passeur* would abandon his responsibilities in the middle of the journey, telling the refugees in his party that his fee only covered his services to that point. Then he would show his band of refugees where they had to go, but leave it to them to get there. You can imagine that that was no easy task—there were no markings on those trails as there are here in our national parks."

"Up there, high up in the mountains, you couldn't be certain where the border was. Sometimes it was marked only by an iron pole driven into the ground or by a cairn of stones. On this side: extreme danger, deportation, and death. On that side: freedom and the possibility of a new life in Palestine. One step forward made all the difference."

"In early October 1942, sixteen Jewish refugees, including eight of our Loosdrecht *chalutzim,* paid the guides their hefty up-front fees and left Holland for Switzerland. They crossed the Netherlands-Belgium border successfully, but when they reached Brussels they were betrayed, turned over to German custody, and transported to Auschwitz. All of them were murdered there."

"You can imagine," Sigi continued, "the effect that the betrayal and murder of our comrades had on us. A mood of despondency, even of defeatism, would have prevailed if it had not been for Joop Westerweel. He demanded of us that we not let ourselves be brought down by this loss, that we harden our resolve. The lesson learned, he told us, was that we could not be as trusting of others as we had been, that we had to rely on ourselves to reach safety and freedom."

"What was Max's role in these rescues?" Renate asked.

"For more than a year Max had been one of the coordinators for the Loosdrecht Pavilion *chalutzim*. The duties that he had had in Holland—of securing hiding places for the *chalutzim* and managing their precarious existence in those places—were now enlarged and extended to cover Belgium and France as well. But now he had the additional responsibility of organizing and pulling off the dangerous journeys across the frontiers, then across occupied France to the border, and then to turn his charges over to the *passeurs*, the mountain guides."

Renate shook her head, solemnly.

"And of course the danger didn't end when you had crossed the border, first into Belgium, and then into France. There was danger everywhere. The last sixty miles bordering on Spain were especially heavily patrolled by the Germans and the French law enforcement officers. To pass through that zone, you had to show special safe-conduct passes, different from the ones that were valid elsewhere in France."

"And when it came to choosing the *passeurs* who were to lead the refugees across the mountains—that was another life-and-death decision. Were they who they claimed to be? Which one of them could you trust to carry out their responsibilities? Which one of them might take your money and then betray the group to the Germans? From Holland to Spain, every move you made was fraught with danger. One misstep could cost you your life and that of the young men and women in your charge."

"That was Max's mission in those days: to bring his charges safely to the Spanish border. It was his responsibility to get expertly forged safe-conduct passes for his charges, to move them from one safe house to the next, and to pay the professional *passeurs* the substantial sums that they demanded. To carry out those tasks, Max, in his new identity as Cornelius Andringa, moved from Holland to Paris and took a room in a *pension*— a lodging house—on the Boulevard St. Michel."

"Now Max had a new name and a new address, and a new life, a double life, if you will. At that time Hitler and his generals were anticipating the Allied invasion of France, across the English Channel. To defend against the invasion, the Germans began in the summer of 1943 to build a massive concrete wall and related fortifications, called the Atlantic Wall, along the western coast of France. The construction of that wall required the labor of thousands of workers, and the contractor, the Todt Organization, could not be choosy about whom it hired. It had to take on, with few questions asked, any able-bodied man who had not been called up for military service. This presented a golden opportunity for Max and me and the other male *chalutzim.*"

"Using our new false identities, and with the papers to go with them, we were taken on in July 1943 as one of the thousands of new Todt employees. Now we had a legitimate reason for being in a place where our presence would not be constantly questioned. Now we had an answer for the question: 'What are you, a healthy young man, doing here on the streets of Paris, in civilian clothes, when you should be in uniform at the front?' Moreover, in our new jobs, we earned good wages, some of which we could contribute to the common rescue effort. Best of all, our jobs put us just a two-hour drive from Paris. As Todt Organization employees, we were issued travel permits that enabled us to travel by train between Paris and the construction site, and elsewhere. If Cor or I were challenged and ordered to show our papers, just showing that permit enabled us to get past the challenge and go on our way."

"I notice that you are now calling Max by his cover name, 'Cor'. Did you do that intentionally?"

"Yes, because from that time on until his last weeks of life, he was no longer 'Max,' he was 'Cor'. That's what we called him, and that's what he called himself."

"Okay, but, so that my readers aren't confused, please continue to refer to him by his birth name, Max. Agreed?"

'Agreed," Sigi answered.

Renate paused, as if turning something over in her mind. "You know, Sigi, I'm thinking about that name that he chose—Cor. It's so fitting, isn't it? *Cor* is the Latin root word for '*heart*,' from which we get words like *courage* and *encouraged*. You get that same sense of 'heart' as a metaphor for courage in expressions like 'he's all heart" and in words like *wholehearted, stout-hearted,* and *heartily.* Is it a coincidence that he chose that name? "No," Renate answered her own question, "it has to be more than a coincidence."

"I agree," Sigi said. "It's as if some Higher Power directed him to adopt that name."

He resumed. "At first, the Frenchmen with whom we worked at Todt, and the slave laborers from other countries as well, were suspicious of us, especially of Max, because of his Germanic looks. But when Max showed them his Dutch identity card and made the point that the Dutch were suffering under the German occupation just as the French were, they warmed up to us. Eventually, we, Max and I, won the trust and confidence of the other workmen. Max started getting tips from our French co-workers, tips on underground safe houses, where to eat, and on how we could move our people from one place to another without being discovered."

Renate interrupted: "How could you and the other *chalutzim* allow yourself to work at those jobs? Didn't that make you an accomplice of the enemy?"

"Of course we had moral qualms about our work. What we were doing, building those concrete defenses, might enable the Germans to repel the Allied invasion and prolong the war. The submarine dry-docks that we were building at St. Nazaire might make it possible for German U-boats to go out into the Atlantic to sink Allied troopships and kill hundreds of Allied soldiers. That was something that we thought about and talked about all the time. We reasoned, on the other hand, that the work that we were doing, the rescue of Jewish children, was also essential. In a way the Nazis were financing our rescue efforts. Still, Max and I were much relieved, our moral dilemma resolved, when we found jobs at Le Bourget, the airport outside of Paris, and no longer had to work on the Atlantic Wall."

"Once we had landed those jobs at Le Bourget, other *chalutzim* followed us there, using their false identity papers. Among them were Max's younger brother Emil, now known by his Dutch name, 'Wim Dalen.'"

"After a few weeks at the Le Bourget job, Max started seeing warning signs of impending danger, a *razzia* by the Germans, perhaps, or by the local gendarmerie. Just as we had had to do so often in the past, we put our heads together and decided to move out. Our destination this time was a tiny village in the far northwest corner of France, Biville la Baignarde, where some of our Loosdrecht comrades were already living and working. On the strength of our experience in the construction of the Atlantic Wall, Max and I both found work there in Biville as carpenters."

"Wherever he went, whether it was in Paris or among the laborers at the Atlantic Wall, Max blended in comfortably in his surroundings, using his forged documents to their best advantage. His French friends marveled at his *chutzpah*, his steel nerves, in moving easily in German circles, using the privileges accorded to him because of his documents."

"In Paris, Max would put on his 'civilian clothes,' as he called them—black jackboots, a black leather coat, and a dark brown fedora—and mingle with Wehrmacht officers without arousing any suspicion."

"He did this, he told us, to obtain information that might be helpful to the movement but also, he said, to train himself in self-discipline and to set an example for us. 'When you're in their presence,' he told us, 'never let them see in you any uncertainty or inner tension.' That should be our motto, the words we live by.'"

"How about the women of the Loosdrecht Pavilion? While you were working as carpenters and pouring concrete for the Atlantic Wall, what were they doing?"

"They were traveling with forged identity cards, too, as non-Jewish Dutch women. Because of their fluency in German, their services were in great demand. They got jobs in the offices of the Todt Organization and even in Gestapo headquarters in Paris. In those jobs, they were in a position to issue 'genuine' travel documents to Max and the other comrades. Using those documents, Max traveled frequently back to Holland, to bring Jewish young people who were still in hiding as *onderduikers* back to France with him. Once they had been relocated to France, they, too, could get work in the building of the Atlantic Wall while awaiting their turn to move toward the border."

"The women of the Westerweel Group performed another vital function for us: that of communicating with each other and our allies. Think about it: How do you get the word out to those who need to hear it? 'Be at such-and-such a street corner at ten o'clock tomorrow night.' 'Be ready with your bags packed at five o'clock this evening.' You couldn't use the telephone, because you never knew who was listening. The safest way was by courier, from one person's mouth to another person's ears, and the women of the Westerweel

Group were the best ones for that job, because they didn't attract attention the way a young man would."

"The women of the Westerweel group carried out another key role as well: They served as escorts, as travel companions, bringing young Jewish children from one place to another along the escape route. They were, so to speak, substitute mothers to these children. Young men out in public, in civilian clothes, were viewed with suspicion. The question on people's minds was always 'Why were they not in uniform as every other young man was?' But a teenage girl, a young woman, didn't arouse suspicions in that way. When the leaders needed to get instructions and forged documents and medicines to one of the *chalutzim*, or to their hosts, they enlisted Loosdrecht women to do the job, and they did it successfully, sewing the documents into the hems of their skirts or cramming them into a wooden goose toy that had been hollowed out for that purpose."

"They also played a key role when the parents of a small child had to deliver that child into hiding. In a crowded space like a train station, the parents would bring their child with its little suitcase, or, if it was a baby in its carriage, and they would walk in one direction, the young Loosdrecht woman in the other. As they approached each other, the 'sender' and the 'receiver' showed by a prearranged signal that they recognized each other. Then as they passed each other, the parents would take their hands from the child, or from the carriage, and the Loosdrecht girl would seamlessly take up the hands of the little girl or the handle of the carriage."

"I can imagine," said Renate, "how heart-rending that must have been for the parents."

"It was traumatic for the parents: They described themselves as 'utterly bereaved', as if the child were dead to them from that time on. And as bad as it was for them when they had to give up their child, for some of them it was even worse after the war, when they were reunited physically with the child, but the bonds of love that link a child to its parents took years to re-establish, and sometimes they never were."

Sigi paused, as if picturing in his mind those forced separations, then continued: "Later, if a small child had to be moved from one hiding place to another, the teenage girls played a vital role there as well. On a train station platform or other public space, no one would question a young woman with a suitcase in one hand and holding a toddler's hand in the other. No one would stop a teenage girl riding a bicycle with a five-year-old on the handlebars. But the leaders, men like Max, were needed to choreograph the handoff, making sure that both the 'sender' and the 'receiver' were in the right position at the agreed-upon time."

He paused, then resumed, "By now, you probably realize, Renate, how the best planning could be frustrated by bad luck, and how, on the other hand, luck could avert what might have been a disaster. You book tickets on the 8:19 train and not on the earlier train. Too bad for you, you end up in Westerbork. You get on your bicycle, and you decide to pedal down this street and not that one, the one you normally travel on. A good thing, too, because that street, the other one, is the scene of a *razzia*, a round-up, and you could have been picked up along with the others. It could work the other way, too: the street you decided to use was the one on which the round-up occurs. It was all just sheer luck. We Jews would say, it's *beschert*, it's inevitable, it's Fate."

Now Sigi's thoughts turned back in time to the painful events of January 1943. Even now, 55 years later, sadness welled up in him as he recalled what happened. But he composed himself and resumed the narrative.

"In that month, January 1943, Max and I and the other *chalutzim* were informed of the tragic death of a mainstay of the Westerweel group, Joachim (Schuschu) Simon. He was arrested as he was trying to lead two women across the Holland-Belgium border and taken to the prison in Breda. There, on January 27, 1943, he was found dead in his cell, having committed suicide. He feared that through the gruesome torture that he had experienced and would continue to undergo, he would ultimately be forced to disclose the names and addresses of his comrades and destroy the rescue movement that was then underway. Faced with that prospect, Schuschu took his own life to protect his comrades."

"I had never before, in all my years as Max's close friend, seen him break down and cry—not when his father died, not when he got the news of his mother's death, and his brother Salo's death. But now, hearing of Schuschu's death, he wept uncontrollably, his grief made even keener by the knowledge of the suffering that Schuschu had undergone before taking his life."

"What effect did Schuschu's death have on the *chalutzim?* I imagine you were very discouraged."

"Schuschu's arrest and suicide was a terrible blow to the men and women of the Loosdrecht *Youth Aliyah*. On a personal level we mourned the loss of a comrade who had been a constant presence in our lives since our arrival in Loosdrecht. But it was more than that. Schuschu's death punched a very large hole in the organization as well. It was as if an army had suddenly lost the general with whom it had been identified. When we speak of the American Third Army in World War II, we invariably speak of its commander, General Patton, in the same breath—it's always 'General Patton's Third Army'. It's the same with the German general Rommel and his Afrika Korps. The two are always spoken of together. That's how we felt when Schuschu died."

"So, yes, it was a huge setback, but we couldn't permit ourselves to cave in. The work had to go on. New leaders stepped forward. There were *chalutzim* waiting to be guided to safety. So we mourned, but at the same time we closed ranks and rededicated ourselves to the goal of bringing the young men and women under our care to safety and to Eretz Israel."

"In the late summer and fall of 1943, other employment opportunities opened up for us. One of our leaders, Willy Hirsch, had established that jobs were to be had in southwestern France in and around Bordeaux, with a Belgian company that was building barracks for German soldiers. So we applied for those jobs and were accepted, no questions asked. With those jobs we were able to get passes that enabled us to travel freely between Bordeaux and Paris, and even return on periodic leaves to the Netherlands."

"Those jobs brought with them an even more important benefit. The rescue movement had established Bordeaux as the jumping-off point for the cross-border movement of the *chalutzim*. From Bordeaux, it was one hundred and fifty miles to the southeast, to Toulouse, where the refugees could spend the next night, and from there another sixty-seven miles to St. Girons, the village in the foothills of the Pyrenees where the trek across the mountains would originate."

"Schuschu's death was not the last of the devastating setbacks to the movement?"

"Tragically, no," Sigi answered. "On October 10, 1943, the German security police, the *SiPo*, raided the apartment in Rotterdam that was being used as a 'headquarters' by our comrades. Kurt

(Nanno) Hannemann and seven other *chalutzim* were arrested and deported. None of them survived."

"So, the leadership ranks of the movement were getting thinner and thinner," Renate commented.

"You're so right," Sigi responded, "but again, we felt we had no choice, those of us who remained, but to forge ahead. These arrests only added a sense of urgency to the work that remained to be done."

Kurt Reilinger

"The following month, November 1943, Max and I were in hiding in the village of Auffray, in northwestern France, with Max's younger brother, Emil, and other *chalutzim*.

"Kurt Reilinger came to Auffray to tell us the good news: that a way had been found to get to the Spanish border undetected and to travel from there across the Pyrenees to safety in Spain. Not everyone jumped at the opportunity that Kurt offered. They felt more secure than they had in Holland, and they were making good money working at the Atlantic Wall. Why give up that safety for a dicey trip across France and the dangerous trek across the mountains? We disagreed: We saw only the positive side of what Kurt had to offer us. If we stayed, there was the risk that those who were now working for Todt would be transferred to labor camps in Germany and from there to the east and to our deaths."

"So Max and I left Auffray as escorts for Emil and four other *chalutzim*. Our immediate destination was Bordeaux, but our intention was to bring these people to the jumping-off place for the trek across the Pyrenees and freedom. From Bordeaux we moved to the southeast, to Toulouse, and from there to St. Girons, that little village that I spoke of before, at the northern end of what came to be called *le Chemin de la Liberté*—Freedom Road."

"The final stop was a shepherd's hut in the foothills. There Emil and the other *chalutzim* were to meet up with the other refugees who were to form the crossing party, and with the guide who was to take them across the mountains. Max and I prepared to say goodbye to Emil and return to spend the night in Toulouse. We embraced, and told each other, '*L'shana haba'a b'Yerushalayim!* —Next year in Jerusalem!"

"Still another parting," Renate observed.

"Yes, it never got easier," Sigi replied. "It should have been—we certainly had enough practice in saying goodbyes—but it never was."

"How was the decision made to include some people in the crossing party and not others?"

"Max and the other leaders made those terribly difficult decisions. Who would go in this group, who would have to wait until the next one?"

"Based on . . . ?"

"Sheer numbers were an important factor. The number of people in each crossing party had to be limited for several reasons: a large number of people would attract unwanted attention. The number of pioneers and other Jews seeking safety far outnumbered the leaders who could help them reach the starting point. And there were not enough *passeurs*, mountain guides, available."

"But how were the individual members of the crossing party chosen?"

"Health was obviously important, because the trek across the mountains was physically demanding. You didn't want one infirm person to slow down the others as they climbed up and down the mountains, and one person needing medical attention might force the whole party to turn back. We gave priority also to the reunification of families: We'd select a young refugee whose parents, spouses and siblings had already made the trek and were waiting for him or her on the other side of the border. And, yes, we gave a preference to our own families. Who, in our position, would not have done that?"

"In an ideal world," Renate mused, "there would be some objective standard by which to determine that this one was more deserving than that one."

"Perhaps," said Sigi, "but we live in the real world, for better or for worse."

"And then, I imagine, you had to tell the refugees who were not on the list to go that they would have to wait until the next crossing or find another way to get across."

Sigi winced, recalling the scene. "That was the hardest part of the job, harder even than confronting our enemies."

"Still another question: With your connections, it would have been easy for you and Max to demand, and obtain, a place in one of the refugee groups and cross over with Emil and the others. And yet you stayed behind. Why?"

"We could have done that, yes," Sigi reflected, "but, honestly, it never entered our minds. We had obligations, sacred responsibilities, to the other leaders and the *chaverim* still waiting to be escorted to the border."

"You were like the captain of a ship, in rough seas, who is duty-bound to stay at the helm until the ship passes safely through the storm."

"An apt comparison," Sigi said. "We couldn't have lived with ourselves if we had betrayed our young charges in their hopes, and perhaps been responsible for their later roundup and death. And for Max, it would have been a breach of that sacred vow he had made to his father at the cemetery in Groningen. So it was completely out of the question."

"In any event," he continued, "it turned out that our goodbyes at the shepherd's hut were not the last ones. Twenty-four hours later, Emil and the other refugees were back in Toulouse. After reaching an altitude of 3,000 feet and halfway across a mountain pass, the refugees were stalled by a sudden snowstorm. The guide, Adrian, made the decision to turn back, and they did, tramping through knee-deep snow. Back in Toulouse, some in the party wanted to stay together in the staging area, so as to make another effort a few days later, when the storm had passed, but Max told them, 'Absolutely not!' The risk was too great that such a large group of young people would be observed and reported to the German authorities. He did allow one young couple, Rolf and Lilo Elsberg, to attempt a crossing, and they were successful, eventually making their way to Palestine."

"What happened to the others in the party?" Renate asked.

"Most of them retraced their tracks to the north and took up their jobs again at the Todt construction sites. Three months later, in February 1944, the weather conditions and all other circumstances were right for another try at a crossing. Now we had in the party of mountain crossers not only the members of the Loosdrecht group who had made the earlier attempt, but also two pilots of Allied warplanes who had been shot down over France and parachuted to safety, and also political refugees and French Jews. So, from St. Girons, that little village south of Toulouse in southern France, this group of twenty-seven young men and women were poised to travel to the northern edge of the Pyrenees. From there a professional *passeur* would guide them across the mountains to Spain."

"On the evening before the planned departure, we had a welcome surprise guest—Joop Westerweel showed up at the inn where Max and I and the party of mountain-crossers were staying. After our evening meal, we gathered outside the inn to hear Joop's parting words to us, words that I have never forgotten:

> *Chaverim,* you are on the threshold of freedom. Soon you will arrive in the land of freedom and will fulfill your goal of building *Eretz Israel* as a homeland for the world's Jews. I wish each of you happiness and good luck, but do not forget your comrades who fell along the road, and who, by sacrificing their lives, paved the way for your journey to freedom. Build up your land and erect a memorial for them, immortalizing their memory. Remember Schuschu and all the other comrades who gave their lives to rescue their comrades. Remember the world's suffering and build your land in such a way that it justifies its existence by providing freedom for its inhabitants and abandoning war.

> You are about to shed a great burden—the burden of being constantly hounded, on the run, the constant fear of being arrested, deported, and killed. You are about to gain, instead, a great privilege, the privilege of living [in freedom] in Palestine. With that privilege comes the great task that awaits you in Palestine: the establishment of a new country, a new society, serving not only the Jewish people but all its inhabitants as well. Through your hard work on the kibbutz, you can help to achieve socialism and the honest distribution of wealth in society.

"Those were thrilling and inspiring words," Renate observed. "It occurred to me, as you were speaking, that by this interview and by the book that I hope will come out of it, we are honoring Joop Westerweel's request: We are honoring the memory of Schuschu and Nanno and the other *chalutzim* who were murdered by the Nazis, and Joop's memory, too."

"That's my hope as well," Sigi replied. "That's what has brought us together, and keeping those words in mind, I'm confident that you will see your book through to completion and publication."

"From your lips to God's ears," Renate said, smiling. "So, did Emil and the others make it across?"

Refugees trudging through the Pyrenees

"Yes, he did, along with the rest of them, but it was no Sunday walk in the park. If today hikers were to duplicate that trek across the mountains in winter, they wouldn't attempt it without wearing several layers of sweaters, a heavy winter parka, and insulated snowboots. Emil and the others were wearing, at most, a woolen overcoat such as you would wear on a cold winter day in the city, and some kind of high boots, uninsulated. So in that knee-deep snow, several of the *chalutzim*, including Emil, suffered frostbite and narrowly avoided losing their toes. But they made it safely across the border. From there, they traveled by train to the southern port of Cadiz, and there they boarded the ship *Guinee* for Palestine."

"Standing around Joop in that open field, we were all of us well aware of the crushing emotional burdens that he was laboring under. His wife Wil had been arrested in December 1943 and was then in custody in the Vught concentration camp; his four children were in hiding. Moreover, knowing that he was a wanted man, and that there were probably photos of him circulating with the police and Gestapo, he had altered his appearance by trimming his hair almost down to the scalp. He told a friend at that time that he felt like the biblical Samson, who lost his strength when his hair was shorn. It must have been that way with Joop, too, because we couldn't help but notice how gaunt he was, how exhausted he looked. He had aged considerably in the three years that we had known him."

"He probably should have stepped down and let others assume the leadership of the rescue movement. It might have restored his health and even saved his life. Instead he threw himself even more energetically into the work, as if realizing that time was short and that every minute was precious. He personally escorted several of the pioneers across the Dutch and Belgian borders to Paris. He met several times with Max and with other leaders in Brussels and Paris to plan for the next moves in the ongoing struggle to bring the *chalutzim* to safety."

"And then, disaster struck. On March 11, 1944, on his way northward from St. Girons, Joop Westerweel was stopped at the Holland-Belgium border and had his papers examined. He had used them many times before at numerous border crossings and routine stops, but this time his papers were his undoing. Why? In choosing a new identity, the person whose name now appeared on his falsified papers,

Joop Westerweel made a mistake that cost him his life. The name he had taken on was that of a Dutchman who was wanted for the murder of a German soldier, and that man's name was on the border guards' watch list. Joop was arrested and brought to the concentration camp Vught, where, under torture, he disclosed his real name. On August 11, 1944 he was shot by a firing squad. In his prison cell, the night before his execution, he wrote what I call his last will and testament:

> There they are . . . all my comrades, standing side by side with me. Together we have advanced along this road to confront the enemy . . . Whether I live or die is now all the same to me. A great light has dawned within me. It is time for silent thoughts. The night is dark and long. But I am fully aglow from the splendor within me.

Sigi closed his eyes and kept them closed. In his mind's eye, he pictured Joop in his cell, writing these words on the last night of his life. Opening his eyes, Sigi was awestruck by the sunlight in the sky in front of him, rays of sunlight streaming through openings in the clouds. It was as if God himself had heard him recite these words, and was now complementing the music of those words with a soul-stirring visual accompaniment.

"Another shattering tragedy," Sigi told Renate, "for the Westerweel family, for us, and for the entire rescue movement. For many of us, Joop had been a father figure, the substitute for the real father whom we had had to leave behind on station platforms in Berlin, Vienna, Hamburg, and elsewhere. Now we had to carry on without him; it was almost more than we could bear."

"Were there other successful mountain-crossings?"

"Yes, many more, by our Dutch comrades, by Allied pilots shot down over occupied France, and others. In May 1944 Kurt Reilinger organized a successful children's crossing, I think of it as a 'children's crusade'. The children were brought to a hostel in Toulouse and from there to St. Girons. For the crossing itself the older children carried the smaller, younger, children on their backs for much of that distance. You can imagine how difficult that was. But the crossing was successful, and many of the children were reunited in Spain with their parents who had crossed earlier."

Sigi returned to the issue of the vacuum in leadership resulting from the deaths of Schuschu Simon in 1943, and now, the arrest and imprisonment of Joop Westerweel. In Holland, Belgium, and France, refugees were still on the move, waiting to be brought to safety in Spain. Who would step in to fill that void in our leadership? It turned out to be Kurt Reilinger. He set up his headquarters in Paris, in a room at the Hotel Versigny on the Rue Letort, and named Max as one of his five deputies, or lieutenants. Max and I took a room at the same hotel. Max's assignment was to welcome the arriving pioneers to Paris, to see to their needs while they were in the city, and then to escort them to the jumping-off place for the crossing of the Pyrenees."

"The loss of our former leaders, the installation of the new leadership, and the new responsibilities imposed on Max did not seem to affect his positive state of mind. He always seemed to find a way around the difficulties that could come up without any forewarning. With his daily reminders, 'Chin up!' and 'Hold your heads up high,' he refused to let us be beaten down or intimidated. No matter how intense the pressures bearing down on him, he always seemed to find a way to keep moving forward. On overcrowded trains, he always managed to find a seat for the two of us. Max always managed—I don't know how—to secure travel passes for us and we got special treatment at good hotels. Oftentimes, as we rode the trains, our spirits were low as we considered our future. At times like those, Max would haul out his harmonica and play the currently popular tunes or the songs that we had learned in the *Blau-Weiss*, songs of the pioneers in Palestine. When German soldiers traveling in our car would ask him about those songs, where they came from, Max would answer, 'They're from South Holland!', and that answer would satisfy them."

"Early in January 1944, Max and I were at the Hotel Angleterre in Brussels with a group of refugees, on our way south to the rendezvous point for the trek across the Pyrenees. We were sitting in the hotel lobby when, to our amazement, one of the Loosdrecht leaders, Tinus Schabbing, came in, escorting two young ladies whom he had that same day brought on foot across the border from Holland. The two young ladies were Betty Britz, whom we knew from the Loosdrecht Pavilion, and Metta Lande, traveling under her Dutch identity as 'Elisabeth Brinkmann'.

Martinus (Tinus) Schabbing

This beautiful girl, who had been so much in Max's waking thoughts and in his dreams since their chance encounter in Loosdrecht almost four years earlier, was now standing just a few feet away from him in this Brussels hotel lobby."

"It was . . . what was that word—*beschert?* Renate asked.

"It was truly *beschert*—predestined," Sigi replied. "Max always believed that this was no chance meeting, that it had been arranged by the angels. Love at second sight, you might call it. It was certainly the most intense relationship Max would have with a woman in his short life."

"There was so much to talk about, to catch up on. Where is this pioneer . . . and that one? Did this one make it safely over the border . . . and that one? What became of him . . and her? By the time the evening had ended, Max had renewed their optimism, lifted their spirits. He pledged: 'Don't worry—I will bring you to safety and freedom!'"

"Max invited Metta and her companion to accompany us to Paris. So within hours we were on the train together, heading for Paris, the City of Lights. For Max, this was routine; he had already been in Paris for months. But, for Metta, it was all new and exciting. After months in hiding, months of constant vigilance and fears for her safety, she was now among friends, men and women whom she trusted, in a place where she could walk freely and anonymously among the crowds, holding her head up high instead of hugging the shadows. She would have liked to have stayed in Paris, enjoying these new freedoms and new experiences, and Max shared that wish with her. He wanted so much to show her the sights of Paris at a leisurely pace, as if they were there in peacetime, perhaps on their honeymoon after the war. But not now, he told Metta: it was too dangerous. They would be safer, he said, if they left Paris and moved in with peasants in Normandy, near Rouen."

"So that's what they did. Max spent as much time as possible with Metta while attending to his work at the Atlantic Wall and to his rescue work for the *chalutzim*. After spending their first night together, Max and Metta announced to us and to the world, 'We're married!' That came as no surprise to us: after all, this was wartime, and we were being pursued, hunted down. A formal wedding ceremony was out of the question. But they did not hide the powerful feelings they had for each other. They made them clear by the loving glances that passed between them, from the way they cuddled next to each other when we had our group meetings in the hotel room, and from their fervent embraces when Max came back to Paris from one of his rescue missions."

"Our stay in Normandy came to an end when our hosts told us that it was time to leave. We didn't argue with them, or try to change their minds. There was too much at stake. After a brief stay with farmers in a village near Pau in southern France, the four of us—Cor and I, Metta and Betty—boarded a train back to Paris. Because the train was crowded, we ended up sharing a compartment with two German officers. Ignoring Cor and me, the officers took a liking to our two female companions. 'It's such a pleasure,' one of them said, 'at long last to meet up with true Aryan women.' Attempting to put the Germans off, the two women said, 'We're Dutch.' 'Doesn't matter,' was the response, 'it's the same race.' Then one of the officers turned to Max and said, 'Hey, you there, what's up with you? You look like you're thinking too hard. Let the horses do that—they have bigger heads than you do.' Without answering, Max took out his harmonica and started playing German folk songs, and soon the two Germans were joining in enthusiastically."

"Max wanted very much to include Metta in the next group that was to be brought across the Pyrenees to safety. But at this point Metta came to another important decision. She would rather stay in Paris with Max, and take her chances on facing the ever-present danger with him. So she returned with Max to the Hotel Versigny, joining three women from the rescue movement who were already living there: Betty Britz, Lolly Eckhardt, and Paula Kaufmann."

Once more, Sigi rummaged through his folder and found what he had been looking for, a letter that Max wrote in February 1944, while on the road in Marseilles. "It gives a sense," he told Renate, "of what his life was like in those days:"

Dear Friends, I'm writing this letter because I was alone all day and had no one to talk to. I had to wait here all day on Sunday because there was no train heading for the Nest [a ski resort area in the French Alps], which is where I have to go. I left Paris yesterday at eight o'clock in the evening, arrived here in Marseilles after midnight, and had to find my hotel. I was stopped by the police at the hotel and they demanded that I produce my papers. I finally got to bed at 2:00 A.M. and fell asleep right away, because I just haven't had much sleep lately. But the next morning, I had to be out of bed by 6:00 A.M.

"Max was traveling constantly between Holland, Belgium, and France, bringing *chalutzim* with him across two borders, living with the ever-present danger of arrest and deportation. In a letter from Paris to two comrades dated March 31, 1944, he wrote that he was enjoying his daily routine: 'Fortunately, I have a lot to do. I say "fortunately" because I find it very satisfying to be able to do as much as possible.'"

"He told his friends that he had just brought three young people with him from the Netherlands to Paris after an eight-hour delay. Why the delay? Because the frequent Allied bombing raids had destroyed much of the track, and when the train encountered a stretch of damaged track, it had to be rerouted to other undamaged lines. And then, of course, there were the long delays at the border crossings while the guards checked each passenger's identification papers."

"That was his routine during those months: every two weeks, another 'delivery' of young Jews on that perilous trip across the two borders. And if the number of persons to be brought to safety on these trips wasn't large—perhaps just two or three on each such trip—you had to accept that, because there was a feeling that time was running out, and every life saved was precious."

Renate interjected: "Wouldn't it have made more sense to wait until a larger group had been assembled? To me, it hardly made sense for the leaders to risk their own lives to bring just two or three people to freedom."

"I'm not surprised that you would say that," Sigi responded. "Most people would. But our Talmud tells us that even one life is worth saving. 'Whosoever saves a life, it is considered as if he had saved an entire world.' So the numbers, whether one or a hundred, didn't matter to us."

Sigi returned to the letter from Max of March 31, 1944. "He ended by commenting to his comrades that 'You can drive yourself half-crazy with the tension, but you can get used to anything, if you have to. You just have to learn to take the unanticipated difficulties in stride.'"

It might have been on one such trip, Sigi continued, from Paris northward to Amsterdam or Brussels, or southward to Marseilles, or Toulouse, or Lyons, or back again, that Max's thoughts turned to Metta, as they so often did, and a poem formed in his mind that showed clearly the intensity of his longing for Metta. Sigi pulled the poem out from his folder and began reading:

The wheels they roll and rattle their song
    on silvery shiny tracks.
A song that pulls me deep into my soul,
    a song of iron on iron.
The night is long and dark and cold
    and tired my spirit and heart
Then, out of this darkest of darknesses,
I suddenly see your face.
Your soft voice whispers into my ear,
    your hand gently caresses my cheek,
    your smile moistens my eyes,
    your mouth kisses mine, passionately.
I feel the kisses go on and on.

But then, with a start, I see daylight.
    With a sigh, I awaken.
Why can't I dream longer?
Why can't I be with you?

Renate absorbed the words, then mused, "So, clearly, his sense of duty motivated him, that vow that he had made to his father on his deathbed, but it seems to me that he was equally motivated by his love for Metta and their mutual yearning for **a** future together in Palestine."

"Like a soldier in his foxhole, or a sailor at sea, thinking of his wife or sweetheart back home. Yes, just like that." Sigi returned to the narrative. "By the spring of 1944, when Kurt Reilinger and Max and the others stepped into the leadership of the movement, their first priority, as I've said, was to continue the rescue operations, moving the young *chalutzim* to the Spanish border. But they took another initiative, too, one which they saw as essential to the first one: They reached out to the *Armée Juive* (AJ), the 'Jewish Army', the umbrella organization for Jewish resistance to the German occupation in France. Schuschu Simon had made the first contacts with the AJ as far back as 1942. Now those contacts were renewed through Adina Simon, Schuschu's widow."

"The AJ was useful—indeed essential—in two ways. First, as its members were native-born French Jews, they could help Max in locating the 'safe houses' where Max and the young people in his charge could spend the night and find secure ways of moving from one safe house to the next. The second important role of the AJ was as a financial intermediary with the Jewish Agency and the American Joint Distribution Committee—we called it the 'Joint'. These two organizations provided most of the money that was needed to cover Max's daily expenses and for the other costs of running this expensive operation."

"Max regularly visited Amsterdam, taking leave from his job with Todt and using the leave papers that he received as a Todt employee. While in Amsterdam, he spent evenings at the home of his loyal friends, Frans Gerritsen and his wife, Henny. It was Frans who, using his skills as a craftsman, created suitcases with false bottoms, and chessboards, cutting boards, stuffed animals, and other children's toys—all with secret compartments—that Max needed to move money and documents across borders and past the police officers and inspectors whom he regularly encountered."

"Until one day . . . Max and I were on an assignment, traveling from Amsterdam to Paris, when we ran into a Loosdrecht comrade, Emil Strander. We decided to travel together. It turned out to be an eventful journey, one that we would have cause to regret. When we reached the French border, we showed our papers to the French customs official who entered our compartment. That should have been enough to satisfy the man and send him on his way. But the customs official's eyes lit on Max's suitcase in the overhead bin. The man ordered Max to take the suitcase down, then, in a peremptory tone, beckoned Max to follow him into the customs house."

"As the minutes ticked by, Strander and I, still in our coach seats, grew increasingly anxious. What could be taking so long? At length, Max came back, trembling, his face ashen. The customs officer, searching the suitcase, had discovered its false bottom and the stacks of bills that were hidden beneath—bills that were intended to be used as payments to the *passeurs*. The customs official threatened to confiscate the money and turn us all over to the Germans."

"Desperately, Max negotiated a deal with the customs officer. 'Keep the money,' he told him, 'but let my friends and me go ahead to our destination'. The Frenchman agreed, and we were able to continue on to Paris, but the money was gone. Nevertheless, we all breathed a huge sigh of relief: Our liberty, our lives, had been spared. Once again, Max's quick thinking had saved his life—and ours."

"There were many such close calls. A year earlier, another Loosdrechter, Norbert Klein, had had to jump out of an upstairs bedroom window when the Gestapo raided the house where he was hiding. He escaped successfully, but he broke his leg in the process. His friends brought him to the hospital, where his leg was set, while his true identity remained hidden. From the hospital he was brought to another safe house, where he was placed in a secret room in the attic. But it wasn't long before Norbert started to react irrationally and violently to his forced confinement in that attic room, and his friends again had to intervene, bringing him to the local psychiatric hospital."

"Responding to that episode, Max wrote a letter to one of his Loosdrecht friends, this one dated March 7, 1943." Sigi read it to Renate, to demonstrate that an important part of Max's role, one that he resorted to repeatedly, was that of morale-builder:

Please don't take this business with Norbert too much to heart. We all have our problems. I certainly have mine. At this very moment, I am carrying many worries in my head, and I know that, right now, things are looking really bad. But then I give myself a good shove, and I tell myself that all those things that are bothering me, they're quite unimportant. We need to resolutely turn our backs on these trivial concerns. There's so much to be done, so much important work awaits us. Shouldn't we suppress our own little difficulties or, as you would put it, our *tsaroth* [troubles]? I believe that's what we have to do. Sure, I have problems, too, but, all in all, we're moving ahead.

Sigi returned to his story. "In 1944, the Easter holiday coincided with *Pesach*, the Jewish Passover holiday. Frans Gerritsen had rented a gypsy wagon—a horse-drawn wagon, like a wooden hut on wheels—in the picturesque town of Nunspeet in central Holland. Max and I and the other *chaverim* came together there for a reunion of sorts, a reunion with a dual purpose. We were there, both the Jews and our non-Jewish friends, to celebrate the holiday, but there was a more somber purpose as well. Schuschu was dead, Joop was behind bars at the Vught concentration camp. Without these leaders, we needed to regroup if we were to continue the important work of rescuing Jewish children and to save our own lives as well."

"Max continued to fulfill his obligations to the pioneers who were seeking to escape across the Pyrenees, and at the same time sought to free comrades who were behind the barbed-wire fences in prison camps across Holland, Belgium, France, and Germany."

"One of our comrades, Kurt (Nanno) Hannemann, was now in prison in Fresnes, the notorious prison outside of Paris." Sigi retrieved from his folder a copy of the letter that Nanno wrote to Max, but, before he could begin reading it, Renate broke in. "Wait a minute, Sigi," she said. "How could Max have received a letter that had been written in prison? I'm sure there was no regular mail service between the prisoners at Fresnes and the outside world."

"Of course not. This letter from Nanno—he gave it to a fellow prisoner who had been released and was about to exit from the prison, and that man brought it out to Max."

"Okay," Renate said, "you've cleared that up. Please go ahead." And Sigi proceeded to read it.

I've received your letter, and was happy to hear from you. We—the other comrades and I—are doing well. I hope your efforts to get us out of this prison are successful. I can't write often, because I don't know how the mail delivery goes, but I can answer [your] questions:

1. I'm not sure if the others are here in Fresnes, but I think so, because I've seen them in the last two weeks.
2. We're all in good health.
3. When I was interrogated, I told them that, yes, I did come to France illegally, but that I worked here for various

companies, and I believe that the others responded in the same way. As far as I know, in the short time since my interrogation, no one has said anything careless or dangerous.

* * *

6. I can't tell you how happy we would be if your efforts to get us out of here are successful.
7. How you get that done, I leave to you. Don't be afraid to use any means possible to accomplish that end.
8. I'm strong enough to get over any disease, and I believe that's true of the others as well.

* * *

12. We don't know who betrayed us. We were all arrested in your rooms.

I hope that you can do everything in your power for us, and hope, if it's at all possible, to hear from you again.

A day later, Cor wrote to Lucien Lublin, his contact with the *Armée Juive* in Lyons:

Dear Lucien,

Let me tell you first that our work on behalf of Nanno and the other *chaverim* is moving ahead fairly well. I received yesterday from Nanno a letter in answer to mine, that I sent to him in his prison. I'm hoping that we'll be able to get him out. I've made that my number one priority. It all depends on your office, in conjunction with the Intelligence Service. * * * As far as the work here goes, I don't have much to tell you, except that it is moving forward. But I need to know from you, as soon as possible, how matters stand with Spain. Have our people left yet? And how can we manage to get our people on the next transports [over the Pyrenees]? Please let me know as soon as possible.

"Is this a good time to stop for today?" Renate asked.

"Just when the story reaches its climax?"

"Exactly. We want you to be refreshed when you tell the most difficult part of the story," Renate assured Sigi. "I'll be back tomorrow, same time, same place."

As she stood in the doorway, ready to leave, Sigi held out his hand to bid her goodbye.

Renate admonished him, "A typical German," she said, "always with the formalities!" And with that, she stood on her tiptoes, gave him a little kiss, first on one cheek, then on the other, and then, with a cheery *"Auf Wiedersehen!"* she headed down the hall to the elevator.

PART 5

The Fifth Day

CHAPTER 5

The Enemy Closes In;
Arrest and Deportation

O n Friday, Renate arrived at Sigi's apartment door at exactly nine
o'clock. *I could set my watch by her arrivals,* he told himself.

It was, once again, a glorious spring day. After Renate had settled
herself on her favorite balcony chair, put down her handbag, and
turned the tape recorder on, she began the fifth day of their interview.

"Sigi, yesterday you mentioned the *Armée Juive*, the AJ—can you
tell us more about it?" Renate asked.

"The AJ was organized in January 1942 as a Jewish militia, an
armed response by Jews to the German occupation of France and its
persecution of French Jewry. Lucien Lublin, the man to whom Max
wrote the letter that I read to you yesterday, was one of its organizers.
In the fall of 1943 the AJ began sending young Jews across the border
into Spain, some three hundred of them. Among them were eighty
Dutch *chalutzim* who had been escorted into France."

"The AJ received generous financial assistance from the Jewish
Agency and from the Joint. Max and the other leaders of the
Westerweel group used some of that money to pay for the movement
of *chalutzim* through France and across the Pyrenees. The exchange
of letters between Max and Lucien Lublin shows that in the spring of

1944 the Westerweel Group was reaching out to other groups— private groups like the *Armee Juive*—to get support for its operations."

"The letter also mentions something called the 'Intelligence Service." What did that refer to?" Renate asked.

"That was the British Intelligence Service, which had parachuted agents into occupied France. They were actively working alongside the *Armée Juive.*"

"Didn't Max understand the risks that he was taking, personally and for his organization, in linking up with the AJ and the Intelligence Service?"

"He certainly did, but with many of its leaders dead or imprisoned, perhaps he felt that the Westerweel Group had no choice—that it needed the help of those organizations if it wanted to continue to operate and continue to move its people across the border into Spain."

Sigi paused, as if trying to frame what he would say next. "So back to the story . . . and it's not a pretty one."

"But it needs to be told," Renate said.

"Quite so. While Max and his friends were celebrating their Easter and Passover holiday in Nunspeet, dancing the *hora* and singing the familiar songs, disaster overtook his fellow *chalutzim* in Paris. Kurt Reilinger, Zippy Frankel, Willy Hirsch, and Susi Hermann were in the pioneers' headquarters in the Rue Letort when the German security police, the *SiPo,* moved in and arrested them. To make matters worse, the *SiPo,* searching the room, found the trunk in which the group kept the fake identity papers and the fake rubber-stamps."

"How did it happen?" Renate asked. "Was it an insider who betrayed them?"

"We still don't know. Max suspected that the owners of the hotel that they were using as their base had betrayed them. It could also have resulted from the arrest of one of the *chalutzim*, Joop Andriesse, at the Swiss border. Either through a search of his luggage or through torture, the Germans learned the address of the pioneers' Paris head-quarters and found out also that there was to be a meeting there on April 27. That's when they moved in."

"Now the whole responsibility for the Paris operation fell on Max and the others who had escaped capture because they had been in Nunspeet at the time of the raid: on Hans Ehrlich, Paula Kaufmann, Judith Markus, Lilo Spiegel, Betty Britz, Metta, Max and me. There was much to be done. We had to find, quickly, another 'safe house' as our headquarters, and we had to re-connect with the AJ. All the while, we had to continue to carry out our mission, the work of bring-ing refugees to safety in Spain. This had become much more difficult because the *SiPo*, when they raided our apartment in the Rue Letort, had found and confiscated the fake travel documents that we had been using."

"The meeting that Max had requested with the British Intelligence Service (the IS) in his letter to Lucien Lublin took place in Nice in March 1944. Lydia Tscherwinska, an attractive and intelligent Russian-Jewish woman, was there to tell us that a friend of hers, Charles Porel, an Austrian Jew, was an agent of the IS and could con-nect us with British intelligence."

"The AJ gambled everything on the prospect of an alliance with the British Intelligence. Such an alliance would offer two important benefits to the AJ: It would give the organization credibility with other Jews and with non-Jews, and it would provide logistical sup-port to the AJ in its rescue-and-resistance efforts. It would also, the AJ leaders thought, give them the inside track in emigrating legally to Palestine after the war."

"We learned from Lublin that he had met Charles Porel for the first time at a secret meeting in Southern France, in Montauban. Lublin had been favorably impressed by the man. He was good-looking, self-assured, and spoke excellent English."

"Never put your faith in outward appearances," Renate commented.

"How true!" Sigi responded. "Porel in turn introduced two other men who, he said, were fellow officers from the IS. To raise Lublin's level of confidence in these men—that they were who they said they were—they showed him their British-made sidearms, Webley MK-IV revolvers. They also showed the AJ people their radio, which, they said, allowed them to remain in constant contact with their offices in London."

"After that first meeting in Montauban, there were more meetings at which the details of their cooperation were ironed out. The negotiations stretched out over many weeks, each side trying to measure the trustworthiness of the other."

"Max must have been under unbearable stress during those weeks," Renate chimed in.

"You're so right, Renate. And we get an idea of what his life was like from a letter he wrote to Adina Simon, Schuschu's widow, on May 21, 1944. Max enumerates in that letter his expanded responsibilities: with so many of his comrades in detention, it was up to him to reorganize the movement so that it could carry out its work effectively. He had to move, or arrange to move, Dutch Jewish children from the Netherlands across the two borders to France, and that wasn't easy because so much of the track had been destroyed by Allied bombings, and he had to continue to move children across France to the Pyrenees. That involved constant traveling: from Paris to Holland, or to Brussels, and southward to Toulouse, to Bordeaux and to Lyons, and every train ride carried with it a heightened risk of discovery and detention."

"Meanwhile, he was doing all he could to enable his comrades, the ones who were now in prison, to escape. He had to continue to see to the ongoing funding that he needed to keep everything running smoothly, and all this against the threat of betrayal and arrest."

"At the time of his letter, he wrote to Adina Simon that he was also investigating the role of the hotel owners in the betrayal and arrest of his comrades while he was in Nunspeet. 'You can imagine,' he wrote, 'what their fate will be if their guilt is proven. We take these measures not out of revenge, because that won't bring our comrades back, but because such creatures should not be allowed to run around freely.'"

"In his letter, he tells Adina that the knowledge of the fate that had befallen so many of his comrades and the weight of his daily responsibilities are almost unbearable, but he knows that he must persevere in the face of every hardship, especially with the war coming to an end. Finally, Max also wrote of his developing contacts with the 'French *chaverim*,' the French Resistance, and his satisfaction with those contacts."

"He was unaware then," said Renate, "that those contacts were to be his undoing, and the undoing of his comrades, as well."

"True," said Sigi. "It makes us want to block his path, put up our hands and say 'Stop! Don't do that!' But that is hindsight, and those of us who were there didn't see it coming."

"Sixteen days after Max wrote that letter, on June 6, 1944, the Allies landed on the beaches in Normandy and advanced rapidly eastward toward Paris. At that point, Henri Pohoryles took over command of the A.J. in Paris, working closely with Max. Everyone in our group was in high spirits. We were certain that Allied soldiers would soon be marching down the Champs Elysées and we would be once again free men and women. In the meantime, with the city still under German control, we assumed a confident air as we carried out our assignments—a confidence that proved to be entirely unjustified."

"What were the women—Metta and Paula—doing during this tense time?" Renate asked.

"They had once again secured jobs that were very helpful to us. Metta was working with Radio Paris. Paula, meanwhile, had put her head in the lion's mouth, so to speak, and carried it off. Using her Dutch assumed name, Els Visser, she marched in with her prepared speech: 'I am a Dutch woman. I was working in Rouen, but my apartment was bombed out, and I had to leave the city. Now I'm looking for a job.' With that little speech, she got a job as a secretary at Gestapo headquarters on the Avenue Foch. And not just any job. She became the personal secretary to the Chief of the Construction Division. In that job she went everywhere with her boss, from the most elegant villas to Gestapo offices and prisons everywhere in the Paris area. She had access to construction plans and other important documents, which she secretly copied. Whenever possible, she tried to be in the company of her boss, because the respect that the sentries gave to her boss rubbed off on her as well, so when they waved him through security, they did the same for her as well."

"Max was now her only contact in the Resistance. Dressed in his jackboots, black raincoat, and brown fedora, he often picked her up at her Gestapo offices. He had also taken to wearing glasses and had grown a mustache and goatee. After the war, Paula, speaking of Max, said 'He looked like one of them.' One day as Paula and Max were talking in the courtyard, her boss showed up. Before the man could ask, 'Who's this?' Paula introduced Max as her fiancé and snuggled up to him. That seemed to satisfy her boss. He turned and walked away."

"Max had found a job as a driver for the SS motor pool, using authentic-looking papers that identified him as 'Aart van Norden.' His papers carried instructions, signed by the SS officer in charge, that required every police officer reading that card to accord all possible protection and assistance, and under all circumstances to let him proceed to wherever he wanted to go. Sometimes, when he reached a checkpoint, he didn't even have to show his pass. All he had to do was say, 'I'm SD!' and they would let him through."

'He looked like one of them.'

"In late June 1944, Porel and his companion, Lydia Tscherwinska, met with Max at his apartment at 6 Rue Jobbè-Duval in Paris. Paula Kaufmann, as secretary to the Gestapo chief of construction, had obtained for Max the secret construction documents for bunkers and for the concrete emplacements for the German V-1 rocket systems. Max and Porel struck a bargain: Max turned those drawings and documents over to Charles and Lydia. In return, they offered Max the in-depth cooperation of the British War Office. Then and there, in Max's apartment, they shook hands and entered into the final agreement."

Max as 'Aart van Norden'

"The agreement provided that the *Armée Juive* was to be incorporated in the British army as the 'Autonomous Jewish Legion' and receive priority in the anticipated postwar wave of emigration to Palestine. The agreement also spelled out that Max's associates in the *Armée Juive*, Jacques Lazarus and Rabbi René Kapel, were to be flown

Jacques Lazarus   Rabbi René Kapel

to London from a secret airstrip outside of Paris. When they landed safely in London, a coded message was to go out over BBC: 'The ducks are lame.' Once that message had gone out, the IS agents and the leadership of the Jewish Resistance would make themselves known to each other."

"Wasn't that terribly naïve on his part? In effect," Renate suggested, "Max gave up something solid—the construction drawings—for a bare promise to do something in the future."

"That's true," said Sigi. "But when you're promised everything you've always wanted, you have to stake everything you have on that bet."

"It's easy to make extravagant promises when you have no intention of keeping them," Renate commented.

Sigi nodded his agreement and continued. "When the young Jews in the Movement heard that the agreement had been sealed, there was a wide range of reactions, from euphoric excitement to melancholy skepticism. On the optimistic side, one of the *chaverim* said, 'Finally, we're being taken seriously. A Jewish Legion as a unit of the British Army—now *that's* an accomplishment! It means there is international recognition for our cause! It will give us influence in France, after the Liberation, and put us in a good position for emigration to Eretz Israel!'

"And the answer from the skeptics came back: 'You can't be serious! Do you think for a moment that the Allies are depending in any way on a handful of undernourished and poorly trained Jews?'"

"What was Max's mood during this time? Was he among the hopeful ones or among the pessimists?" Renate asked.

"Of course, he was aware of the risks that he, and all of us, were exposed to every day, every hour, but with him his mission, the mission of saving the lives of Jewish children, was always uppermost in his mind. As the circle grew ever smaller, instead of retreating or withdrawing altogether, he accepted that he had to reach out, to grow ever bolder in the actions he was willing to undertake. There was another element to it, too. Kurt Reilinger had worked hard to keep the rescue activities of the Movement entirely apart from active resistance. That was, after all, something that we were entirely untrained for. Now, as the end of the war seemed near, our group was increasingly drawn into the armed resistance activities of the AJ. That may have been the price that the AJ exacted from us in exchange for its support of our rescue mission."

"In those heady weeks, as the Allies advanced toward Paris, Max struck a positive note. For him it was always 'Chin up! Don't let them get you down!' We tried to reassure ourselves and each other that way. Metta would quote her father, who was always telling her: '*Tapfer bleiben, Mut erhalten*' Stay strong, hold onto your courage.'"

Renate listened, then commented: "I think it's called 'the power of positive thinking.'"

Sigi smiled at the familiar phrase. "To be sure, that phrase wasn't current back then, but the attitude certainly was."

Renate tried to sum up. "So, until the very end, Max was hopeful, upbeat."

"Yes, he, along with the other pioneer-leaders had a very clear vision of what the future would look like, the future that he hoped to build in Eretz Israel."

"And then," Renate said, "the hammer fell on the anvil."

". . . the hammer fell on the anvil," Sigi repeated. "On the evening of July 17, 1944, all of us were in Max's apartment with the radio tuned in to Radio London. Dozens of coded messages went out over the airwaves. Then we heard: 'The ducks are lame.' That was it! Max and Metta fell into each other's arms, embracing each other passionately. Everyone was hugging and kissing in wild elation. 'René and Jacques have landed in London! We've done it!' Max picked up his harmonica and started playing '*Hatikvah*,' the song of hope. Now it's the Israeli national anthem."

"In the early afternoon of the following day, Max left the room he shared with Metta in the Rue de Courcelles. He was on his way to a meeting with AJ leaders in an apartment on the Rue Erlanger. Metta would have gone with him, had planned to attend the meeting, but she was feeling ill with a chest cold that day, and Max urged her to stay home. I picture them sharing a parting embrace—"

"—their final embrace," said Renate.

"—their final embrace, yes," said Sigi, "and Max telling Metta, 'Take care of yourself, dearest. We need you healthy, for yourself and for our team.' Neither of them could have known then that it was Max who was in peril. Neither of them could have known that this was to be his last day of freedom, that, indeed, they would never see each other again."

"Go on, please," said Renate. "What was the purpose of that meeting?"

"We were trying to firm up the organizational ties between our group and the AJ."

"And who was at the meeting?"

"André Amar, Henri Pohoryles, Ernst Appenzeller, Cesar Chamay, Maurice Loebenberg, and Max. And I."

"And then?" Renate asked. She knew what was about to happen, but she wanted to hear it from Sigi's lips.

"At exactly five o'clock there was a loud knock on the door. We knew. Only the Gestapo pounded on a door that way. Ernst got up to open it. Standing in the doorway were twenty Gestapo agents with their pistols at the ready."

"'Hands up!' they shout**ed**. 'Up against the wall! You're all under arrest!'".

"I stole a glance at Max. He had a resigned look on his face, as if he had expected this to happen right along. He had played out the string. His luck, and ours, had run out."

"It was *beschert*?" Renate asked quietly. "Looking back, Sigi, what, in your opinion, went wrong? What could have been done differently?"

"As you can imagine, I've given this a lot of thought over the last fifty years. There was no one action on our part that I can point to. The cards were stacked against us from the beginning. We were up against an implacable enemy. We didn't realize until it was too late that we would be hunted down until we were either dead or in captivity."

"Can you be more specific?" Renate asked.

"We were amateurs, they were professionals. They had an expert counter-intelligence operation, and they were able to get vital information about us—names, addresses, associates, and so on—by brutal interrogation, and by traitors, German and Dutch."

"What would cause a man or a woman to inform on you? Was it money?"

"Sometimes it was money, that bounty that I mentioned earlier. Sometimes, the Germans would arrest someone and offer a cruel bargain: If you tell us what we want to know, and if you work for us from now on, we will spare you and your family. If you don't talk, we will shut down your business, torture you, and kill you and your family. Sometimes, the motive was a false patriotism: If we spill the beans on this Jew, or these Jews, the Nazis will take our cooperation into account and deal lightly with our village, our province, or with the entire nation. And sometimes, it was just perverse sadism: the pleasure of working your way into someone's confidence and then betraying him."

"So you were too trusting in your contacts, in those with whom you shared information?"

"That was a big part of it. Another reason was our overconfidence, and—I have to use the word—our gross negligence. It was almost as if we were thumbing our noses at the Nazis, daring them to do their worst."

"And then, in the spring and summer of 1944, when they rolled you all up, they showed that they were up to the challenge."

"You could say that, yes." Sigi replied and picked up the story. "After we were arrested, the Gestapo agents pushed us roughly down the stairs and shoved us into the black vans that were waiting at the curb. After a short ride, we arrived at the notorious Gestapo interrogation center at Rue de la Pompe 180."

"Please spell it out for my readers. What do you mean when you refer to it as an 'interrogation center'?"

"Rue de la Pompe 180 was, to be exact, one big torture chamber, the infamous place where hundreds of French Resistance fighters were tortured in the most horrible ways and broken."

" . . . and Metta?"

"When Max had not come home that evening, she started to feel a high level of anxiety. She got dressed, went out, and looked for him in all the neighborhood cafés and other hangouts. On her way back to their rooms, Metta, increasingly distraught, passed the open front door to the apartment on the floor below, the apartment occupied by two *chalutzim*, Hans and Eva Ehrlich.

"'Get away from here—fast!' they told her. 'Everyone's been arrested. Max, too. The concierge told me that the Gestapo has already been here, looking for you. They're sure to return, so leave—now!'

"Metta didn't need a second warning. She turned around and headed for the Metro a block away. As she went down the Metro steps, she turned and saw the black vans of the Gestapo pulling up in front of her building."

"So Metta had to go underground again. There was more to it than that: knowing that Max carried her photograph in his wallet, she had to change her appearance. In a different part of the city, where she was not known, she stopped at a beauty salon and had her hair dyed and her hairdo changed, no questions asked."

"So," Renate said, "the obvious question. Someone betrayed Max and his comrades. Who was it? I think I know the answer: that Charles Porel and Lydia were not who they claimed to be. Am I right?"

"Half right. The man who called himself Charles Porel was in reality Karl Rehbein, an agent for the German counterintelligence service, the *Abwehr*. He was a smooth-talking double agent, working also for the British Intelligence Service, offering his services to both sides, and paid by both. The woman with him was who she claimed to be, Lydia Tscherwinska, a Russian Jew in exile in Paris, and well known in Jewish circles there. She claimed after the war that she had no knowledge that her associate, Rehbein, was playing a double game."

"So the skeptics who had voiced their pessimism a day earlier were right, yes?"

"Yes, they were, but I don't dwell on that. It doesn't mean that we should not have made the attempt. We tried valiantly, and good men lost their lives, yes, but even today looking back, I feel that we did the right thing."

"How so?" Renate asked.

"We did our utmost to carry out our mission, rescuing Jewish children, saving them from deportation and death, even until the last minute. Who can fault us for falling short of our goal?"

"You get no argument from me on that score," Renate said.

"And it wasn't only the seven of us who had been in the apartment on the Rue Erlanger whom the Gestapo arrested. On that same day, Paula Kaufmann was also arrested elsewhere in Paris. And on the following day, Paul Wolf and Ernest Asscher. They, too, were brought to Gestapo headquarters on the Rue de la Pompe."

"Did those arrests finish off the rescue activities of the Westerweel group?"

"To a large extent, yes. Metta and the others who remained free tried to carry on. So did Frans Gerritsen and his wife and other individuals. But the organized effort ended with the rollup on the Rue Erlanger."

And then Renate asked "What was it like, once you were all under Gestapo control in the Rue de la Pompe?"

"We were all put into a luxuriously furnished salon in the mansion. Perhaps it had at one time been the drawing room. In one corner a man in civilian clothes was playing pieces by Bach on a baby grand piano. He would break off every once in a while to talk endearingly on the telephone with someone he told us was his daughter. He spoke knowledgeably about Jewish history. All this was intended to put us at our ease. 'Relax, you will not be harmed.' That was the message they were trying to convey."

"Those attempts at 'relaxation' ended when Friedrich Berger, a veteran agent of the *Abwehr*, entered the room. He had made it his personal mission to roll up the Resistance, and now it seemed he had succeeded. Berger started shouting at us about 'the Jews,' about how the Resistance had perverted its idealist principles, and told us of his intention to protect the Wehrmacht from what he called 'Jewish terrorists.'"

"While Berger was berating us upstairs, Max and other Jewish arrestees were in the cellar of the mansion in the torture chambers, being flogged with leather straps and undergoing other brutal punishments. The torturers had no time for time-consuming techniques such as sleep deprivation. They needed to break the prisoners down quickly so that they could move them out and make room for others."

"What were they looking for?" Renate asked.

"The *Abwehr* tried to get out of us by torture and other inhumane methods the information that we wouldn't provide voluntarily. So, to answer your question, what did the *Abwehr* try to squeeze out of us? To begin with, our true identities and our addresses. Who else lived there with us? Did we know so-and-so? Where were we on such-and-such a day? And so on. And then they built more questions on our responses to the first ones. When they got Max by himself in that torture chamber, they demanded that he tell them who the pretty girl was whose photo they had found in his wallet. His answer: 'She was a friend of mine in Holland. I don't know where she is now'"

"Not every one of the *chalutzim*-prisoners had the physical stamina to stand up to the torture. Maurice Loebenberg, a close associate of Max's, died from the beatings. A few days later they found his body dumped in a forest outside of Paris."

Renate asked. "Did you ever find out what happened with Jacques Lazarus and René Kapel, with the airplane flight that was supposedly taking them to London?"

"We heard about it from Jacques while we were all in in the basement of that building on the Rue de la Pompe. It had been decided between the two of them and Charles Porel that they would leave for London on July 17, 1944, and that they would meet at six o'clock in the evening at the Cafe de la Regence with the man who was to accompany them on the trip. Everything went according to plan. They all got into the car, René and Jacques in the back seat, their contact in the front seat next to the driver."

"When they had traveled no more than a few blocks down the Rue St. Honoré, the contact turned around in his seat to face the Frenchmen, pointing a gun at them, and commanded, 'Hands on your head!' So they realized it had all been a well-planned setup, an elaborate act, and they had fallen for it. They faulted themselves for their naïve stupidity, for their readiness to put their trust in strangers. The driver made a sharp U-turn and brought them to the Rue de la Pompe."

Renate waited for Sigi to continue.

"After three days of deprivation, torture, and interrogation at the Gestapo headquarters there on the Rue de la Pompe, we were all taken on July 20, 1944, to the notorious prison at Fresnes, some ten miles to the south. That was the day, coincidentally, on which an attempt was made on Adolf Hitler's life by placing a bomb under the table at which he was conferring with his top generals at his field headquarters in East Prussia. When we prisoners heard the news through the prison grapevine, we were elated. Certainly, the death of the Führer would bring this terrible war to a quick end, or so we thought. But then just hours later our mood changed when we learned that the Führer was alive—shaken up, yes, but alive. The heavy wooden conference table had shielded him from the force of the explosion. Our deliverance, if it came, would have to come from some other source."

"What was it like in Fresnes?" Renate asked, to move the story along.

The cellblock at Fresnes

"A living hell. The noise was unbearable, and there was no let-up at night. We constantly heard the clanging of hobnail boots on the steel floors, feet tromping up and down the stairs, cell doors opening and closing with a bang. And the guards and prisoners contributed to the uproar: the guards barked out orders, and the prisoners at all hours yelled back and forth to each other, from one cell to another. Twice a day, we stood in line for our meager rations: a watery soup with a few vegetables, two slices of bread, some *topinambour*—you may know it as a Jerusalem artichoke or earth apple—and on Sunday, a little bit of meat that I couldn't identify. You can imagine that we quickly lost weight and body strength on that diet."

"The nights were the worst. Night after night as we lay awake in our cells, we heard those jackbooted guards approaching. 'Is it my turn?' I would wonder. 'Is this the night that they come for me?' And then the steps continue on, past my cell, past Max's, and stop at the cell of some other unfortunate soul. Who is it this time? That man, the unlucky one, will be marched down to a holding cell to spend his last hours there. Then at daybreak he will be led out into the yard, tied to a stake, blindfolded, and shot."

"And back in the cellblock, when the tromping boots of the guards escorting the doomed prisoner are no longer heard, a soft humming comes from one of the cells. Others pick it up and join in, and it gets louder and louder. The song they are singing is '*La Marseillaise*,' the French national anthem, the song of free men everywhere. We were singing it to express our defiance of our captors. The song ended, and then came the cry, from one cell to the next, until it resounded through the building: '*Vive la France!*'"

"I imagined that Max, lying there on his bunk, was thinking of all his comrades in the Westerweel Group, the ones who were still alive and those who had perished. And of his close family, the ones who had died in the camps, and of his sister Ruth and the two brothers who had survived, Emil and Isi, who were now in *Eretz Israel*. Max never learned, and I found out only after the war, that his brothers, when they reached Palestine, volunteered for the Jewish Legion, a unit of the British Eighth Army. They were on the front lines fighting the Germans in North Africa, and in that way gained a small measure of payback for what the Nazis had done to the Windmüller family."

"And, of course, there was Metta, always Metta, in his waking thoughts and in his dreams. And as much as she was on his mind, he was on hers. Their days and nights together . . . there had been so few of them, but they were so sharply etched in his memory and hers! They had spoken ardently of living together as husband and wife in *Eretz Israel*, and of the children they would have together. Would that day ever come? With his characteristic optimism, he wrote hopefully:

Right now, darkness prevails. But the day will surely come when the clouds disappear. Then the sun will bring light into the hiding places and the doors of the prisons will be opened. A new life is waiting for us and a new task. If one of us does not come back, someone will take his place and continue the effort. That day will come when we achieve victory.

"I notice," Renate said, "how that image of light prevailing over darkness comes up repeatedly in his letters and in his diary entries."

"You know the adage," said Sigi: 'It's always darkest just before the dawn.'"

"Trite but true," Renate commented. She turned toward Sigi, looking directly at him. "Sigi, did he ever express disappointment with his life, that he had not achieved his dream of *Aliyah*, and was now behind those prison walls?"

"Not to me, no, never. I once asked him that, as we stood outside in the prison yard at Fresnes. He smiled wanly, and shook his head from side to side, as if to chide me for even suggesting that. 'You know, Sigi,' he said, 'so many men die without ever having truly lived. With no mission, they drift aimlessly on the tides, with no control over their destiny. I found my cause by the time I was fifteen, and I never let go of it. I had my mission, my direction in life, before I was twenty-one, and I lived my mission, carried it out and achieved my objectives, all before I was twenty-five. How many men can say that?'"

"His rescue mission, yes, his dream of reaching Eretz Yisrael, no," Renate commented.

"True, tragically. But still, he was right. We remember him today for the goal he did achieve, for saving the lives of so many others."

Sigi continued. "On Friday, August 11, 1944, after twenty-two days at Fresnes, Max and I and the other resisters were called out of our cells and ordered to assemble in the ground floor hallway. On our way down the steel stairs, we saw that our friends from the *Armée Juive* had also been called from their cells: Henri Pohoryles, Ernst Appenzeller, Jacques Lazarus, René Kapel, and Paula Kaufmann, too—fifty-one men and women in all."

"When we were assembled in the hallway, the notorious Alois Brunner came out, smartly dressed in his black Gestapo uniform, and told us. 'You are all headed for Drancy. From there, you will be deported to the Reich, where death awaits you.' Two of his deputies were waiting to escort us out of the prison into the waiting trucks. Handcuffed in pairs, we were pushed onto the trucks and taken to Drancy, about six miles northeast of Paris. This enormous prison had been built before the war as an apartment complex for low-income families. Later it was converted into police barracks, and still later, it became an internment camp where Jews and political prisoners were held until they were shipped to the extermination camps in the east."

Drancy prison

"The following day, our first full day at Drancy, was a Saturday, the Jewish Sabbath. On that day, something like a miracle took place. René Kapel, an ordained rabbi, conducted Sabbath services for the political prisoners in the open cellblock. The service was followed by the *Oneg Shabbat*, the traditional after-services repast. From the miserable prison rations, we managed to put together and serve something like an elaborate meal. Remember, Max and most of the others in our group of Jewish pioneers had not been raised in religious households. That was true of the Communist prisoners with whom we shared the cellblock. In earlier years, many of them could hardly be brought to acknowledge that they were Jews. With my religious upbringing, I was the exception. But now, in these terrible conditions in the Drancy camp, we all came together under Rabbi Kapel's guidance, and sang the traditional *Shabbat* songs with incredible fervor, and, at the end of the service, joined in singing *'Hatikvah.'* It was a soaring, spiritual experience that has stayed with me all these years."

Rummaging in his folder, Sigi found the moving letter that Max wrote to one of the *chalutzim* on August 19, 1944, just before they were both deported to Buchenwald. It's an important letter, one that Sigi wanted to read, almost in its entirety, to Renate. By way of introduction, he told her: "All of us—you and I and every thinking person—are well aware of our shortcomings. We all have our moments of doubt: Are we up to the job? That's the question we're constantly asking ourselves. Max asked those questions of himself, too, but, in his case, they were more meaningful, because they involved issues of life and death. Max and his comrades might well have asked themselves, 'Have we suffered this pain for nothing? Or can we point to something on the positive side, something that we have contributed that makes this suffering, in the end, worthwhile?"

With that introduction, Sigi turned his eyes to Max's letter and began to read:

I have looked forward to your letters, but I must say that there is a point where I do not agree with you. You write that you are lacking in courage. Rest assured, I have not always been courageous, either. I, too, have tried to shove the responsibility onto others and have left people in the lurch. I tried not to do that, to do it as seldom as possible, but it was impossible to avoid it completely. Now I am charged with espionage, with falsifying papers and resistance; these are serious accusations.

We have committed many errors. We were instructed never to retain documents that would incriminate us if they were found. This time I had hidden the papers carefully, so they did not find them. But it would have been better to destroy everything. We all have made many mistakes and if it were possible to start again, we would do it differently.

When I found myself in Gestapo quarters, with my hands tied behind my back and on my knees for 24 hours, I thought about a lot of things. Was it all worth this pain? I asked that not because I was arrested, but because so many people were rolled up along with me. But I also thought about all the comrades who are now in Spain; if we had not done what we did, there would be more victims and even more of our comrades would have been deported to Poland. I think this fact alone gives us satisfaction.

"That's a beautiful letter," Renate murmured. "So revealing of his true nature."

"Yes, he's saying that he's not a god, not infallible. He has made mistakes, as we all do. He admits that he lacked courage in some situations. We feel shame, too, when, in some instances, we don't step up to do what is asked of us. But after everything that Max had undergone, all the pain, physical and emotional, he could look back and say that his labors had not been in vain, that he saved the lives of countless people, and that, yes, it had been worthwhile."

"The fact that he admits those shortcomings, admits that he wasn't always what he wanted to be, but strove to become a better man, that makes him an even bigger man in my eyes," Renate said. Sigi nodded in agreement, and went on:

"Over the prison grapevine, we learned that the Allies were at the gates of Paris. The city would fall within a matter of days. Drancy, close by, would surely fall to the Allies a few days later. What was SS

Hauptsturmführer Brunner likely to do? Would he gather his prison staff and, together with them, take a train back to Germany, leaving the prisoners behind to welcome the Allied soldier-liberators? That, it turned out, was wishful thinking on our part. Some of them he did indeed leave behind, but the Jewish inmates, the ones he labeled 'political prisoners,' he made sure were deported to the east. We were, after all, his prize 'booty.' He would under no circumstances leave us behind. When the Allied troops arrived at Drancy, they found not one of us remaining within its walls."

"On Thursday, August 17, word got around that a train was being prepared to bring Brunner and his staff back to Germany. Later that day, one of Brunner's deputies passed on his orders: We political prisoners were to fall into formation and get ready to board the train that would take us, along with Brunner and his prison guards, back to Germany. A half-hour later, we were standing in the courtyard with our knapsacks and the few clothes we were able to bring in, a blanket, and perhaps items that the other prisoners had given us on the sly, things like toiletries, that they thought might be useful to us."

"As we left the courtyard and exited through the prison gates, the remaining prisoners called out to us, '*Shalom l'hitraot*' and '*auf Wiedersehen*' and '*adieu*'! Outside, a small crowd of people was waiting; many of them appeared to be family and friends of men and women in the column of marchers, or looking to get information from us about the prisoners who were still inside."

"Marching out alongside Max, I noticed that he was looking here and there, scrutinizing the faces in the crowd. Perhaps, I thought to myself, he was hoping to see Metta in that crowd so that he could get a last look at her. No, he probably hoped that she would not be there, that she would even at that moment be somewhere in southern France on her way to safety in Spain."

"Under the watchful eyes of the prison guards, we were marched in a ragged column to the nearby rail depot at Bobigny. There, standing on a railroad siding, was the train that was to take us to Germany. History has recorded that we were among the 20,000 Jews and others who were shipped to the camps from this little village, and that we men and women from Drancy were to be the last French prisoners deported to Germany."

"What happened to those who remained behind in Drancy?" Renate asked. "Do we know?"

"Of course, I wasn't there, but we have read about it from survivors' accounts. As we were marched out of the prison gates, and Brunner and his guards got into their cars to drive away, wild delirium broke out among the prisoners who were left behind. Shouts of 'The Germans are gone!' and 'Tear off your Jewish star. We're free at last!'"

"So," Renate says, "for them the war was over. They had survived."

"Right, they had survived. But for us, the fifty-one prisoners who were being marched to Bobigny, the days and weeks ahead were only a continuation of the horror, and it would get worse, not better. When we arrived at the train siding in Bobigny, our hearts sank."

"We had not expected to ride in first class, of course, but what we saw was beyond belief. Directly behind the locomotive was a freight car—more specifically, a cattle car—and, painted on its sides in large white letters, a description of its cargo: 'Jewish terrorists'! That was us, the fifty-one prisoners who were to be confined in that car, like so many head of cattle, on the journey eastward. Directly behind were the two passenger cars in which Brunner, his deputies, and other prison staff could sit in comfort on the same journey. Behind the coach were flatbed cars loaded with tanks and other combat vehicles and artillery, and bringing up the rear, more coaches carrying German soldiers in retreat from the advancing Allies."

"We learned after the war that this train was originally designated to carry only the retreating soldiers and their equipment. Brunner, a skilled bureaucratic infighter, had managed through considerable pressure to have three cars added to the train: two comfortable coaches for him and for his staff, and the third for his prized possession, the fifty-one of us."

"We prisoners were rudely shoved into the waiting cattle car. The younger men—Max, a few others, and I—reached down to help lift the older men up into the car. What we saw inside was utterly dispiriting: straw was scattered on the floor of the car, evidently to serve as our beds. At one end, curtained off with some rude cloth hung from the ceiling of the car, were the buckets that served as our toilets."

"Typical," Renate commented. "The Nazis cared nothing for the prisoners' survival, for their lives. Whether you lived or died was of no importance to them. But they cared enough about your privacy to put a curtain in front of the slop bucket."

"Yes, it shows how warped their values were."

"So," Renate urged, "go on with your description of that cattle car."

"Even in daylight, in the bright sun, the only light that entered the car came through slats in the siding. Two kerosene lights provided the only illumination after nightfall. Each of us, on boarding, had been given our rations, which had to last for the entire trip: fifteen small boiled potatoes, five and a half ounces of bread, and an ounce of sausage."

"That's the equivalent of, maybe, two meals," Renate commented. "Tell me more about these fifty-one prisoners. Who were they?"

"There were, more or less, three sub-groups, with some overlap. There were, first, the French resistance fighters, like Jacques Lazarus and Rabbi Kapel. Max and I were in the second group, the one that the French group called 'the Dutch,' although we weren't Dutch at all. We were all of German or Austrian origin. Our loyal friend, Paula Kaufmann, was among the 'Dutch' resistance fighters in the cattle car. She had not been among those originally rounded up when the prisoners were assembled at Drancy, but she had called out: 'Wait! I'm part of that group. I'm going with them,' so she was added at the last minute to the list of deportees."

"In the third group were the VIPs, the high-profile prisoners. We called them the 'prominents.' There were fifteen of them, including Armand Kohn, who had been the director of the Rothschild Hospital in. Paris, with his wife and their four children; a Russian princess, Olga Galitzine; a Mr. Mizrachi, a rich Jewish merchant from Salonika; and Marcel Bloch. After the war, Bloch, who had taken the name Dassault, became famous as the designer and manufacturer of the French Mirage fighter plane, but to us in that cattle car, he was simply 'Monsieur Bloch.' The 'prominents' were not shoved onto the train and otherwise mistreated, as we had been. 'Trade bait,' Max whispered to me as he watched them boarding. He meant that the Germans would dangle these wealthy and famous individuals as hostages, to be exchanged, perhaps, for high-ranking generals or highly placed Nazi officials held by the Allies. As for the rest of us, it's been speculated that Brunner wanted us back in Germany so that he could feed his ego by putting us in the dock in a highly publicized show trial."

"Finally, the heavy doors of our car were slammed shut, and we were pitched into that near-complete darkness. We put our knapsacks and our blankets down and tried to adjust to these primitive conditions. It brought to mind all the trains that Max and I had traveled on in the four years since the invasion of France. It never occurred to me, during any of those train journeys, that I would someday return to my homeland, and Max's, on another such train, this time traveling not in a comfortable coach but in the close confinement of a cattle car."

"As the train proceeded slowly across eastern France, we in that first car knew nothing of what was going on outside. We were confined in this prison cell on wheels."

"Wait," Renate urged. "I want to be clear. What you're about to tell me comes not from your personal experience but from someone else, from other sources?"

"That's right." Sigi told her. "As a good historian, you will want to verify what I tell you from those other sources."

"Of course," Renate said with a smile.

"So the train we were on would indeed be the last shipment of deportees to the east. Brunner, seated in his comfortable coach, must have felt very pleased with himself. He had made sure before boarding that the large wooden crates with his name on them were also on board, the crates loaded with valuable booty that he had appropriated for himself over the last four years. More important than his personal possessions, he had been able to carry out with ruthless efficiency the orders he had received from his higher-ups in Berlin, to round up every Jew in his jurisdiction, keep them under guard, and to send them to the camps in Germany and Poland to be killed. Babes in arms, small children, teenagers, adults, older people—age didn't matter. Nationality didn't matter. They were Jews, and that was all that mattered."

"This train, it might have occurred to Brunner, was symbolic. It carried an army in retreat—its officers and men, its guns and rolling stock—but even as men and arms were moving to the rear, away from the enemy, space was found in this train for Jewish deportees. That was true on the grand scale as well, from the beginning of the war until the day of the surrender: Nazi Germany diverted manpower and precious resources away from the fight against its armed enemies and into the dirty business of killing unarmed civilians, Jews mainly, but millions of other as well."

"Brunner had ordered this train to be assembled, and the cattle car with its human cargo attached, in breach of an express agreement that he had reached just hours earlier at the Hotel Majestic in Paris with the Swedish consul in Paris, Raoul Nordling, and with the local Wehrmacht commander, General von Choltitz. He had solemnly assured them that all prisoners then in SS prisons in the Paris area would be dealt with humanely in accordance with the terms of the Geneva Convention. It was to Brunner's advantage to come to terms with the Swedish diplomat and with von Choltitz, but it was never his intention to carry out this agreement. His goal instead was to treat us like human garbage, to debase us in every way possible, and then have us killed."

"And, after the war . . . ?" Renate asked. "How did the Allies deal with him? How did they punish him for the atrocities he had committed during the war?"

"Sad to say, Brunner was one of the lucky few who never got what was coming to him. He was tried and convicted by a French court, but only in absentia. He was not present in court. At the end of the war, he escaped to Syria, where he lived a long life under the protection of successive Syrian dictators. He was well into his nineties when he died."

"And he never expressed remorse for his terrible deeds?"

"Never. On the contrary, he was proud of his efficiency in breaking the back of the French Resistance even after it was clear that from a military standpoint, Germany would be defeated. Sending, all told, 140,000 Jews to the gas chambers, including the 24,000 whom he had deported while he was the superintendent at Drancy from June 1943 to August 1944—he considered these his proudest accomplishments. Far from being remorseful, he said after the war: 'I have no regrets and would do it again.'"

Renate shook her head. "A lovely man," she said, her voice heavy with sarcasm.

"A thoroughly disgusting man," Sigi agreed. "The only thing that gives me satisfaction is the knowledge that from his home in exile in Damascus, Syria, he had to watch, over a period of fifty years, the dynamic growth of the State of Israel. The survivors and the children and grandchildren of those whom he had sent to the gas chambers became Israelis. There in Tel Aviv, just one hundred thirty-two miles away, and three years after the war ended, they became a new nation."

"I like to think of Brunner gnashing his teeth in frustration as he saw the people of this new land fight for and win their independence, and then repeatedly push back the combined armies of Syria and other Arab nations. We, the survivors, have prevailed and have become strong, militarily and economically, in the Middle East, a democratic success story. As for Alois Brunner, he, too, has left a legacy: History curses him for what he did."

There was quiet while both of them contemplated what Sigi had just said. Renate broke the silence. "So, Sigi, go back to the train and its cargo—you and Max and the others."

"The fifty-one prisoners in the cattle car knew nothing of the high-level negotiations that had taken place among generals and ambassadors. We knew only the four walls of the cattle car. First, we organized ourselves into those three subgroups that I mentioned: the French, the 'Dutch,' and the 'prominents,' and gave each of those groups a 'territory' in the boxcar. After that, we allocated what little straw was on the floor of the boxcar, so that everyone would have enough to sleep on. And we set up rules for the use of the latrine. Max unrolled his blanket at one corner of the car, next to me. Across from him along the other wall, were our comrades, Ernst Asscher, Kurt (Nanno) Hannemann, Alfred (Zippy) Fränkel, Willy Gerhard Sperber, Paul (Seevi) Wolf, Paula Kaufmann, and I.

"Even then, as we were rolling eastward, one mile after another, closer and closer to Germany, optimism prevailed. 'This craziness can't last much longer. The war will be over in four weeks, and then our future, our future in Eretz Israel, will be secure!' Oh, that those fond hopes had been realized! How many lives, Max's and others, would have been spared! But the war continued for nine more months, and thousands lost their lives during that period."

"During those weeks that we were confined in the cattle car, the train made painfully slow progress toward its destination. A strike among the railroad employees caused long delays. Then, too, much of the track in eastern France had been damaged or destroyed by Allied bombing raids or sabotaged by the French Resistance, and that meant further delays and detours."

"The train stopped first at Pavillons-sous-Bois, just nine miles from Paris. The guards, rifles at the ready, opened the sliding doors to the cattle wagon. In the darkening sky, the prisoners breathed in fresh air for the first time in days. Looking westward toward Paris, we saw the sky lit up across the horizon by orange-colored flames. We believed that the entire city of Paris was ablaze, and we mourned the destruction of that beautiful city. But it wasn't the city of Paris that was on fire. What we were seeing were the fires from the steel mills of Pantin, outside of Paris. We know now that Hitler had demanded that Paris be set afire by the retreating German forces, but the commander in Paris, General von Choltitz, had defied the Fuehrer's orders. His forces had retreated eastward, away from Paris, without setting a single building on fire."

"On the following day, the train was on the move again, but soon came to a halt once more. It was Friday, August 18. Toward evening, Rabbi Kapel, true to the traditions of our faith, recited the prayers for the start of the Sabbath, and we passed what few rations we had among us to celebrate the arrival of the seventh day, the Jewish holy day. We, the fifty-one of us in that cattle car, had every reason to believe that God had forsaken us, but we persisted in our faith that He was there, at our side, and would help us through this. We were still optimistic that in a few hours we would be meeting once again in a Paris synagogue. We ended the evening singing, with conviction and spirit, the French national anthem, '*La Marseillaise*,' and our own anthem, '*Hatikvah*.'"

"But before that, Rabbi Kapel recited two psalms that spoke powerfully to me, with those of us who knew them joining in. The first one was Psalm 121: 'I lift up my eyes unto the mountains, from whence cometh my help.' And then he spoke the words to Psalm 130: 'From out of the depths I call upon thee, O Lord.' You know, there's a motet by Orlando de Lassus on that theme, in Latin: "*De profundis clamavi ad te Domine*.""

"I can well imagine," said Renate quietly, "how powerfully moving it was to hear those words there in the cattle car."

They were both quiet, picturing in their minds that unforgettable scene, then Sigi continued.

"We got underway again the next day, then stopped, then started again. Some of us had the impression that we were simply going around in circles. But we were moving eastward. We were in Soissons, some 37 miles from Paris, and we stopped in a tunnel to protect the train against Allied air raids. To keep our spirits up, we sang the familiar songs of our childhood in the many languages that were represented in our cattle wagon. Then we ended with the song that all of us knew, the song that expressed our pain, and also our hope, the song of the 'peat bog soldiers':

But for us there is no complaining
Winter will in time be past
One day we will cry rejoicing
Homeland, dear, you're mine at last.
Then will the peat bog soldiers
march no more with their spades to the bog.

"We didn't know it at the time, but the tunnel that the train had stopped in was directly under the building in Margival-Vauxillon that housed the headquarters of the German Army in France. In that very building a few weeks before, Hitler had met with his generals, Rommel, von Rundstedt, and Blumentritt, to plan the Wehrmacht's defense against the invading Allied armies."

"The train resumed its slow journey eastward. At Laon, it encountered still more bomb-damaged tracks. The locomotive had to be decoupled from the train and the cars reorganized for the further journey eastward. When we got underway again, the position of our car had been changed. It was now the last car in the train, and that opened up what would be our last opportunity to escape."

"The French prisoners in our car—Jacques Lazarus, Ernst Appenzeller, René Kapel, and the VIP prisoners, with the exception of Monsieur Mizrachi, the Greek merchant from Salonika, and Marcel Bloch, signed on to try to escape."

"Max and I and our friends were undecided. If some of us escaped, what would the SS do to the ones who were left behind? Chances are they would shoot them all. If we escaped, could we then live with the knowledge that we thought only of our own survival? And even if we escaped successfully, how would we get back to Paris through territory still held by the Germans, without proper papers? We thought to ourselves: 'We're on the last transport back to Germany. The war will be over soon, and we'll find ways to survive.' We were so wrong!"

"We 'Dutchmen' could not come to an agreement among ourselves, but in the end, we were given, and accepted, a few extra rations, and a number that established our place in the line of jumpers. We were to make that escape at the next available opportunity."

"Ernst Appenzeller, on leaving Drancy, had managed to smuggle out in his backpack a hammer, a screwdriver, and other such tools. His plan was to use those tools to pry out a plank from the rear wall of the wagon and create an opening that would be large enough to squeeze out of and to jump from. Our hearts sank, though, when, at the next stop, we heard people on the outside hammering extra nails into the loose slats. The only chance that was left now was to bend the iron slats in the single vent in the wall to create an opening large enough for one person at a time to escape."

"In the early morning hours of August 21, near the village of St. Quentin, northeast of Paris, Max and I and our circle of *chalutzim* were stunned to realize as we woke up that we were almost the only ones remaining in the car. The members of the French Resistance, most of the 'prominents' and one 'Dutchman,' twenty-seven in all, were gone. 'They've jumped!' someone shouted. From Paula Kaufmann, I heard, 'We've been betrayed.' Paul Wolf answered: 'Betrayed, no, but abandoned, definitely.' Zippy weighed in: 'I drew number twenty-three. I wanted to jump. But they saw us as almost-Germans. We irritated them, and they thought that we would be a burden to them as they tried to get back to Allied-held territory.' It was true. From the minute that we had boarded the train, there had been unspoken tension between the French Resistance fighters and our group of German-Dutch *chalutzim*. Each group mistrusted the other."

"Moments later, the guards on the outside pushed the door open and screamed at us: 'You're all going to be shot as accomplices. You helped the others to escape. And it was all in vain, because we'll catch them anyway.'"

"The doors slammed shut again. Through the slats we heard the sound of gunfire and excited voices: 'Command executed! All refugees liquidated!' And we heard the order given to dig a pit. It seemed obvious to us that the escapees had been captured and that, once the pit had been dug, they would be shot and their bodies buried in that pit."

"Then we heard another loud voice, the voice of someone accustomed to giving orders. Evidently it was the voice of the officer in command of the train

This train is under my command until it arrives in Kassel. What you do with the prisoners, once the train gets to the camp, is your responsibility. But until then you follow my orders. We in the Wehrmacht do not shoot civilians. Anyone who shoots these civilians in violation of my orders will be dealt with in accordance with martial law. You're all idiots, Attaching the car to the end of the train—you should have known this would happen. It's all your fault.'

The guards, muttering under their breath, yielded to the officer's orders, and returned to their car."

"The twenty four of us remaining in the cattle wagon heaved a collective sigh of relief. Our comrades, those who jumped, had not been caught and there would be no mass shooting. But what was their fate, the ones who jumped? Those of us who survived found out after the war that the rifle shots we had heard were all a mock shooting. All of the 'jumpers' escaped and survived the war. Those of us who stayed behind were less fortunate. That decision to stay behind, in solidarity with our fellow *chalutzim*, cost many of us our lives."

Again Sigi dug into his folder and pulled out a copy of letter, written by Rabbi Kapel in 1981, posing to himself and to history this question:

How did it happen that [Max] and his Dutch comrades were not among those who jumped from the wagon that day, but stayed behind? What happened at the last minute?

"Rabbi Kapel goes on to answer his own question:

The fact is that [Max] and the members of his group voted not to participate in the escape attempt. If only we had known, we would have tried the impossible and sought to convince them to make the try with us. It is likely that the behavior of [Max] and his comrades was caused by a fatigue of a physical and moral nature that had broken them. And there may have been another reason, which was entirely unjustified: that these five people, coming from their German-Jewish background, felt a bond with each other, but felt like alien outsiders to those from other backgrounds who had decided to make the attempt. They hadn't known us very long and didn't feel entirely at ease with us.

In the situation that we found ourselves in, the slightest sound would have aroused the guards and frustrated our plans. You had to have full control of your nerves. You had to be wide awake and calmly wait for your number to be called, when it was your turn to jump."

"And he closes by saying:

The way it all happened, these unfortunate events were devastating to us, but, nevertheless, none of us felt that we bore a personal responsibility for what happened."

Renate broke in. "Do you feel that that's an accurate account of what happened? Was Rabbi Kapel justified in absolving himself and the other escapees of any guilt for leaving Max and you and the others behind?"

There was a long silence between them as Sigi considered the question. Finally he answered, choosing his words carefully. "What Rabbi Kapel wrote was true to a certain extent, but it's not the whole story. From the weeks of near starvation and mistreatment at the hands of the Germans, Max had lost a great deal of weight. He was seriously physically weakened, and he no longer had the mental sharpness that was so characteristic of him. That night, the night of the escape, I was awakened by the commotion. The ones who were participating in the escape had lain on their straw pallets that night, fully clothed, and now they were lining up in the order of their numbers. Jacques Lazarus, seeing that I was awake, came over and whispered, '*Êtes-vous avec nous? C'est l'heure de partir*' [Are you with us? It's time to go']. My first thought was of Max. I nudged him to try to waken him. But he was in a deep sleep. Every time I nudged him, he pushed back, turned his back to me and fell back asleep. It became clear that I would not be able to wake him, let alone to get him into that state of watchful awareness that he would need to make a successful escape."

"When it became clear to me that I would not be able to get him up and fully awake, I realized that I had a life-and-death decision to make: I could get in that line with the other escapees, leaving Max and the others behind, or I could let them go and stay with Max, facing with him whatever destiny had in store for us. When I asked myself the question that way, the answer was easy: I would stay. Max and I had been through so much together for so long that I could not abandon him now. It would be a betrayal of the trust we had in each other. If I had joined in the escape attempt, leaving Max in his sickly condition lying in the straw in the cattle car, I would carry the guilt of that betrayal on my shoulders for the rest of my life. I couldn't do it. From my kneeling position next to Max, I whispered to Jacques: *'Je reste ici. Vous allez sans moi. Bonne chance.'* ['I'm staying here! Go on without me. Good luck!'] He looked at me quizzically, then shook his head regretfully, and rejoined the others."

"But," Renate persisted, "hadn't you already made up your mind the night before when the vote was taken whether to jump or not?"

"That's true. In that vote, the so-called 'Dutchmen' were lined up on one side, the Frenchmen and the VIPs on the other. We Dutchmen looked to Max for leadership, and there was no sign from him that he wanted to join in the attempt. I was torn and went to sleep that night hoping that Max would change his mind, and that we could escape together."

"And, looking back on your role in the affair, do you feel that you made the right decision?"

"Yes, thank God, my conscience is clear."

"Do you feel, as some of your comrades did and maybe still do, that you were betrayed by the ones who escaped?"

"I can't find it in my heart to feel that way. The others made their intentions clear, and we had every opportunity to join in. Like so many other times in life, we came to a fork in the road. They chose one path, and we chose another."

"Rabbi Kapel . . . what was his judgment of Max? Did he respect him or hold him in contempt for his failure to act?"

"I'll let him speak for himself. After the war, he recalled Max as 'an exceptional man, [who] showed in many circumstances intelligence and unparalleled courage.' Jacques Lazarus, the head of the French contingent in that cattle car, said of Max that he 'was an exemplary fighter in the Jewish Resistance. He gave up his life for the ideal of freedom, and for the protection and survival of the Jewish people.' I believe that everyone in that cattle car held Max in the same high esteem."

"Those are powerful testimonials, certainly," Renate said. "Please go on with the story."

"The very next day, the cattle car was recoupled amid the other cars, and the train got underway again. Our last chance for escape had passed. Shut off in near darkness in the cattle wagon, we were completely unaware of what was happening in the outside world."

"Max never knew, and I found out only after the war, that Metta, frantic to get Max out of his predicament, had rented a car with two friends and tried to stay on the road alongside the train as it chugged through eastern France and then into Belgium. Perhaps she hoped that when the train stopped at some way station, she would be able to free him. But it was all in vain. At the outskirts of the city of Liege, in eastern Belgium, Metta and her friends in the car were prevented from going further because Liege was at that time still in the combat zone. They wept in distress when they realized that despite their best efforts they would be unable to rescue Max from the prison train. Sadly, tragically, they turned around and made their way back to Paris."

"The prison train crossed the German border and reached Kassel. There, the Wehrmacht turned over control of the train to the SS. The cattle car was decoupled from the Wehrmacht train to a new locomotive, heading in a southeasterly direction, toward Buchenwald."

"We arrived at the camp on August 25, 1944, the very day that Paris was liberated by the Allied armies—certainly a day of joy in Paris and around the world, but for us, newly arrived at Buchenwald, a day of pain, of foreboding for what lay ahead."

"As we prisoners were marched from the train siding into the camp, we saw on the horizon an enormous cloud of dense smoke rising from the ruins of what had once been a factory where 3,500 slave laborers had worked, building controls for the V-2 rocket. Bombs from an Allied air raid had destroyed the factory the day before. Seeing that enormous mound of debris raised our hopes. Perhaps the entire camp administration was now in a similar state of disarray and the day of liberation was near."

"But then as we entered the camp our hopes were dashed, as they had been so often in the past. We saw, on a rise in front of us, the undamaged SS quarters, and below, the miserable inmate barracks. The placement of the two, the SS barracks above and the inmate barracks below, seemed to symbolize the master and slave relationship between them."

"Minutes later, we encountered for the first time the brutality of the men and women who ran the camp. Arriving at the processing center, we passed by a group of SS men lounging around outside. Our presence seemed to stir them out of their lethargy—they greeted us with shoves and kicks and blows and drove us into the office where we were to provide our personal information. There, under penalty of death, we were made to provide our true names and other data."

"The man we had known for the past three years as Cornelius Andringa—Cor—had to drop that name and take up again his real name, Max Windmüller, just as I became, once again, Sigmund Kirschner. Max was classified as a stateless Jew, with the occupation, 'agricultural worker.' He was further classified as a political prisoner, tattooed with the number 54573 on his forearm, and given the red chevron, symbolic of his political prisoner status, to be worn over the yellow triangle that signified that he was a Jew."

"With our information transcribed onto file cards, we were instructed to gather our belongings and marched to our barracks. When we got there, we were made to stand with our faces against the barracks wall, our hands clasped behind our heads. We could not see who or what was behind us. Soon, we heard a shrill voice, a man's voice, screaming at us. He was reciting a list of camp rules, the violation of which was punishable by death. Then we were forced to trot, double-time, to the bathhouse, where we were made to strip off our clothes. I was shocked to see how gaunt Max had become during his imprisonment at Fresnes and Drancy and then on the eight-day train trip to the camp. He was nothing now but skin and bones. I was stockier than he to begin with, and although I had lost weight, it seemed to me that I was still in better physical condition than Max was."

"By some God-sent miracle, the respiratory problems that had kept me off the *Dora* had long since cleared up and had not recurred. When we were naked, we were led to the barber, who shaved off all of our hair, from top to bottom, except for a little cockscomb strip at the top of our heads. The barber couldn't create that strip on Max's head, because he was already largely bald. From there it was on to the disinfectant baths, where we had to step into a large cauldron of filthy disinfectant solution that burned like crazy on our exposed skin."

"The next stop was the clothing room. There, the clerk behind the counter threw at us the gray-and-black striped uniforms, without regard to size, that we were to wear at the camp. For many inmates, these were the clothes that they would be wearing at their deaths. We had to turn over all our valuables and other personal belongings; they were placed in a bag bearing our prison number. We were told that the contents would be turned back to us on our departure from the camp."

"What was Max's state of mind during this process?" Renate asked.

"He let this whole ritual of dehumanization and degradation play out without any outward response on his part. He had trained himself to be stoic in the presence of the SS thugs, to hide his true self from them."

Sigi moved on. "Most of the inmates in our barracks were what we called the 'Reds' because, as Communists and Socialists, they wore a red triangle on their uniforms that signified their leftist political affiliation. They had a great deal of sympathy for us, as younger men, and because of our record as rescuers and resisters in France, and they gave us strong moral support and practical advice. They urged us to step forward as soon as possible to volunteer as skilled workers for one of the numerous calls for slave labor details outside the camp gates."

"Like the other new arrivals, Max and I and the other men in our group were housed in the Little Camp, seventeen barracks arranged like horse stalls. We slept in triple-tiered bunks laid out on each side of a central aisle. The only source of light and ventilation was a small wire-reinforced hatch in the ceiling. Fifteen hundred to two thousand men lived in these conditions, in a building which, if they were stables, would have housed no more than fifty horses. Latrines and washing facilities were primitive, and you had to get up earlier than everybody else, or go to bed later, to be able to use the facilities before the others did. If the wash facilities were broken, they weren't repaired. If the latrines were filled to overflowing, they weren't emptied. You simply had to adjust to your conditions."

"Day after day, the bodies of those who had died during the night were brought out of the barracks block. During the morning *Appel*—the roll call—they were placed in the front of the formation of prisoners still living, because, alive or dead, they still had to be accounted for. Sometimes the corpses lay there for hours before they were carted away."

"The barracks supervisor was scarcely able to maintain order and discipline, especially at the mealtimes when the meager rations were distributed. Hunger and misery turned formerly civilized men into beasts. Everyone tried to protect his food bowl, his cap, his blanket, and his sleeping place."

"Taking the older inmates' advice, Max and I responded as soon as we could to the call for slave laborers outside the camp walls. On September 16, 1944, we were in a group of six hundred inmates from Buchenwald who were transported to Bochum, to work at the *Deutsche Ausrüstungswerke AG* (DAW), an ironworks factory that fabricated armor plate for tanks and other vehicles. The name makes it sound like a private corporation, but it was in reality an enterprise organized and operated by the SS, with 'corporate' headquarters in Berlin."

"Our new workplace in Bochum was just a two-and-a-half hour drive from our hometown, Emden. Our supervisor, learning that we were from Emden, told us that two weeks earlier, on September 6, Allied planes, in a massive bombing attack, had destroyed the city. Eighty percent of it now lay in ruins. Max wondered if the building where he had grown up, at 44 *Mühlenstrasse*, was still standing. He tried to imagine how it would look, in ruins."

Renate interjected, "So was that house in fact destroyed?"

"Miraculously, the building was untouched by Allied bombs. For all I know, it is still standing."

"Perhaps I will get to see it on my next visit to Emden," Renate said. "Okay, Sigi, please continue."

"Metta was never far from Max's mind. He pictured her in Paris at the time of its liberation, sharing in the joy of the Parisians as soldiers of the Free French army marched under the Arch of Triumph and down the Champs Elysées. Was she perhaps even now on her way to Palestine? Had she met up again with Frans Gerritsen and his wife, Henny? And where was Paula now? Which camp had she ended up in? Max was unaware that, even as he was thinking of them, Frans and Henny had him very much on their minds. When their baby daughter was born, after the war, they named her Corrie Pauline. 'Cor', you recall, was Max's cover name, and Pauline, after Paula Kaufmann."

"As you can imagine, Renate," Sigi went on, "Metta had Max very much in her heart and on her mind, too, in those weeks and months. She worried endlessly over his fate at the hands of the Nazis. Every day, she wrote letters to him in her diary. The letters survived the war, but Max never got to read them. She wrote poems, too, which speak to us powerfully of her state of mind during that time." Sigi retrieved one of the poems from its folder, and paused, as if asking for permission to read it. Renate nodded.

"It's dated December 28, 1944. Max was working as a slave laborer in Bochum on that day."

The people are unfamiliar and far away.
Inside I am sad, almost hopeless, and cold.
I would so much love to be happy!

But I cannot be happy and laugh like they,
When so many of the best are suffering.
I believe we can never be like them
Because there'll always be a difference between us.

Now you are my only happiness,
Though I know you are far away.
What else gives me this strength to endure,
If not thoughts of you, night and day.

Whenever I travel by train,
My boy, I think of you,
Since oftentimes your work. .
found you travelling that way too.

During time spent alone on the train,
your thoughts likely dwelled
on the times in the past, long ago,. . . .
that you remembered so well.

Still I'm hoping with all of my heart,
with all the love that I feel,
that after this pain is over
you will be given back to me.

Renate was pensive. "So poignant," she said finally. "It expresses the feelings of every woman, since time immemorial, who is waiting for her husband or lover to return safely from the battlefield, or from some other form of mortal peril. Think of Penelope, back in Ithaca, waiting for Ulysses to return from Troy."

"And, of course," said Sigi, "for us the poem is made all the more poignant by the knowledge that her ardent desire—that Max be given back to her—was not to be fulfilled."

Sigi resumed his narrative. "On March 7, 1945, American troops, after heavy fighting, crossed the Rhine River at Remagen. Now they had a clear path into central Germany. Buchenwald lay just 200 miles to the east. On that same day, we were ordered to leave our workplaces in Bochum and brought back to Buchenwald. Now, back once again in the prison barracks, Max and I were reunited with our comrades: Paul (Seevi) Wolf, Jacques Rothman, and Leo Weil."

"Less than a month later, on April 4, 1945, the camp commander, Hermann Pister, ordered all Jewish prisoners to prepare to evacuate the camp. On that same day, coincidentally, American troops of the 89th Division liberated Ohrdruf, a satellite camp of Buchenwald, twenty-three miles to the southwest."

"On the morning of April 10, American fighter-bombers strafed military targets on the Ettersberg, just a few miles away from the camp. Minutes later, we prisoners heard the order that we most feared: 'Roll call! All Jews are to assemble immediately in the central *Appel*.'"

Knowing what this might lead to, we did our best to avoid turning out for that roll call, but the SS guards combed the barracks, rounding up the Jewish prisoners, or whoever they thought was Jewish, to force them into the assembly area. We—Max, Paul, and I—were in that group."

"With nearly 5,000 other prisoners, mainly Hungarians, Poles, Russians, Ukrainians, and a few Dutch Jews like us, we were force-marched the seven miles to the train station at Weimar. On that march, sixty prisoners were shot and killed."

"When we arrived at the loading yard at Weimar, we saw an enormously long train, sixty cars in all, waiting on the track. Some of the cars were enclosed freight cars, some were open coal cars. I guess they grabbed cars wherever they could in those last chaotic weeks. They loaded us onto the cars, up to two hundred men in each car. Max, Paul Wolf, and I found ourselves in one of the open coal wagons, so tightly packed together that there was no room to sit, much less to lie down. We had to stand shoulder to shoulder in that wagon, with an inch or more of coal dust at our feet. We were doled out rations that had to last us for the entire journey: fifteen small potatoes, five-and-a-half ounces of bread, and an ounce of sausage."

"Then the train got underway. Its destination, as we were soon to find out, was the Flossenburg concentration camp, near the Czech border. The train, with its human cargo, encountered endless delays and was forced to take many time-consuming detours, because of damage to the tracks caused by Allied bombing raids and to avoid the advancing Allied troops. You can imagine that because of those delays, hundreds of prisoners were dying every day of exposure to the weather, of disease, and, mainly of thirst and starvation. From time to time, when the train was stopped, details of prisoners came into our car to remove the corpses. Paul Wolf told me later that as he stood in the crush of prisoners, he realized that the man next to him had turned cold. Dead. He would be pitched out of the wagon at the next stop, to join the many other corpses along the way."

"The transport with the Jewish prisoners on board—Max, Paul, and I among them—lumbered slowly forward on branch lines past Naumburg, toward the Flossenburg camp. In the village of Zeitz, the train was the target of Allied bombs. Four hundred prisoners were killed, and three hundred were wounded. The three of us took the opportunity to flee into the woods, but Max was too weak to get very far, so we were captured and brought back to the train. For a half-day after that, the train sat at a freight depot. There was no medical care available for the severely injured. The corpses of the dead were simply stacked alongside the railroad tracks."

"Finally, the train moved on. Sick, hungry, and thirsty, we had lost all sense of time. Had three days passed or four? Standing shoulder to shoulder in the crush of other men and with intense pain in our legs and feet from standing constantly, we had only one thought: 'When will it all finally end?'"

"On our arrival in Flossenburg, we found no relief from our suffering. The concentration camp had been built for 4,000 prisoners. Now it housed four times that many. Whereas Buchenwald had been run by the SS, this camp was run by professional criminals and 'asocials'—we called them the 'Greens', because of the green patches on their uniforms. The camp was descending into chaos. A typhus epidemic had broken out and was spreading rapidly; there was no way to control it. The whole camp was one big infirmary."

Flossenburg concentration camp

Renate interrupted Sigi's narrative. "My readers may not know what typhus is. Can you briefly explain what it is, how you contract it, and how it spreads?"

"Typhus is an infectious disease that can spread very quickly, especially in a confined space like the concentration camp barracks. Its victims develop high temperatures, wracking headaches and joint pains, and painful skin rashes. If it's not treated effectively, the mortality rate for typhus is near one hundred percent. And don't forget that in the camps, the prisoners' resistance to the disease was already low because of malnutrition, exposure to other diseases, and poor hygiene. Your readers today have not encountered it, because, thanks to antibiotics and modern standards of sanitation, outbreaks of typhus in the western world are now few and far between."

"Once the disease became established in the camps, it spread rapidly from one prisoner to another. Anne Frank was a victim of the disease, and so were hundreds of thousands of others in German prison camps all over Europe. During and after the war, vaccines were invented that prevented the disease, but good hygiene is still fundamental in preventing it."

"Thank you, Sigi. Please continue."

"We were well aware that the advance units of the American army were approaching rapidly against only light resistance. Hopes mingled with fear: Were we all to be killed? Lined up and shot? Or would they leave us to starve and die? Will the Americans bomb the camp?"

"The SS guards didn't want to get infected by the typhus epidemic, so they mostly stayed out of the camp. The commandant, Max Koegel, designated 400 German prisoners as 'camp police', dressed them in Italian uniforms, and gave them side-arms. When the call went out for volunteers for this unit, we did not step forward; we didn't want to be seen as collaborators with the prison administration in its final hours."

"On April 16, 1945, as the Americans advanced rapidly toward the camp, the SS abandoned Flossenburg, but not without first scooping up and dividing among themselves all the prisoners' valuables and their shoes, clothing, alcohol, and cigarettes. As we watched the last of the SS leave the camp, we broke loose in cheers. We were free at last!"

"But our joy was premature. The SS came back the following day and resumed its brutal domination of the camp. History records that the Gestapo chief, Heinrich Himmler, had sent Koegel, the camp commandant, the following order: 'The surrender of the camp is out of the question. You are to evacuate the camp. Not one prisoner is to fall into the hands of the enemy.'"

"On April 19, 1945, all prisoners who were not bedridden were forced to leave Flossenburg under guard. The destination: Dachau, 134 miles away—on foot! We three—Max, Paul Wolf, and I—were among the marchers. Max was now gravely ill, feverish He was no longer eating, he was seriously undernourished, and wanted only to drink. He appeared to have typhus. He traded his meager rations for medications that he hoped would reduce his fever."

"At five o'clock in the afternoon we set out from Flossenburg in what history records as a death march, one of many in the final weeks of the war as the Nazis emptied out the concentration camps that lay in the path of the Allied armies."

Death march to Dachau, April 1945
Source: Yad Vashem Museum, Jerusalem, Israel

"We continued on foot all night long and throughout the following day, pausing only for the briefest of rest stops. Prisoners who could no longer keep pace with the other marchers were killed without mercy, shot where they had fallen. At the tail end of the column of marchers there was a detachment of prisoners with shovels who would gather the corpses and bury them right there at the side of the road."

"The younger and stronger prisoners dragged the sicker and weaker prisoners along, hoping to prevent them from being shot by the guards. Oftentimes prisoners fell to the ground in bunches and were immediately shot."

"What was that march like for the three of you, for Max, Paul, and you?" Renate asked.

"Those were days I will never forget. We were so weak from hunger and thirst that we could not lift our feet to walk, as men normally do. We more or less pushed ourselves forward, every movement requiring enormous effort on our part."

"We were moving forward in a column, in rows of three, Paul at the left, I on the right, and Max in the middle. From the outset, as soon as we left the prison gates, I was concerned about Max, more so than for myself. His gait was unsteady, his upper body bent at the waist. It was clear to me even then that it took every ounce of effort for him to keep pace with us and the other marchers. If it was difficult for us, who had not endured the torture that Max had endured, whose bodies were not wracked with typhus as Max's was, how much more difficult must it have been for him?"

"Looking now to my right, past Max to Paul, I saw that he shared my concern for Max. Once I had Paul's attention, I made a slight gesture, slight enough to escape the guards' attention. I cupped my hands and made an upward motion, nodding toward Max. Paul understood. Furtively, we brought our hands up under Max's armpits, and in this way tried to help Max to move at our pace. Soon, my arms and shoulders ached from the weight of Max's body. How long would

I be able to drag him along like this? Could Paul continue to support Max's weight on his side?"

"In the hour that we had been underway, we had covered less than two miles, and there were men in the ranks in front of me who simply dropped in their places. Nothing could be done for them. The man directly in front of me, a French Jew whom we knew as André, fell to his knees in exhaustion. The rest of us, those who were still on our feet, stepped around him and moved forward. What else could we do? He was beyond help at that point. Minutes later, when the column had moved on, we heard a single pistol shot. We did not turn our heads; we knew what that meant. One of the guards had delivered to André the *coup de grace*, a bullet in the back of the head."

"For three days we trudged down the road, moving always in a southerly direction, sometimes in the hot sun, sometimes with the wind and rain in our faces. The first shooting was followed by many more as men collapsed in the roadway. Sometimes there was no shot fired, as if it wasn't worth expending a bullet to put the man away when he was already done for."

"As we marched, we passed through many small towns and villages in the *Oberpfalz*, the Upper Palatinate region of Bavaria. I can't recall for you the names of those places, and it doesn't matter—one was like the other. I do remember that in every village we passed through, we were met with utter silence. Yes, I saw occasionally on the face of a villager an expression of sympathy, but what I saw on most of the townspeople were expressions of indifference, even disgust and contempt, as if we were a plague that the villagers dared not expose themselves to."

"To those onlookers, we must have seemed like ghosts, with our blankets wrapped around our heads and bodies, our arms clutched around our chests to try to maintain our body warmth. But were we not fellow human beings, deserving of sympathy and support? Evidently not: it seemed that we were not much more than animals in the eyes of most of these people. They wanted nothing to do with us."

"On the evening of April 20, a heavy rain prevented us from moving forward. We were ordered to stop in a freshly planted field, where we sank to our ankles in mud. The three of us found shelter under a tree, which gave us some protection from the rain. Squeezing together like a couple in love—that's how Paul remembered it—that's how we spent the night. Max could not get to sleep because of his high fever. It seemed to us as if scenes from his life were passing across his eyes. He kept on murmuring the names of those nearest and dearest to him—his parents, his brothers and sisters, and, of course, Metta. 'Will the Americans ever get here?' we heard him ask. That question was uppermost in our minds, too."

"At 5:30 the next morning, we were ordered to get underway again. Paul and I took up our positions, on either side of Max, with one arm under each of his armpits, dragging him along in that fashion. At that point, we had walked some 43 miles, less than halfway to our destination."

"We were all extremely weak and suffered from unbearable thirst. Again and again, prisoners in the column would kneel down to quench their thirst with water from the rain puddles. When the SS guards saw a man doing that, they would come up and shove their carbines or pistols in his ribs and order him to get up immediately."

"On the outskirts of Winklarn, on the way to Rötz, it was clear to me that Max was in great distress. He was breathing with difficulty, gasping for air. He whispered to us, *'t is allemaal voorbij*. It's all over.' 'Don't say that, Max', I begged him. 'Please don't say that.' And he answered, barely whispering, *Ik kan het niet meer aan, jij gaat nu door zonder mij.'* 'I can't go on anymore. You go on without me.' And with a slight twisting of his torso, Max slipped out of our grasp. He no longer had the strength to stand up. Wordlessly he knelt down at the edge of the road and bent over to get water from a rain puddle."

"Glancing to our left over our shoulder, we saw the SS guard approach Max with his pistol drawn. *'Aufstehen! Sollst bewegen!'* 'Get up and get moving!' There was no response from Max. Then we heard the gunshot. The bullet in the back of the head. Max fell to the ground, dead. It was April 21, 1945, at two o'clock in the afternoon. Max Windmüller's mortal struggle was over. He died one day before we were to be liberated."

"Paul and I were no more than six feet away when it happened. Stunned by what we had just seen, we stood, frozen in place, until the SS guards, with a shove from their rifle butts, got us moving again. What else could we do? So, with tears streaming down our faces, Paul and I rejoined the other marchers."

"So," said Renate, "for the two of you, and for Max, this was the final goodbye."

"'The last goodbye,'" Sigi echoed. "And there was no final embrace, as I so much wanted. My goodbye had to be whispered from a distance. For all the years since, I have had to live with that painful image, still fresh in my mind, of Max sprawled face down in that rain puddle on that country road in southeastern Germany."

"And then . . . liberation?" Renate asked.

"Liberation was still some hours away," Sigi replied. "The death march continued all through that night. Finally, on the following day around noon, outside the village of Stamsried in the vicinity of Cham, an American tank came down the road toward us. The guards fled into the woods. We were free . . . free at last! Paul and

I embraced, leaning weakly against each other, weeping tears of joy. Our long agony was finally over. Together, in quavering voices, we recited the traditional Jewish prayer of thanksgiving, thanking the One who granted us life, sustained us, and enabled us to reach this occasion.' If ever there was cause to give thanks to God, that was it."

Again, Sigi resorted to his folder. "On April 25, 1945, four days after Max's death, Metta wrote this final poem and entered it in her diary:

I don't know why it happens
    that I feel so empty inside
My heart is anxious;
    I want to know: where are you now?
When I look through the window
    I see mountains and sunshine
Only one thing is missing for my happiness:
    You should be with me again!
No use to me are Spring and warmth
    They make it twice as hard for me.
I can think only of how much
    you would want to be here.

But something quietly
    gives me strength and courage,
Knowing that God's will
    can make things good again.

This I will go on thinking
    with all my love for you
    and keep on writing to you,
God will not abandon us!

"So tragic," Renate murmured, "that Metta's hopes had already been dashed, even as she wrote these words." Then she asked "Sigi, if Max had been alive on the day of your liberation, do you think he would have survived?"

"It's hard to say. He was mortally ill, his body reduced to a skeleton and ravaged by the typhus bacteria. With heavy doses of antibiotics, he might have lived, but it's an open question."

"It's been estimated," Sigi went on, "that more than 7,000 men and women died on that death march from Flossenburg. After 1957, as more and more of the temporary burial places of the dead were found along the road, the corpses were exhumed and reburied in a burial ground at the Flossenburg camp."

"Do we know where Max lies buried?" Renate asked.

"Not really. There is no grave marked with a headstone that bears his name. His remains are interred with sixty-seven others in a mass grave at that Flossenburg cemetery."

"So," said Renata, with an air of finality in her voice, "the story of Max Windmüller ends with his violent death, a pistol shot in the back of the head, the fallen body in the rain puddle, on a country road somewhere in Bavaria."

"His life ended there, to be sure, but he left a legacy that I believe will live forever. I want to read to you what I like to think of as his last will and testament. It's an excerpt from his diary, written on July 18, 1944, shortly before his arrest:

The small group [of *chalutzim*] that is left has bonded more closely together and is fighting for its existence. We are not the only ones who have had to go underground. The enemy is pursuing the youth of all nations to exploit them and to weaken them.

We must think seriously about the symptoms of the war. Hundreds and thousands face death daily. It is not just the military who fight; many others risk their lives in the struggle behind the front. Hundreds are waiting for their liberation from the clutches of the monster. Millions of children are suffering from hunger. The daily struggle is a struggle for life and death.

We must renew ourselves, not only to get through this period, but with a view to the future. We do not want to return to the days of injustice and war. Let's now live a life of cooperation and equality. Let's start with our self-education and eradicate our mistakes.

Over the past two years I have made the acquaintance of many people. I am happy to have met them. They were a source of faith for us, and the idealism that has stimulated them created bonds of friendship between them and us. It's good to know that we are not alone. We are continuing our path and, God willing, we will not forget them.

We feel solidarity everywhere, with those in hiding, in the attic, behind the barbed wire, in the camps. Every day they lock our people in the camps, but they cannot defeat us. We know our mission; we think of Schuschu [Simon], who sacrificed everything for us. We have a single goal: freedom! We will prove that we are worthy of it.

Right now, darkness prevails everywhere. But the day will come when the clouds disappear. Then the sun will shine in the hiding places and the doors of the prisons will open. A new life is waiting for us and a new task. If one of us does not come back, another will take his place and continue the action. That day will come and we will achieve victory.

Sigi gave Renate time to let the words sink in. "More of that darkness and sunlight imagery," she commented, her words barely audible. Finally she said quietly, "Such noble ideals! It was a great loss, not only to Israel but to all of us, that he did not survive to help us build on the firm foundation that he laid for us." After an interval spent in thoughtful silence, Renate resumed: "And how about those who survived the march? Tell us what happened to you and Paul when the Americans arrived."

Sigi responded with passion. "I will never forget it, and for the American soldiers who freed us, it was a scene they would never forget, either. As I said, some of us, the stronger ones, cheered, we embraced each other, we cried for joy. Others just collapsed, unable to go on even a single foot onwards. The soldiers tried to give emergency care to those who were the worst off. Soon after that, American trucks arrived and those of us who were able to climbed up onto the trucks; the others were lifted up on stretchers. They drove us to Dachau, which had been liberated by then. The stronger ones were taken directly to a mobile army field hospital. I could never express enough gratitude to the doctors, the medics, and the nurses who treated us there. Over time, we got our health back and our strength. I should say, we got our *physical* health back, but the emotional scars, getting over what we had experienced and seen, the loss of our friends and loved ones—I'm not sure that we ever got over that."

" . . . and Metta?" Renate asked. "My readers will want to know. I assume that after they had to end their efforts to keep up with the train that carried Max and his fellow prisoners to Germany, Metta and her friends headed back to Paris. What happened to her after that?"

"You're right. She returned to Paris and helped her friends—those who hadn't been arrested and deported—to bring Jewish children to safety."

"How did Metta find out about Max's death?" Renate asked.

"She learned about it from Frans Gerritsen, Max's good friend. He and Max had made a pact that if either of them died, the one who survived would take care of Metta. Immediately after the end of the war, Metta sought to reunite with Max. She was standing in line at a train station in Paris, planning to buy a ticket to Amsterdam for that purpose, when she felt a tap on her shoulder. Turning, she saw a familiar face. It was Frans. He told her not to buy that ticket, and conveyed by his quiet stare and a soft waving of the hand, back and forth, that the planned reunion with Max was not to be. Metta fell into Frans's arms, weeping inconsolably."

"Metta had earlier said, 'I want to live only if Max is alive.' Now it was up to Frans and his wife, over the next days and weeks, to try to restore Metta's will to live and to help her to envision a future without Max. It took some time, but eventually Metta came to realize that she would have to carry on without Max, that this was, in fact, what Max would want her to do. Four months after the war ended, on September 9, 1945, Metta was able to reach Marseilles and board one of the illegal transports, the S.S. *Mataroa*, bound for Haifa with 175 other young people, survivors of the Holocaust, on board. She settled in Tel Aviv and has lived there ever since."

There was silence between them. Then Renate spoke: "And you, Sigi, what's your story? How did you get back on your feet, physically and emotionally?"

After Liberation: Forgiveness and Reconciliation

The question surprised Sigi. For the past four days his conversation with Renate had focused on Max. Now Renate was asking very directly about his, Sigi's, postwar life. Hadn't Max's story ended with his death? But Renate's question suggested that she was interested in Sigi's postwar story as well. It wasn't that he was reticent about himself; he simply wanted to understand what Renate was getting at with that question.

He looked at Renate intently. "I'm puzzled. I thought your book was to be about Max, about his life, and about the people around him."

She smiled disarmingly. "Of course, this is Max's book, and he is the central character. But I believe I owe it to my readers to give them the entire story of the years after the war ended, how thousands of Jewish survivors moved from Europe to Palestine, and you as one of those survivors can tell that story, at least a small part of it. I see you as traveling the path that Max would have taken had he lived. My intention is also to write of the many ways in which Max's memory has been kept alive over the past fifty years, and you have participated in that effort. Think of it as an extended afterword, if you will."

Sigi weighed what Renate had just said. She had traveled more than 1,700 miles to listen to him. He had firsthand knowledge of these events. She, not he, was to be the author of this book. Who was he to judge what its content should be? Who was he to decide what would be within the scope of the book and what lay outside its scope? That was a matter to be decided by Renate and her editors. He decided to cooperate and give her the information she needed, so far as it lay within his experience to do so.

"Okay," he said, with an air of decisiveness. "I'll tell you some of my own story, and of what I know from what friends have told me, and what has come to me from other sources." Renate smiled broadly and repositioned the tape recorder.

And he began. "Like the other survivors, it took me many months to put the pieces of my life back together again. I was in poor health, not just my body but my mind and spirit, too. There were long periods when I wondered if I had the strength to see it through. And I wasn't the only one. You know, in the months and years after the war ended, thousands of former prisoners died of typhus and other causes; even though they were now free men and women, they were so sick from their mistreatment in the camps that no amount of medical care could save them. I read the account of an American priest, an army chaplain, who was among the first to arrive at Buchenwald after it was liberated. He wrote that 3,000 prisoners died on that first day of liberation alone. And that was how it was in those first days; hundreds of prisoners dropping every day. It was as if they had never been liberated. It was really heartbreaking."

"And then?"

"Over time, my health returned. I was in the field hospital for a month. The American doctors and nurses were wonderful. And lying in that hospital bed, I felt like I needed to get on my feet again, to find Metta again, and tell her how it went with Max. She would want to know, of course. And I had to decide where my future lay, how I would spend the rest of my life, and where. For me that was not a difficult decision. I had been a committed Zionist since childhood. As I've already told you, Max and I had been in the *Blau-Weiss* together, and then in the *hachsharah,* so Palestine was the only destination. I never considered emigrating to America or anywhere else."

Sigi paused, looking intently at Renate's clasped hands, trying to form the words to say next.

"You know, as I've already said, I came from a religious family, and I grew up with the strong belief that *HaShem* puts each of us on this earth for a reason. And so, lying in that hospital bed, I came to understand that God wanted my life to continue, that He had spared me from death for a reason. Why had I lived, when, everywhere around me, men and women were dying? It made no sense otherwise. And I decided then and there that God's plan for me was to go to Palestine, where they needed young men like me, and to work in some endeavor where I could be of use to the people who were pouring into the Jewish homeland from every corner of Europe, Jews like me, Jews who had survived the camps or who had been in hiding. I hadn't yet settled on a career in medicine, but that was my thinking."

"How did you get from Germany to Palestine?" Renate asked.

"Like thousands of other survivors, Jewish and non-Jewish, we made our way to displaced persons (DP) camps, where we could unite with other survivors and receive the care and assistance we so urgently needed, and get ready for the next stage in our lives. Many of these DP camps had been German concentration camps, Buchenwald was one of them. That's where I ended up. It's where I was hospitalized and nourished back to health. And it's where I met Minna, my future wife. I had known her for only a month before I proposed to her, right there at Buchenwald. That's where we were married, too, by a real rabbi, a U.S. Army chaplain. After that, we decided on a wedding trip, you might call it: We decided to leave immediately for Palestine. It wasn't until eleven months later, in January 1948, that we were lifted off Cyprus and brought to Haifa. Home at last!"

"Tell me more," Renata urged, "about your arrival. What was that like?"

"I remember that we all rushed to the bow for our first glimpse of the Promised Land. None of us wanted to miss this historic moment. We knew that we would be telling our children and grandchildren about this, our first sight of Palestine. We stood at the ship's rail, transfixed, overwhelmed. After all we had been through—after all that, our dreams had been achieved."

"You thought then of Max?" Renate suggested.

"Of Max, yes, of course. It was as if he were standing there at the rail alongside me. And I don't mind saying it, the tears flowed freely as I thought of Max, and Joop, and Schuschu, and the two Kurts, Hannemann and Reilinger, and the other rescuers, and of our liberators, the American GIs, and all the others, Jews and non-Jews, who made it possible for the rest of us to be here now, within sight of Palestine, *Eretz Yisrael*. That is a debt that we can never repay."

Sigi sat silently, sipping his coffee, waiting for Renate's next question. It wasn't long in coming. "It's been fifty-three years now since the liberation. Have you been back to Germany since then, back to Buchenwald?"

"To Buchenwald, no. I haven't the courage to do that. But I have been back to Germany many times. I went for the first time in January 1971, when Germany's postwar economic expansion was already well underway. And on that occasion I visited Emden. My city, the city where I was born and raised, had been heavily bombed, first by the British Royal Air Force in March 1940, and finally by a raid on September 6, 1944 that destroyed almost eighty percent of the houses in the city's center. I found out on that first trip that many of the houses on the *Judengasse* had been destroyed."

"I had felt some concern, even some fear, about returning to Emden, but I have to admit, it felt good to be home again, back in the *Heimat*, the homeland, after thirty-eight years. Pushing aside the negative memories of Nazi flags flying from the city hall, of the brown-shirt thugs parading down the *Neutorstrasse*, of the young bullies beating up Jewish boys in the schoolyard, I found myself looking forward to a reunion with the men and women who played a large role in my upbringing. Fearfully, timorously, they asked about Max, about Hanne and Sarah and the other children from the *Judengasse*. I told them what I knew, as delicately as I could. After all, I had not asked them, nor had they volunteered the answer to the unspoken question: 'What did you do in the war?'"

"Then, six months ago, last November, I went back to Emden. I hadn't planned on it, but out of nowhere came in the mail an invitation from the city government, an elaborate engraved invitation. They were getting ready to honor Max on Sunday, November 8, and asked if I would be their honored guest, all expenses paid. I couldn't believe it! The invitation said that I could bring another guest, too, at the community's expense. I thought long and hard about that. In the end, I asked my rabbi in Haifa to accompany me, and I invited my children to come, too, at my expense. It was important to me that they understand our family's roots. It turned out that every surviving member of what had once been Emden's Jewish community had also been invited. There weren't many of us left, just twenty-five or so. But I came, and so did Metta—now Shulamith Roethler—and Isi Windmüller's two sons, Aryeh and Yaron, and Emil Windmüller's grown children. There were fifteen of us altogether from Israel, but also from South Africa, England, and the U.S.A."

"In late afternoon on the following Sunday, we gathered at the site where the synagogue had stood. It had been burned to the ground during *Kristallnacht* and had not been rebuilt. The town authorities had erected a grandstand for the important guests. Every seat was filled, and there were many more people standing in the plaza in front. The mayor, Herr Brinkmann, was the featured speaker. He turned to face us, the former Emden Jews, and sincerely welcomed us back, told us with conviction in his voice that what he called the new Emden had arisen out of the ashes of the old, and that that was true not just of the buildings, but of the hearts and minds of all Emdeners. He earnestly asked us, the survivors, to forgive the townspeople of Emden for the cruelty and indifference they had shown us before the war. I was powerfully moved by those words, let me tell you."

"Then it was my turn to speak. On our arrival in Emden, the survivors had asked me to prepare some remarks in response to the mayor's welcoming speech. So I had already given some thought to what I would say. I rose and approached the microphone. I could have yielded to anger and chastised the people of Emden for their complicity in the Nazi regime, for their passivity in the face of the deportations of men, women, and children whose families had lived in their midst for generations. I could have reminded the Emdeners of their city's important role in the *Kriegsmarine,* of the shipyards where U-boats were built that would later go out and sink scores of warships and commercial vessels, killing hundreds of sailors and civilians. All these words I could have spoken, hoping in that way to shame the assembled Emdeners, to remind them of their guilt for what had transpired fifty years earlier. But that's not what I did."

"After thanking the mayor for his words of welcome, I began speaking in the *Ostfriesische* dialect, bringing warm smiles to those on the platform and those standing in front of me."

My standing here today, among the people of the town I called home, the city of Emden, marks the end of a journey for me, a journey of more than fifty years. For many years, I admit, I was filled with hatred and bitterness for Germany and its people, and all things German. I vowed never to buy a Volkswagen or an Audi, and I even avoided speaking German. When I heard German spoken on the streets of Haifa, I cringed. But then it came to me, not all at once, but over time, that my hatred served no purpose. My rage made me a lesser person, a person whom I didn't want to be. And I asked myself: What would my dear friend Cor, whom we knew in Emden as Max Windmüller—what would that man want from me? And the answer was clear: Cor would have said, 'Sigi, it's over. Let it be over for you, too. You and I have been together all these years. I am still with you in everything that you think, say, and do. This hatred is not serving you.' So I made a conscious effort to cast off my feelings of hatred, and in their place move to forgiveness. To forgive is to heal, to heal the wounds of the past and move on. If I were to meet the young Sigi of the past, the Sigi who was consumed by hate, who vowed vengeance, I would tell him what I am telling you now: 'Drop it! Your bitterness drives people away from you. It makes you smaller in my eyes, and in the eyes of the people who know you. Sigi, cast off those musty old clothes of hatred and resentment, and don the new mantle of love and forgiveness.' And so I come here today to tell you all, 'I forgive. I, Sigmund Kirschner, now Shimon Kirschner, forgive you for the acts of your fathers, your grandfathers, your great-grandfathers.'

"I have to say, though, that, even as I said those words, I felt a twinge of guilt and hypocrisy. Who was I to grant absolution to these people, to forgive them their iniquities? Only *HaShem* can do that. Does He not tell us in his holy Bible, 'To me belongeth vengeance, and recompense'? To Him, and not to us. And will these Germans not challenge me, as other Germans have done, telling me that 'we suffered terribly, too; don't forget that.' But I forged onward in my remarks."

Whatever your forefathers did during the Nazi regime, has nothing to do with you who are standing here today. The warm, caring reception you have given me and my companions makes it that much easier to put the old wounds behind me and embrace you all. Standing here on the street that my ancestors walked, across the many generations, I am filled with pride that I can call myself an Emdener, and will be so until I die.

"At that, the audience on the platform and standing in the square burst into enthusiastic applause. The mayor then took the podium and told the audience: 'Please direct your attention to the street sign over there,' pointing to the corner of what had been, in my time, the *Judengasse*. At a signal from the mayor, Aryeh Windmüller, standing beside me on the platform, pulled down the black cloth covering the street sign and the new street sign came into view. What had been for centuries the *Judengasse*, the street that the Nazis had renamed the *Webergildestrasse*, or Weavers' Guild street, was now renamed for my comrade-in-arms, the *Max Windmüllerstrasse*, Max Windmüller Street.

"I was overcome with emotion and cried tears of joy, and I wasn't the only one up there on the platform who was smiling through tears."

Former *Judengasse*, Emden, Germany

"But there was more to come. The mayor turned to Metta and asked her to do the honors. She pulled the cord, the black cloth fell off, revealing a monument, about shoulder height in size,"

And Sigi showed Renate the photo of it in the album in front of them:

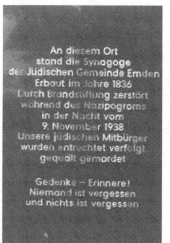

Here's the translation:

At this place
stood the synagogue
of the Jewish community of Emden
Built in the year 1836
Destroyed by fire
During the Nazi pogroms
On the night of 9 November 1938
Our Jewish citizens were deprived of their rights,
Chased out . . . Tortured . . . Murdered

Think back on it. Remember it.
No one is forgotten
And nothing is forgotten.

Sigi continued. "Again the tears came to my eyes. The faces of the dead came before my eyes, as if in a solemn procession. My Vati and Mutti, and my adored sisters, my aunts and uncles, my cousins, and then Max, big as life, grinning that big wide grin of his. And then I saw in my mind's eye the photographic images of the chimneys at the death camps, spouting their thick gray spumes of smoke. Perhaps it was those same chimneys, those same plumes of smoke that carried toward heaven the ashes from the burning bodies of my family, and of millions of others."

Out there, on his balcony, Sigi squinted into the setting sun. He and Renate bathed themselves in its warming rays. That man who was born Sigmund, who had survived years of hatred and violence almost unto death—the man who now called himself Shimon—paused once more, turned toward Renate, and speaking in a soft voice, almost wistfully said: "Wouldn't it be a wonderful world if we could put aside our hatreds, our grudges, and find it in our hearts to forgive? After all, if *HaShem* could forgive the Israelites for worshiping the Golden Calf, if Jacob and Esau could embrace at Isaac's death, who are we to nurse our hatreds?"

Conclusion

⁓

Moments later, they stood in the open doorway to say their goodbyes.

"You know," Renate said, "you have shown me that Max's mission was to save as many Jewish children as possible from certain death. But," she continued, "it went beyond that. Max's mission was about more than saving lives. His objective was to get these young people to Palestine, so that they could be pioneers in the establishment of the new State of Israel. That's what drove him. And, of course, Max had a personal vision of his own happiness with Metta in what was to be the Jewish homeland."

"I understand," Sigi answered, thoughtfully, "why you are excited about writing this book and telling Max's story. But why should young people be receptive to Max's story? Why should they want to read it?"

"Perhaps because I want our young people to identify with Max, to identify with someone who had a grand purpose in life outside of his own well-being. Too many of our young people have no purpose in life, believe in nothing. They live from day to day. If they are students, they go to classes, they party, it's all about having a good time. When they think about their future, it's very hazy. It's about getting married, establishing themselves in a career, maybe having children, and so on. Very few of them have a sense of mission that goes beyond their own personal success and happiness. Hopefully, when these young people read Max's story, they will identify with those who stood in opposition to the Nazis. Max and his comrades stood for life. They were life-affirming."

Sigi paused, as if considering his next words. "Life affirming," he repeated. "Renate, to me, that's the purpose of this book that you're writing. I'll be happy if even one person, after reading it, fixes his or her sights on something life-affirming, something outside of his or her own life to contribute to. That would make this effort, our joint effort, all worthwhile."

Sigi was struck with a sudden thought. "Renate, would you be interested in visiting with me the Joop Westerweel Memorial Forest in Ramat Menashe? I have been there many times. It's a just a little more than a half hour from here. We can do it if we don't dawdle."

Less than an hour later, they stood together at the entrance to the park. It's not a formal garden, such as one might see on the grounds of a European park or palace. It's a scrub landscape, typical of the area.

They approached the first memorial, Sigi using his cane for support. Moments later, they were standing at the memorial, inscribed in Dutch and Hebrew, to all the men and women, Jews and non-Jews alike, who gave their lives in the cause of protecting and saving the lives of Jewish children.

They moved on to another memorial, this one bearing the names of nine of the martyrs: eight German Jews and their mentor, Joop Westerweel, with their dates of birth and death. Sigi called Renate's attention to the lower right-hand corner of the plaque, to Max's name.

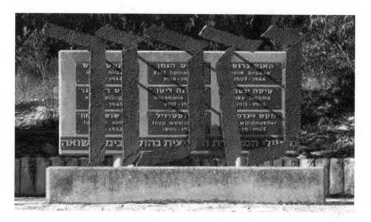

Memorial to Joop Westerweel and the Loosdrecht *chalutzim*

"What do those Hebrew letters mean?" Renate asked, pointing to the large bronze letters standing in front of the names.

"It's the Hebrew word, *zachor*," Sigi pronounced it for her. "It means 'remember.' We are enjoined never to forget what these young people did for us, and to remember that they gave their lives in service to others, Jews and non-Jews."

Pointing to the monument, Sigi commented, "There is no tombstone in Flossenburg to mark Max's grave. This is that tombstone—2,360 miles from the place where his remains are buried." On the top of the granite marker, a few loose stones were scattered. Sigi bent down with difficulty and picked up some stones, placing them there on the marker to join the others.

"Putting stones on the monument—is that a local custom?" Renate asked.

"Jews all over the world do it. When we put these stones on the grave marker, we are in effect helping to enlarge the size of the headstone. In this way, we are doing our part to memorialize the dead. It is also like leaving a calling card as evidence that the mourner visited the tomb."

Renate stooped down to pick up some stones and added them to the pile atop the memorial. She turned toward Sigi and said, "I felt a strong connection with Max when I did that."

"You are joining the hundreds, maybe thousands, of others who have stood here and felt that same strong bond," Sigi told her.

The two of them, Renate and Sigi, returned to the car and drove in silence back toward Haifa. Renate broke the silence. "Sigi, right now I'm picturing the two of us on your balcony, and Max is there, facing us, leaning back against the railing. Of course, he hasn't aged. He's still that cheerful guy, singing his German folk songs as he brings in the crop on the Koekoek farm. What questions would you have for him? And what message do you think he would have for you?"

Sigi found that a response came quickly to mind. So often, when he was at Max's side, first when they were youngsters together in Emden and later on, doing their rescue work in Holland and France, he had thought of himself as Max's sidekick, his helper, Sancho Panza to his Don Quixote, Dr. Watson to his Sherlock Holmes. The world, he thought to himself, would remember Max Windmüller, honor him for his good deeds; Sigmund (Sigi) Kirschner would have to look elsewhere for acclaim. But he also knew that Max wouldn't be buying that pessimistic, that "I'm-not-worthy" way of thinking.

Sigi gave it some more thought, then began. "He'd be saying something like this:

Sigi, you can look back at your life with a feeling of great satisfaction and enormous accomplishment. Look at what you have achieved, first, alongside your *chaverim*, your comrades, during the war, and then here, in Eretz Israel. . . . Esteemed professor, dean of a well-thought-of medical school . . . father, grandfather . . . and this!' And I picture him waving his arms, encompassing the view and my seaside apartment. A long way from the *Judengasse* in Emden, that's for sure! Out of the ashes of a destroyed Europe, you and the other survivors built a new nation, the State of Israel! Isn't that what you and I were fighting for, wasn't that our *tikvah*, our hope?'

"I imagine him clapping his hand on my shoulder, congratulating me. 'Adolf Hitler and his gang of thugs, they're down there in Gehenna, in Hell, gnashing their teeth in frustration. *Am Yisroel Chai*, comrade! We Jews have prevailed. And you made it happen! You have every right to be proud!'"

"And then I picture him turning away, ready to go out the door, but at the last minute, he looks back at me over his shoulder, flashing that big grin that I remember so well, and his last words are, *"Hab' Mut!* Chin up, brother! *Shalom l'hitraot!* [Peace! Until we meet again!] . . . and, with that, he disappears."

There was silence between them again, as if Renate was digesting those words. Then she spoke with intense emotion: "That was beautiful, Sigi. Everything that you imagined Max telling you—I could imagine it, too. And if I needed any greater motivation to get this book written, you've given it to me now."

After an interval, Renate spoke again. "You know, Sigi, earlier, back in your apartment, you questioned whether your post-Liberation story tied in to this book that I'm writing about Max. Hearing that story, I'll give you another reason why it's appropriate." And she continued:

"Think of your post-Liberation story as the story Max would have told me face-to-face, if he had lived—how he would have sailed on one of those 20 Aliyah ships with Metta and the two of them building a life here in the new nation. It didn't happen, to be sure, and we grieve for him, and for Metta, that it didn't. So picture yourself, Sigi, as stepping out of your sidekick role and carrying on his legacy. You're no longer Sancho Panza, or Doctor Watson. I see you more as Joshua, Moses's disciple. Moses couldn't reach the Promised Land, but Joshua did. You are that man, a 20th century Joshua."

Max smiled inwardly. Unlike Joshua, he led no army into hostile territory. He had only Minna to accompany him. But if that was how Renate pictured him, he would not contradict her. "Thank you; I like that," was all he said.

Back in Haifa, they stood alongside her rented car in front of Sigi's apartment building to say their goodbyes. Renate said,

"Thank you, thank you, thank you, Sigi, for all your help, and all your kindnesses. I've come to realize in the last five days that, in helping me to understand Max, you've also helped me to gain a new understanding of myself."

"It was my pleasure," Sigi responded, "and I say that with the utmost sincerity. I'm the one who should be thanking you, for bringing Max to the reading public, and for helping me to restore my confidence in myself, and in my future." And Sigi added, as an afterthought, "You'll send me a copy of the book?"

"Maybe even two or three," she replied, with that disarming smile that Sigi had come to know so well. Moments later, standing at her car, they embraced warmly, and exchanged a light-hearted kiss. Renate stooped to get into her car, and Sigi headed for the door of his building with an optimism, a new outlook, that he hadn't felt in many years.

Sigi reminded himself of his thinking in his earlier depressed state, before that fateful telephone call from Renate, of how he had likened himself to a piece of flotsam that had been cast onto the riverbank, left to dry out in the searing-hot sunlight. He felt only intense satisfaction and elation: that piece of flotsam had been dislodged and was once again caught up in the current and hurtling downstream. In the elevator, heading up to his apartment, he said aloud to no one in particular, and to the world, "Max, my dear friend, my *chave*r, my comrade, I owe it all to you. You have transformed me, made a new man out of me. You're still performing miracles, fifty-three years after your death. *Todah rabah*! I can't thank you enough!"

Epilogue

~⌐

H istory—the teaching of it and the learning from it—has many
purposes and uses.

There are some who would turn their backs on that history and
dismiss it, especially if it's a history of violence. There are also those
who read history selectively, taking from it only that which supports
their preconceived ideas, rejecting anything inconsistent with them.

Then there are those who forthrightly say "Yes" to their history,
adhering to the Biblical injunction:

Remember the days of old. Consider the years of all generations. Ask your father; he will inform you. Ask your elders;
they will tell you. (Deut. 32:7)

Countries around the world celebrate important dates in their national history as occasions for rejoicing, with parades, fireworks, patriotic
displays, and so on. But not every anniversary is cause for celebration.
We have a parallel duty to remember the less-attractive chapters in
our national history, the ones that we would like to turn our backs
on, pretending that they didn't happen, even seeking to justify them.
It is this very human impulse that community leaders in Emden,

Germany, have worked for forty years to counteract. In 1978, they organized the *Arbeitskreis Juden in Emden*—the Jews in Emden Study Group (AJE)—for that purpose. The AJE evolved in 2012 into the *Max Windmüller Gesellschaft* (Max Windmüller Society).

In the late 1970's and early 1980's, individuals in Emden began to reach out to Jews now living in Israel who had lived in Emden before their forced emigration during the Hitler regime, and to the descendants of those men and women. The Emdeners were Marie Werth, head of the Society for Christian-Jewish Cooperation in Ostfriesland; Professor Siegfried Sommer; and Marianne Claudi and her husband Reinhard, the then-director of the *Volkshochschule*, the Adult Education School. Their primary contacts in Israel were Max's cousins, the sisters Auguste Nussbaum Hartogsohn and Sophie Nussbaum van de Walde. They in turn undertook to reach out to other Jewish Emdeners then living in Israel.

The first institutional links between the two groups took place on November 9, 1978, the fortieth anniversary of *Kristallnacht*. Some 100 people gathered at the Jewish cemetery in Emden for the unveiling of tablets commemorating that anniversary. A year later, Marie Werth met in Israel with Israelis who had ties to Emden, to lay the groundwork for continued contacts between the two groups. Those exploratory meetings led to the reunion, three years later, with 60 former Emdeners who came back for a week of celebration and commemoration. Among them were Max's brother Isi, and his wife, Roshel (Shoshana), and their two sons, Yaron and Aryeh, and the Nussbaum sisters named above.

After the destruction of the Great Synagogue in 1938, no Jewish house of worship remained in Emden. To enable the Israeli visitors to Emden on that weekend in 1978 to hold Sabbath services, the town authorities set aside a room in the town hall for those purposes, and a Torah was brought in from Groningen, the same city to which the Windmüller family had emigrated in 1933. The services held in that room, using that Torah, marked the first public Torah reading in Emden in more than 40 years.

The AJE had two overarching goals:

⁂ To make future generations of Emdeners aware of the historical presence of Jews in their city and of the fate of those Jews when the Nazi regime came to power, and

⁂ *"Nie wieder*—Never again"; to work unceasingly to prevent another Holocaust.

To implement those goals, the AJE had as its programmatic objectives:

⁂ To stay in touch with survivors of the Holocaust and other Jews from Emden who left before 1940.

⁂ To organize commemorative events.

⁂ To collaborate with schools in Emden to heighten student awareness of the historical events that ultimately led to the Holocaust.

⁂ Education for tolerance and against anti-Semitism.

Those first contacts led to ever-closer ties on a personal level between individual citizens of Emden and the once-and-former Emdeners now living in Israel. But there were communal actions, too, to keep the light of memory burning after those who have the personal memory of the Holocaust have passed from the scene. Some of them are listed below:

- On November 9, 1988, and on November 9 of each year since then, the City of Emden has held a public event marking the anniversary of *Kristallnacht*.
- The *Arbeitskreise* figured prominently in the restoration of the Jewish cemetery on the *Bollwerkstrasse*, which had fallen into disrepair. Norbert Tillman, head of the city's planning department, placed at the cemetery gates a monument to the former Emden Jews who had fallen victim to the Holocaust. Students of the city's vocational high school helped to rebuild the cemetery gates.
- In 1997 Emden's historical municipal library, the famous Johannes a Lasco library, organized and displayed an exhibit on the life of Max Windmüller.
- To honor Max's memory, the Town Council on July 9, 1998 voted to rename the street that had for centuries been the *Judengasse* the *Max Windmüllerstrasse*. Dr. Jürgen Hinnendahl, director of City Administration in Emden in the mid-1990s, had become a member of the AJE. His support for the renaming and his influence in the City Hall, were major factors in the decision to rename the street for Max.
- Another important element in the work of the organization has been the production of books and films using interviews with Holocaust survivors, former residents of Emden. See the attached bibliography for a list of these books.
- On April 21, 2015, the 70th anniversary of Max Windmüller's death, a *Stolperstein*, a brass memorial stumbling block or plaque placed in the sidewalk there to cause pedestrians to stop and pay attention, was unveiled in front of the family residence at Mühlenstrasse 44.

Max Windmüller *Stolperstein*

❧ Most recently, on October 7, 2015, the Gymnasium, roughly equivalent to an American high school, was renamed the Max Windmüller Gymnasium, by vote of the faculty and the students and their parents. The Max Windmüller Society expressed the hope that the students of the Gymnasium would dedicate themselves to the ideals for which Max lived and died.

Faculty, staff and students in front of the
Max Windmüller Gymnasium, Emden, Germany

In 2012, when the directors of the AJE decided to change the name of the organization to the Max Windmüller Society, the objectives of the organization remained the same, but there was a shift in emphasis, a concentration on programs centered on education, on working with, and within, the Emden schools. One outcome of this new emphasis was the Lodz-Project, initiated in 2012. This project researched the fate of Jews of Emden and the surrounding areas who were deported to the Lodz (Poland) ghetto in October 1941. Under the direction of Dr. Rolf Uphoff, the principal in Emden, the two sets of students, from Emden and Lodz, produced a book entitled: *Eine Reise nach Lodz [Podróz do Lodzi] (A Journey to Lodz]* (2013).

Through the activities of the men and women mentioned in this Epilogue, and with the strong support of successive civil administrations in Emden's city hall and in its schools, new generations of Emdeners have been made aware of the stain that the Holocaust represents, for their city and for their nation. They have learned about and have gained in respect and affection for their hometown hero, Max Windmüller.

Bibliography and Recommended Reading

Books and Articles in English

Chanan Arnon, "Jewish Resistance in Holland: Group Westerweel l," in *Judaism: A Quarterly Journal of Jewish Life and Thought*, Fall 2000.

Chanan Arnon. "Paula Kaufmann and Berri Asscher: Two Stories of Young Jewish Rescuers," in. http://www.holocaustchild.org/wp-content/uploads/2011/12/JRJ_Presentation_at_09_conf_ChanaArnon.pdf

Haim Avni. "The Zionist underground in Holland and France and the escape to Spain," in Yisrael Gutmann and Efraim Zuroff (eds.), *Rescue Attempts during the Holocaust*. Jerusalem, 1974.

Yigal Benjamin. *They were our friends; A Memorial for the Members of the Hachsharot and the Hechalutz Underground in Holland Murdered in the Holocaust*. Jerusalem, 1990.

Jacob Borut. "Antisemitism in Tourist Facilities in Weimar Germany," http://www.yadvashem.org/download/about_holocaust/studies/borut_full.pdf (January 20, 2016)

Frank Caestecker and Bob Moore (eds.). *Refugees from Nazi Germany and the Liberal European States*. New York: Berghahn Publishers, 2010.

Larry Collins and Dominique Lapierre. *Is Paris Burning?* New York: Pocket Books, 1965.

Jozien J. Driessen-Van Het Reve and Bert-Jan Flim. *Saving the Children: History of the Organized Effort to Rescue Jewish Children, 1942–1945.* Capital Decisions, Ltd, 2004.

Free Online Library. *Jewish Resistance in Holland: Group Westerweel and Hachshara.* November 22, 2014.

Peter Hayes and Jeffrey Diefendorf. *Lessons and Legacies VI: New Currents in Holocaust Research.* Evanston, IL: Northwestern Univ. Press, 2004.

Patrick Henry, Y. Lindeman and H. DeVries, eds. *Jewish Resistance Against the Nazis.* Washington, DC. CUA Press, 2014.

Michael Hirsh. *The Liberators: America's Witnesses to the Holocaust.* New York: Random House, 2010.

Inge Windmueller Horowitz, Rita Janet Windmueller, and Ida Stein Windmueller. *Windmueller Family Chronicle.* Richmond, VA: Windmill Press Associates, 1981 (1st ed.), Suppl. 1984.

E. H. (Dan) Kampelmacher. *Fighting for Survival.* New York: Yad Vashem and the Holocaust Survivors Memoirs Project. 2006.

Alex Kershaw. *Avenue of Spies: A True Story of Terror, Espionage and One American Family.* New York: Crown 2015.

Mark Klempner. *The Heart Has Reasons: Holocaust Rescuers and Their Stories of Courage.* Cleveland: Pilgrim Press. 2006.

Raymond-Raoul Lambert. *Diary of a Witness, 1940–1943: The Experience of French Jews in the Holocaust.* Paris: Librairie Arthème Fayard, 1985, English translation, Chicago: Ivan R. Dee, 2007.

Ellen Land-Weber. *To Save a Life: Stories of Holocaust Rescue.* Champaign IL: Univ. Of Illinois Press, 2000.

Walter Z. Laqueur. *The Fate of Young Jewish Refugees from Nazi Germany.* Hanover NH. University Press of New England, 2000.

Michael R. Marrus, ed. *The Nazi Holocaust, Part 6; The Victims of the Holocaust, Vol 2.* DeGruyter, 1989.

Rochelle Mass, ed. *Youth Takes the Lead: The Inception of Jewish Youth Movements in Europe* (Sionah Kronfeld-Honig, transl;). Givat Haviva, Yad Yaari, 2014.

Bob Moore. *Survivors: Jewish Self-Help and Rescue in Nazi-Occupied Western Europe.* New York: Oxford University Press, 2010.

Bob Moore. *Victims and Survivors: The Nazi Persecution of Jews in the Netherlands, 1940–1945.* Hodder Educational Publishers, 1997.

Renée Poznanski. *Jews in France during World War II*, tr. by Nathan Bracher. Brandeis Univ. Press, 2001. Originally published by Hachette Livre, 1994, as *Les Juifs en France pendant la Seconde Guerre Mondiale.*

Jacob Presser. *Ashes in the Wind: The Destruction of Dutch Jewry.* London: Souvenir Press, 2010.

Peter Romijn. "The 'Lesser Evil': the Case of the Dutch Local Authorities and the Holocaust," in Peter Roman, et. al. (eds.). *The Persecution of the Jews in the Netherlands, 1940–1945.* Amsterdam: Vossius Press, 2012.

Andre Stein. *Quiet Heroes: True Stories of the Rescue of Jews by Christians in Nazi-Occupied Holland.* New York: New York University Press, 1991.

Werner Warmbrunn. *The Dutch under German Occupation, 1940–1945.* Stanford, CA: Stanford University Press, 1963, 1991.

Bernard Wasserstein. *The Ambiguity of Virtue: Gertrude van Tijn and the Fate of the Dutch Jews.* Cambridge, MA: Harvard University Press, 2014.

Susan Zuccotti. *The Holocaust, the French and the Jews.* New York. Harper Collins. 1993.

Internet Links
in English

http://wwii-netherlands-escape-lines.com/library/netherlands/. (December 3, 2015)

http://en.tracesofwar.com/map/63309/

http://www.humboldt.edu/rescuers/book/Pinkhof/yaari/sophie1.html

http://www.humboldt.edu/rescuers/book/Pinkhof/p.contents.html

http://www.germanjewishsoldiers.com/

http://www.tbesoc.org/So%20You%20Will%20Remember%20manuscript%20(DeLiema).pdf

http://www.chicagoreader.com/chicago/on-exhibit-a-jewish-artist-confronts-the-swastika/Content?oid=883318

ttp://www.hassia-judaica.de/Lebenswege/English/Floersheim_Hans_Chanan_English/ChananFloersheim_He_Who_Dares_Wins.pdf

http://www.dutchjewry.org/drieluik/jacobus_henricus_kann/jacobus_henricus_kann.htm

http://www.dutchjewry.org/drieluik/deventer/deventer.shtml

http://www.jewishgen.org/yizkor/terrible_choice/ter001.html.

http://www.danielabraham.net/tree/katz/toni/dora.asp

http://www.wertheimer.info/family/GRAMPS/Haapalah/plc/8/9/bc8a7be864e71822098.html

https://www.questia.com/magazine/1G1-68738710/jewish-resistance-in-holland-group-westerweel-and *hachshara*. (December 5, 2015)

http://www.infocenters.co.il/gfh/notebook_ext.asp?book=136934&lang=eng&site=gfh

http://collections.ushmm.org/search/catalog/irn45946

http://www.humboldt.edu/rescuers/book/Pinkhof/yaari/sophie1.html
http://www.godutch.com/newspaper/index.php?id=295. (timeline of Dutch-and Jewish history in 1930's and 1940's):
http://www2.humboldt.edu/rescuers/book/Strobos/Conditions. Holland.html
http://digitalassets.ushmm.org/photoarchives/detail.aspx?id=1158295
https://www.jewishvirtuallibrary.org/jsource/Holocaust/Vught.html
http://www.jcpa.org/jl/vp412.htm
http://www.yadvashem.org/yv/en/righteous/stories/westerweel.asp
http://sowe.fho-emden.de/windmueller/ebilder7.htm
http://www.bunkermuseum.de/bunkermuseum_texte/bunkermuseum_english_190304.pdf.

Websites, Books and Articles
in Other Languages

[Hebrew] Yigal Benjamin. *Faithful to Their Destiny and to Themselves: The Zionist Pioneers, Underground in the Netherlands in War and Holocaust.* Yad Tabenkin/ Beit Lohamei Hagitaot, 1990.

[Dutch] Ineke Brasz and M. Pinkhof. *De Jeugdalijah van het Paviljoen Loosdrechtsche Rade, 1939–1945.* Hilversum: Uitgeverij Verloren, 1987.

[German] Marianne Claudi. *Under every tombstone a story: the Jewish cemetery in Emden.* 2008.

[German] Marianne und Reinhard Claudi. *Die Wir verloren haben: Lebensgeschichten Emder Juden.* Aurich, Ostfriesische Landschaft. 1988.

[German] Reinhard Claudi, ed. *Eine Stadt erinnert sich: Siebzig Jahre nach der Kristallnacht, 1938–2008.* Emden: Stadtarchiv Emden und Arbeitskreis "Juden in Emden." 2008.

[French] Raphael Delpard. *L'Armee Juive Clandestine en France, 1940–1945*. Ann Arbor, MI: Univ. of Michigan Press, 2002.

[German] Hans Florsheim. *Über die Pyrenaen ist die Freiheit.* (Published in English as *He Who Dares Wins*). Konstanz. Hartung-Gorre Verlag, 2007.

[German] G. Janssen: *An example of love to humanity, the story of the Israelite community in Emden before the Holocaust*, 2006.

[French] Lucien Lazare. *La Résistance Juive: un combat pour le survie*. Paris, 1987.

[German] Klaus Meyer Van Dettum. *Max Windmüller: genannt Cor—ein Retter im gewaltfreien Widerstand, 1920–1945*. [Max Windmuller, Named Cor, a Rescuer in Non-Violent Resistance]. _____

[Dutch].Hans Schippers. *De Westerweelgroep en de Palestinapioniers: Non-Conformistisch Verzet in de Tweede Wereldoorlog*. Hilversum, 2015.

[German].Werner Teuber. *Jüdische Viehhändler in Ost Friesland und in nördlichen Emsland, 1871–1942*. Cloppenburg, Verlag Runge. 1995.

[German] *Max Windmüller—Der jüdische Widerstandskämpfer.* . . . https://www.youtube.com/watch?v=NvNDwpDLBOk

[German]. http://www.mwg-emden.de/

[Dutch] ttps://www.joodsmonument.nl/nl/page/716/introduction

[Dutch] http://www.joodsmonument.nl/person/459549?lang=en

http://joodsebegraafplaatsassen.nl/essays/jonge-idealisten-op-het-assense-zeijerveld

Glossary

⸺⸷⸻

L isted below, in alphabetical order, are words and phrases, in languages other than English, which appear in this book. In most instances, but not in all, the translation appeared in brackets immediately after the foreign word or phrase, but they are shown below, so as to collect them all in one place.

A

Aliyah (Hebrew). Literally, "the ascent." The carrying out of the Zionist ideal, the emigration from elsewhere in the world to Palestine/Israel.

Abwehr (German). Literally, "defense." During World War II, the German military service responsible for espionage, counter-intelligence, and sabotage.

Am Yisroel Chai (Hebrew). "The people of Israel live!"

B

Beschert (German). Literally "given." Generally used among Jews in the sense of "predestined."

"Bis Morgen!" (German). Literally, "until tomorrow" or "See you tomorrow."

Blau-Weiss (German). Blue-White, the earliest Zionist youth movement, established in Germany in 1912, inspired by the culture of outings and hikes prevalent in the German youth movement.

Buitenstaander (Dutch). Outsider.

C

Chalutz, pl. chalutzim (Hebrew) Pioneer(s).

Chaver, pl. chaverim. (Hebrew), friend(s), comrade(s)

D

E

Eretz Israel (Hebrew). The Land of Israel.

F

G

Grote Markt (Dutch). In many Dutch and Belgian cities, the central market square,

Guten Morgen (German). "Good morning!"

H

Hab' Mut (German). Have courage.

Hachsharah (Hebrew), hachsharoth (pl.) Training, preparation.

Hakenkreuz (German). Literally, the hooked cross, the Nazi symbol.

HaShem (Hebrew). The name (of God). Used by Orthodox Jews because the second commandment prohibits the use of the Lord's name in vain.

Hatikvah (Hebrew). The hope. The song *"Hatikvah'* was informally adopted as the national anthem of the new state of Israel in 1948.

Hauptsturmführer (German). An SS rank, equivalent to the rank of captain in the US Army.

Hechalutz. A Zionist youth movement founded in 1905.

Hinaus (German). Get out!

Hitler Jugend (German). Hitler Youth, the German Nazi youth organization.

I

J

Jude ist unser Unglück, der (German). The Jew is our misfortune.

Jüdische (German). Jewish.

Judengasse or **Judenstrasse** (German). Jews' street. In many European cities, the street on which Jewish homes and businesses were concentrated.

K

Kashruth (Hebrew). From the Hebrew word, *kasher*, meaning fit (for consumption). The set of Jewish dietary laws which prohibit certain foods and dictate how meats are to be prepared.

Kindertransport (German). Literally, Children-transport. The organized movement which brought thousands of Jewish children out of Germany and Austria to safety in other countries between 1938 and 1940.

L

M

Macht nichts (German). It doesn't matter.

Mann denkt, Gott lenkt (German). Man proposes, God disposes.

Melamed (Hebrew). Teacher.

Mezuzah (Hebrew). Doorpost. A container holding parchment inscribed with verses from the Torah, which Jews are commanded to affix to their doorways (Deut. 6:9, 11:20).

Muss (German). Must.

Mutti (German). The affectionate shortening for *Mutter,* mother. Akin to Mommy.

N

Nationaal Socialistische Beweging (Dutch). National Socialist Movement. In Holland, the pre-war fascist movement.

Nieuwsblad van het Noorden *(Dutch).* Newspaper of the North.

O

Oma, Opa (German). Terms of endearment for grandmother, grandfather.

Onderduiker (Dutch). Diver. Term used for those who went "under water," hiding during World War II.

Onkel (German). Uncle.

Ostfriesland (Germany). Adj.: Ostfriesische. East Friesland, that part of the German state of Lower Saxony that borders the North Sea, just to the east of the border with the Netherlands.

P

Q

R

S

Schutzjude (German). Literally, "protected Jew." A Jew who had received a written guarantee of protection from the local ruler.

Sei stark (German). Be strong!

Seudat havra'ah (Hebrew). Literally, "meal of condolence." The repast eaten by the family of a deceased and other mourners on their return from the cemetery.

Shalom l'hitraot (Hebrew). Peace! I'll be seeing you.

SiPo (Sicherheits Polizei)(German). Security Police—an arm of the Nazi security apparatus.

T

Tante (German). Aunt.

Tzedakah (Hebrew). Charitable donations to the less fortunate, a Jewish religious obligation.

Todah rabah (Hebrew). Thank you so much!

Tsaroth (Hebrew). Troubles. In its more familiar Yiddish form, *tsuris*.

U

V

Vati (German). Familiar term of endearment for *Vater*, father.

Viehhändler (German). Livestock-dealer.

Volksschule (German). A primary school for those who do not intend to go further in their education.

W

Wandervogel (German). Wanderbirds. A youth movement founded in 1896 to bring German youth into the countryside.

X

Y

Z

11/17

77258596R00186

Made in the USA
Columbia, SC
25 September 2017